Homebodies

Homebodies

*Performance and Intimacy in
the Age of New Media*

L. Archer Porter

THE UNIVERSITY OF MICHIGAN PRESS · ANN ARBOR

Published in the United States of America by the
University of Michigan Press
First published February 2026

A CIP catalog record for this book is available from the British Library.

Library of Congress Cataloging-in-Publication data has been applied for.

ISBN 978-0-472-07784-7 (hardcover : alk. paper)
ISBN 978-0-472-05784-9 (paper : alk. paper)
ISBN 978-0-472-90545-4 (open access ebook)

DOI: https://doi.org/10.3998/mpub.14524406

The open-access publication of this book was supported by
The Eugene B. Power Fund.

The University of Michigan Press's open access publishing program is made
possible thanks to additional funding from the University of Michigan Office of
the Provost and the generous support of contributing libraries.

Cover image: Meagan Willoughby

The authorized representative in the EU for product safety and compliance
is Easy Access System Europe, Mustamäe tee 50, 10621 Tallinn, Estonia,
gpsr.requests@easproject.com

Contents

Digital materials related to this title can be found on the Fulcrum platform via the following citable URL: https://doi.org/10.3998/mpub.14524406

Illustrations

Acknowledgments

I have to admit—I scoured the acknowledgments sections of countless books in hopes of unearthing some well-worn template for how to express my profound gratitude. Turns out, no blueprint exists to instruct me on how to capture the sprawling network of colleagues, mentors, advisers, friends, and family who helped shepherd this project into being, from doctoral coursework and dissertation drafts to fully fledged manuscript. *Homebodies* indeed owes its shape to many wonderful human beings, alongside a few institutional frameworks, algorithmic oddities, and heroic amounts of caffeine. Doing so amid a global pandemic, when private corners doubled as professional stages and human connection often glimmered solely through pixels, only underscored the depth of this collective support. To everyone who kept me steady before, during, and after that surreal landscape of shifting ground, I offer my deepest thanks—and a grateful salute to the subreddits, Zoom grids, and cups of coffee that sustained me along the way.

At UCLA—the conceptual birthplace of this project—I owe much to the environment that both nurtured and challenged my thinking. Professors who shaped my approach to performance and media include Aparna Sharma, Janet O'Shea, John Caldwell, Sue Ellen Case, and Todd Presner. Thank you for holding intellectual space where I could safely (and sometimes clumsily) flesh out my ideas.

My dissertation readers were exemplary dance partners in navigating this intellectual choreography: Kathleen McHugh, whose attentiveness and abundant insights into domesticity and screenic representation helped me see paths where I only saw walls, and Anurima Banerji, who, with her encyclopedic knowledge of performance discourse, sharp critical insight, and generous spirit, taught me to "follow the object."

To my advisers and mentors, I cannot express enough appreciation. Harmony Bench provided thoughtful feedback, and her provocative questions guided me through conceptual thickets and into more expansive intellectual territories. Also, I give my thanks to Harmony for bringing me into the fold of her advising group at Ohio State University, where her community-building efforts offered me both academic rigor and camaraderie. And Susan Foster likely did not know until reading this that she had been quietly co-choreographing this project since I stepped foot on UCLA's campus in 2015. Susan's remarkable ability to *read* (read bodies, students, research, situational subtexts, and *me*) often left me feeling as though I was being guided by a benevolent sorceress of critical theory. She knew where my work was headed before I did, putting words to my unformed thoughts and modeling exceptional analytical insight. Her wisdom, wit, and patience carried me through the sticky parts of this endeavor.

My peers at UCLA deserve their own standing ovation: Johanna Kirk, Jingqiu Guan, Melissa Melpignano, Sevi Bayraktar, Mika Lior, Shweta Saraswat, Zena Bibler, Ajani Brannum, Christina Novakov-Ritchey, Arushi Singh, and Jackie Davis—to name just a few. You provided dialogue and companionship, from week 0 curiosities to week 10 existentialisms.

To my University of Nebraska–Lincoln colleagues Katie Anania, Gloria Flores, Hye-Won Hwang, Susan Ourada, Ash Smith, and Jesse Fleming—I appreciate your dynamic insights into performance and the mediatized body. Your collective brilliance often made me think, "Is it too late to rewrite this entire chapter?" (Spoiler: It was.)

To my students in Emerging Media Arts and Dance, and to Mariela Hernandez, Tasha Russell, and Vanessa Uriostegui, in particular: thank you for helping me choreograph my way through a theory-practice entanglement.

Permission to reprint key parts of this research was generously granted by *Performance Research, Etudes, International Journal of Screendance*, and *communication +1*. Your willingness to allow this research to find a home on new pages is deeply appreciated.

Harmony Bench and Alexandra Harlig, who coedited a special issue of the *International Journal of Screendance*, offered incisive feedback on the concept of the "homebody." I'm grateful for your careful attention and for your ability to not flinch at my affinity for language play (i.e., corny puns).

Artist and architect Meagan Willoughby lent her skilled hand and keen eye to create the beautiful images that grace this book. Her work is proof that home dance media can have a brilliant life outside the hollow chambers of social media.

Finally, I wish to thank my parents, Tom and Debbie, who have always supported my affinity for dance (and didn't question me when I quit pre-med to pursue a master's degree in dance). And to my core compadre, Z, whose support, humor, and willingness to stage impromptu dance parties reminded me that even as I studied everyday choreographies online, the reality of my own situation was still the richest stage of all.

To all of you, thank you. You've helped me refine the question, follow the object, analyze the body, critique the platform, and choreograph the text—and, ultimately, you've helped me find my footing in this unprecedented journey.

Preface

I started collecting data for this project in 2016, just as Facebook (now Meta) transformed Instagram's feed from a straightforward chronological list into a "relevancy sorted" stream of images. This algorithmic pivot allowed the platform to identify patterns in users' online behavior and predict what they might want to see next, subtly yet significantly altering how people navigated media, related to one another, and created their own content. Then the COVID-19 pandemic arrived, collapsing the boundaries between public and private spheres and turning homes into our primary stages of social life. Screens became portals for both broadcasting ourselves outward and welcoming others inward, all while these predictive algorithms continued to fine-tune what we encountered online. In this way, the decade between 2010 and 2020 captures a poignant arc in digital culture—a period when the rapid normalization of predictive curation met an unprecedented reliance on digital intimacy, exposing new fissures in our collective sense of authenticity, belonging, and self-presentation.

You might ask, What does all this have to do with dance? The dancing body is skilled at absorbing its environment and then responding with movements that are both situational and socially inscribed. It takes cues from others, sensing subtle changes in tone, atmosphere, and rhythms, and transforms them into a physical language that is at once deeply personal and communicatively rich. In an era when social media platforms assume the role of choreographer—arranging our feeds, assembling our communities, predicting what we might want to see next—our gestures and movements are increasingly guided by invisible forces. These systems, like dance partners we never chose, alter the contours of our digital embodiment, the ways we position ourselves within an ever-shifting cultural terrain.

Homebodies: Performance and Intimacy in the Age of New Media emerges from this interplay between bodies and technologies, between the self and the algorithm, between the person and the platform. It investigates how personal spaces, movements, and narratives circulate through platforms that are always watching, always guessing at our next inclination, desire, or need. By placing the dancing body at the center of this inquiry, I reveal how movement practices—ranging from carefully choreographed sequences to spontaneous, everyday gestures—negotiate visibility and invisibility, presence and absence, authenticity and artifice in digital realms.

This book thus speaks to a complex moment in the evolution of social media and performance, where lines between private and public, internal and external, and physical and virtual have become ever more fluid. Amid these transformations, the dancer's body becomes a powerful metaphor and a literal site of engagement. It gestures at the promises and perils of algorithmic curation: how we learn new steps in response to unpredictable partners, how we move in sync or fall out of rhythm with the feed, how we try—and sometimes fail—to resist the shaping forces that guide our online expressions. Ultimately, dance, as a bodily practice, offers a counterpoint to the disembodied logics of new media. It offers a language of motion that can challenge, complicate, or complement the strategic sorting and filtering of human experience by increasingly potent digital systems.

In the chapters to come, I track how these dynamics played out in the culturally and temporally specific context of 2010–20—a period that might, one day, be recognized as the formative decade of "curated intimacy." By the end, I hope to show how the dancing body offers a lens through which we might understand both the constraints and the creative possibilities that lie at the intersection of performance and platformed life. In this way, *Homebodies* seeks not only to document a decade in flux but also to propose that through understanding the dancing body's responses, we might learn to navigate our own online environments—algorithmic and otherwise—with greater awareness and agency.

Introduction

"If intimacy is the answer, then what is the question?"
—Henrietta Moore

Anthropologist Henrietta Moore may not have been referring to new media when she posed this question during a keynote address in 2014, yet her query captures the ways in which intimacy has become a panacea for the social, cultural, economic, and political woes brought on by the internet and its proliferation of new media platforms. Indeed, intimacy is frequently deployed as a solution to some state of isolation, a touchstone for cultivating connections across distance, and an amelioration of the trials of a network society. Its frequent deployments may be observed in the term's appearance in titles across a range of disciplines, from psychology to architecture, philosophy to sexuality studies, and sociology to marketing studies—texts that address both a lack in and a discovery of intimacy on or through the internet.[1] Across its deployments, however, the term often eludes definition, garnering a commonsense appeal via its effusiveness. The suggestion of this frequency-without-grounding is that intimacy is so innate to a universal human experience that it requires no definition, no explanation, and no discussion of its mechanics.

This book works against the presumed innateness of intimacy by unpacking its underlying mechanisms through a study of home dance videos on the social media platform Instagram. Such an investigation reveals how intimacy is not only actively constructed but also produced through a tension between the unseen and seen, the interior and exterior, the private and public, and the familiar and unfamiliar. I theorize the notion of *intimaesthetics*—or the aestheticization of intimacy—to capture the phenomenon wherein intimacy is choreographed and harnessed into an image, particularly toward the cultivation of closeness in and through media. The maneuvers of the performing body in the domestic environment, and its subsequent mediatizations, are especially instructive in revealing the aestheticization of intimacy. Once on Instagram, however, the intimaesthetic image becomes enveloped in a system of algorithmic determination, data collection, and neoliberal commodification: maneuvers that are largely obscured from the user. This study on the production of intimacy thus highlights a tension between performer agency and platform control, wherein the performer gives themselves to the platform without a clear sense of how their intimate data might be used, whom or what it may be serving, and what exactly is being transacted. It thus reveals the bait-and-switch logic that defines everyday, twenty-first-century new media praxis.

Intimacy and Its Aestheticization

Rooted in the Latin *intimus*, meaning "inmost," and *intimare*, meaning "to impress, to make familiar," intimacy reflects a multifaceted interiority. In other words, the two roots "inmost" and "impression" both require some notion of inside, yet one that is conceptually expansive. For instance, intimacy appeals to spatialities of closeness or enclosure; conceptions of an inner, human experience; and the possibility of close intersubjectivities.[2] These various conceptions point to how intimacy operates along three registers: spatial, psychological, and sociocultural—all of which are undergirded by some sense of interiority. Of course, by connoting a multifaceted interiority, intimacy inadvertently references notions of exteriority, as an *inmost* can only exist in relation to an *outermost*, and an impression relies on an outside entity impacting one's inner state or form. The logic of this etymology suggests that intimacy is bound by, and wound through, the binary of interiority and exteriority—a binary that is linked to myriad other modernist dualities, such as privacy and publicity, body and mind, and nature and culture.[3] In the introduction to their anthology *Intimacy in Cinema*, David Roche and Isabelle Schmitt-Pitiot reflect on intimacy's reliance on this system of dualities. They state, "As a concept, intimacy is problematic—and stimulating—because it begs to be defined and delineated in terms of binaries that are themselves unstable, such as inside and outside (Lebovici 19, Clam 11), hidden depth and visible surface (Clam 20), public and private (Boyer 72), and self and other, and from a Lacanian perspective, the intimate and extimate."[4] The qualification of this foundation of dualisms as already "unstable" is telling of intimacy's effusiveness in the popular imagination: it is able to shape-shift across its various deployments because its foundation is composed of an unsteady and already troubled logic of binary order.

The concept of intimaesthetics draws on intimacy's associations to interiority, while also revealing the mechanisms that bolster such associations—mechanisms that, like Roche and Schmitt-Pitiot's qualification of intimacy, are also "problematic" and "stimulating." While an understanding of intimacy is foundational to the concept of intimaesthetics, this neologism also relies on a particular understanding of aesthetics. Indeed, intimaesthetics fuses "intimacy" and "aesthetics" to name the twenty-first-century formalization of qualities *around* intimacy. The incorporation of "aesthetics" in the term identifies the processes by which one *creates an image* of something. The intellectual history of aesthetics, with its discourses and debates on beauty—symmetry, proportion, and so forth—is not as relevant to the mechanisms of intimaesthetics as are the processes of defamiliarizing the familiar. In this respect, intimaesthetics draws on an emerging discourse of everyday aesthetics, which is situated as oppositional to classical models of aesthetics. As opposed to focusing on "surprise, shock, and wonder," the field of everyday aesthetics attends to extraordinary dimensions of the functional, familiar, ordinary, and mundane.[5] As Yuriko Saito summarizes, everyday aesthetics is attentive to activity rather than object.[6] Sianne Ngai echoes this sentiment in the naming of "everyday aesthetic categories," which provide a "more direct reflection on the relation between art and society" than classical aesthetic categories like the sublime and beautiful.[7] For Ngai, these categories revolve around some sort of "triviality" that results in an ambiguity of judgment.[8] Drawing on this discourse of everyday aesthetics, intimaesthetics reflects Saito's sense of an "aesthetic texture of ordinariness," in that it emphasizes bodily action and familiarity, and Ngai's discussion of triviality and ambiguity, in that it captures a "deficit of power" within the scheme of cultural production. Thus, to aestheticize intimacy means to harness a semiotics of everyday interiority through one's actions.

Aligning intimaesthetics with a discourse on everydayness reveals a performer's resourcefulness in a situational context. The concept of choreography, I maintain, is foundational to this work, as it emphasizes how intimacy is activated in and through the body and steeped in one's quotidian situation. In other words, to create an *image* of intimacy—or to engage in a process of aestheticization—one must arrange, orchestrate, situate, and sequence the individual parts in their world. This process gestures toward the *mechanisms* of intimaesthetics, which entail the choreographies of body, space, and media. A review of each of these facets will further contour the notion of intimaesthetics and establish an understanding for how images might cultivate a sense of closeness with viewers on new media.

Mechanisms of Intimaesthetics

Unpacking the production of intimaesthetics through the body relies on an understanding of what I call the *homebody*. More than merely a person who finds pleasure in staying at home, the homebody is the product of the dialectical relation between the *habitat* and the *habitus*. That is, the home is a space where individuals cultivate and rehearse the habits they inherit from and carry out into the world. It subtly, over time and space, embodies social structures, which through the homebody's movements ultimately feed back into those structures. This give-and-take process results in a body defined through what Bourdieu terms the habitus, or a "system of transposable dispositions."[9] The homebody, extending Bourdieu's concept of the habitus, is a corporeal manifestation of social constructedness—the everyday, micro-developments of gender, class, race, sexuality, ability, and so forth that are cultivated through domestic space and expressed through the body. However, the homebody also reimagines itself in the confines of its space, testing its limits and tweaking its habits. This figure moves in and through the home, secured by the familiarity of its surroundings yet excited by the world beyond its walls. Though it is subject to normative patternings, it is also compelled by the possibility of deviation. In this way, the homebody is not just public/private and personal/social but also reiterative/subversive.

The homebody is indeed paradoxical. Not only does it embody the structures of its environment, thereby enmeshing itself into social fabrics, but it also interfaces with the public through screens. For the twenty-first-century homebody, in particular, screens have become an apparatus of habitualization: the homebody maneuvers itself in front of screens, just as it becomes the image on screens. In fact, it may be argued that *it is only through images and screens that the homebody may appear in the first place*—since, once it exits its domestic world, it becomes evacuated of its defining characteristics. In other words, the homebody cannot *be* outside of the home. However, by remaining in its habitat, positioning itself in front of a camera, and pressing record, it may mediate and transmit itself and its choreographies. Through screens, then, this figure comes to know the world, just as the world comes to know it. Its production and consumption of media then make up its habitual exercises—voices, bodies, and scenes from afar are drawn into its habitat and shape its habitus. Though this figure indeed "stays at home," it is shaped by and expressed through the various interfaces that enable it to engage with the wider world—broadcasting itself out to that world, while also bringing the world to it.

The homebody engages many tactics when creating and screening images of its person and space. It may draw the viewer into its world by playing with the quality with which it moves; the repetition and rhythm of its movement; its interaction with or mere relation to the objects around it; the direction and expression of its gaze; the clothes it wears; its posture; and its assumption of "casual," "cute," "innocent," "authentic," or any other affective quality that suits its purposes. Each gesture—seemingly insignificant in itself—is part of a larger choreographic thrust to produce some essence of intimacy in image form. For instance, by flailing the arms, casting the head from side to side, and generally ignoring the camera, the homebody might suggest a sense of abandon or carefreeness that is associated with solitude, privacy, and the sphere of unseen activity—it may, in other words, indicate how it is "dancing like nobody's watching." It might move toward and away from the camera or remain completely stationary as a way to emphasize closeness (or merely play with the *possibility* of closeness). Perhaps it engages in the quotidian activity that would normally take place in its space (e.g., sweeping, mopping, scrubbing, and cooking), thereby playfully visibilizing labor that might otherwise go unseen. In each of these circumstances, the homebody attends to the cultivation of intimacy in a unique manner, yet all via the dispositions, movements, and techniques of its corporeal entity.

The face, head, and gaze are especially integral to the homebody's efforts to choreograph intimacy through bodily movement. While these three components operate in tandem to construct meaning, they also harness distinct discourses in relation to faculties of communication and imbrication in power structures. The gaze, in particular, is steeped in robust discourses surrounding the politics of looking.[10] Borrowing from gaze theory, as developed and articulated in feminist film studies, the performing subject might attend to the powers of the gaze to subvert the capturings of both the camera and the viewer. These techniques are especially profound for the dancing body, considering prevailing constructions of the dancer as an object that moves to satisfy the pleasures and desires of the viewer and to be *consumed* by both the viewer's eye and the eye of the camera.[11] The gaze of the dancer might just as well lend itself toward docility—docility toward the camera, the cameraperson, or the viewer.

While the gaze has been construed and applied in varying contexts to refer to different techniques and structures of capture, its relation to the homebody articulates the performer's ways of looking, including those in both agentic and reiterative fashions. Using the gaze to choreograph intimacy might include closing one's eyes so as to demonstrate (and possibly to achieve) introspection—or, quite literally, the experience of looking inward.[12] The performer might also look toward the camera to cultivate a more direct connection with their viewer-to-be. Alternatively, they might keep their eyes open but not look at the camera at all, performing as though their movements would never be seen.[13] Though not an exhaustive catalog of the ways in which the homebody incorporates the gaze to choreograph intimacy, these instances capture a few primary techniques of the intimate gaze.

Like the gaze, the face, too, works to construct meaning and cultivate intimate sensibilities. Smiles directed toward nothing or no one in particular, grins aimed at the camera, glimmers in the eye, laughter, and even stoicism all subtly function to compose a sense of closeness. Such efforts resemble what Sherril Dodds calls "facial choreography," or an emphasis placed on facial expressions, as enabled through cinematic framings and video editing. This choreography of the face draws from performance vocabularies, as well as everyday codes and conventions, but is ultimately produced through the screen apparatus. In an essay detailing the concept, Sherril Dodds and Colleen Hooper recall Deleuze's notion of the *abstract machine of faciality*, which they characterize as a force that produces "legible messages that resist ambiguity, polyvocality, and heterogeneity."[14] In this way, facial choreography, they argue, becomes incorporated into hegemonic structures of capture.

Extending this perspective, the process of aestheticizing intimacy entails the choreography of one's face so as to construct and perform an unambiguous closeness. While Dodds and Hooper engage the concept of facial choreography in relation to the politics of the close-up, particularly regarding dance on reality TV, the notion also applies to everyday, self-produced videos online. The new media performer—though they are directly involved in the choreography of the face rather than being the subject of another's production—produces their videos with the knowledge and consideration of an impending viewer. As such, they work within codified systems of communication, including that of the face, head, and gaze, to choreograph an image of intimacy.

Alongside the choreographic work of the body, intimaesthetics also involves the choreography of space. The space of the home in particular is central to the ways in which intimacy is aestheticized, as it is already imbued with a sense of familiarity, habituation, and autobiography. However, as a *kind* or *type* of space, the home itself requires delineation before unpacking its semiotics and the ways in which it is choreographed and aestheticized. According to Mary Douglas, the home is "always a localizable idea." It is "located in space," Douglas continues, "but it is not necessarily a *fixed* space."[15] Linda McDowell takes Douglas's argument further by claiming that, if the home is considered to be a *place*, it "is defined not as a bordered container but a locus of exchange and interactions across different spatial scales."[16] Notably, in offering these distinct positions on the home, it becomes evident that Douglas uses the term *space*, suggesting the home's abstractness (i.e., through describing it as an "idea"), while McDowell uses the term *place*, articulating the home's cultural, economic, and political dimensions. While a home certainly possesses qualities around its geometries and materials of construction, it is ultimately socially determined.[17] *Homebodies* thus rejects any notion of the home as abstract. It is, as McDowell underscores, economically and politically charged, with a propensity for exchange and interaction. Extending McDowell's position on the home as place, while also remaining oriented toward the social construction of space, I utilize the term *homespace* throughout this book to refer to the locationally specific, socially constructed, and politically charged qualities of the domestic environment.

Of course, the ways in which the home is conceptualized in the public imagination determine its social life through images and other cultural products. So, while the home is never abstract, never universal, and always political, the semiotics of the home rely, to some degree, on its ability to convey a ubiquitous familiarity. The notion of *dwelling*, for instance, pervades popular conceptions of the home. Martin Heidegger's proposition of dwelling as a space of consistency, neutrality, and staticness for the development of human perception speaks to this sense of how the home might be perceived.[18] In concert with Heidegger, Gaston Bachelard's manifesto on the home presents another sense of this space as one that nurtures imagination and protects its inhabitants (who, as Bachelard describes, are "dreamers").[19] The respective positions of Heidegger and Bachelard should be read with criticality, as they both propagate an essentializing sensibility of the home. At the same time, these perceptions of the home persist in the public imaginary, as they anchor popular conceptions of the home apparent in phrases like "home is where the heart is," "my home is your home," "there's no place like home," "home is not a place, it's a feeling," and "with you, I am home." Such conceptions of the domestic setting not only extend Heidegger's and Bachelard's sensibilities of the home but also allow their deceits of universality to circulate through public discourse, thereby sustaining a popular, essentializing notion of the home.

The popular conception of the home as universal facilitates its ease of imaging, its wide circulation, and its mass reception. It may, for instance, serve as a backdrop to a range of quotidian activity, thereby enabling whatever performance it houses to catch the limelight. Conversely, the home may intermingle with the performer's extraordinary performance in a way that calls attention to itself. The homespace, then, though it relies on a certain conceptualization of ubiquity, is also actively constructed by the producer of that image. That is, the creator of an image set in the domestic environment choreographs their space in particular ways. In preparation for the production of a home dance video, for example, the performer may consider the conditions of the homespace and how they might effectively achieve a particular aesthetic or affective sensibility. Such considerations might include the cleanliness of the space (*Should my dirty laundry be visible?*); the appearance and semiotics of objects that are hung on the walls, situated on the tables, magnetized to the refrigerator, or placed on the bookshelf (*Do I really want "Birdwatching for Dummies" resting on the coffee table?*); and the natural or artificial lighting of the space (*Do I want to be backlit and hide my face?*). These considerations reflect a series of transformations that the performer-producer initiates so that their living quarters might temporarily become a staged set primed for viewership.

In conjunction with these stylistic decisions to transform the homespace are the practical and coincidental dimensions of that space. However meticulous the subject's choreographies may be, the image also results from the limitations, specificities, and practicalities of the space. Homes of all kinds are designed and constructed for the purposes of cooking, eating, sleeping, bathing, and other fundamental, life-sustaining activities. So, converting the home into a stage might require practical considerations, as well as create openings for the appearance of unplanned elements. For instance, on the practical side, the performer might determine the room in which to record based on its existing lighting capabilities. They might respond to the suitability of the floor, as hardwood and tile are better for swift movement but not traction. Or, they might decide that they need to reconfigure their furniture to create more space, so they do not hit anything while moving. On the more coincidental side, the performer might not realize that their calendar is visible on the refrigerator behind them, thereby exposing their travel schedule. They might not care to address the stack of books on the table or the photos on the shelf behind them. They might not realize that the cat is hiding under the bed behind them. In this way, the performer's choreographies of space are met with a certain degree of disregard, as well as practicality—elements that, once imaged in video, shape the significations of intimacy.

Just as the performer aestheticizes intimacy through their orchestrations of space and body, they also consider factors of the recording device and the image it creates. Such factors include the setting up of the camera, the relation to or interaction with it, the review of footage, the use of a *filter* to add a certain aesthetic to the image, and the trimming of the video. This work enables the dancer to frame, quite literally, their intimate scene, so as to offer an image of interiority and to cultivate a sense of closeness with the viewer. Of course, the concept of the frame is theoretically rich, and that richness informs the meaning of the frame for its work toward intimaesthetics. A frame is at once an object, a rhetorical device, a technique of communication, and a boundary around an image. In each of its manifestations, the frame carries the power to visibilize and, also by extension, the power to invisibilize. Susan Sontag notably addresses this power that is embedded in framing, focusing in her case on photographic framing. As Sontag writes: "The photographic image, even to the extent that it is a trace (not a construction that is made out of disparate photographic traces), cannot be simply a transparency of something that happened. It is always the image that someone chose; to photograph is to frame, and to frame is to exclude."[20] In this view, the idea of capturing an image demonstrates, on the one hand, the mechanism of preserving a moment and, on the other hand, the power structures involved in harnessing some place, object, or person in image form—and what is left out of that image.[21]

While Sontag focuses on photography, her articulation of the power inherent in frame-based inclusion—and by extension, that of exclusion—just as well applies to other modes of mediation, in particular that of video. In the case of the home dance video, a choreographic approach toward the production of an intimaesthetic product foremost entails the placement of the camera: shall it be held, or shall it sit in a stationary place? If in a stationary place, what room should it be in, and how should it be situated? How high and how close to the dancer should it be placed? If the camera is held, who shall hold it and with how much movement? These decisions provide a wealth of information that structures the resulting semiotics around intimacy. In determining the placement of and the degree of interaction with the camera, the performer-producer identifies what elements of domestic life should be visible within the frame and what should be excluded. The camera movement, or lack thereof, also articulates the contours of some relationality. If the frame is moving, however subtly, the suggestion is that someone else other than the performer is involved in the production of the video. Conversely, a completely motionless frame suggests that the performer positioned the camera themselves ahead of time. The semiotics of the frame differ depending on the image and the other information it offers. Thus, discussions of framing remain integral throughout *Homebodies*, as they provide major clues as to *who did what*.

The ways in which the performer orients themselves toward the camera, moves in particular ways, crafts their space, and frames the scene contribute to a product that pictures their world from the inside looking out and the outside looking in. Through these choreographies, they leverage a multifaceted interiority and manifest a sense of familiarity for circulation and consumption. This process results in a blurring of not just publicity and privacy, or interiority and exteriority, but also text and context—a central feature of intimaesthetics. That is, while body, media, and space are choreographed into the creation of a product that reads as intimate, the home dance video simultaneously suggests a lack of preparation, a degree of the unchoreographed, and an indication of one's contextual world. As is the case with many staged performances, viewers do not glimpse the preparations involved in the production. However, because the home dance video is set in a quotidian space that already evokes familiarity, the ultimate product reads as a reflection of one's life, thus prompting a con/fusion between text and context. The viewer might not glean the specifics of the stories behind the artifacts on the shelf, for instance, but the mere presence of those artifacts nonetheless suggests facets of some untold personal history. In this sense, the frame of the image is porous: the image is constructed, but its boundaries are leaky with personal information and off-screen quotidian activity. The intimaesthetic production, in other words, suggests a world that is *more beyond* the frame—a concept that is threaded throughout *Homebodies*.

While intimaesthetics represents a blurring of text and context, this reading is nonetheless contingent upon the media's encounter with an audience. The ways in which the home dance video circulates on new media amplifies the social, cultural, economic, and political intricacies of intimaesthetics. This circulation not only activates the image's semiotics of interiority, familiarity, and authenticity but also opens the homebody, homespace, and media object out to the logic and whims of the platform. In particular, the social life of intimaesthetics is shaped by the forces of the market, the gaze, and the algorithm.

Though the intimaesthetic product reveals the performer's choreographies of body, space, and media, its life on platforms like Instagram amplifies its political and economic charge. Neoliberalist constructions of the individual as a consumerist product, in particular, color this charge by announcing the marketability of all corners of human activity, however seemingly private and personal. Boltanski and Chiapello maintain that "the new enterprise mechanisms . . . demand a greater engagement and are based on a more sophisticated ergonomics . . . [and] precisely because they are more human in a way, also penetrate more profoundly into people's interior being." Actors within this new spirit of capitalism, they continue, "are expected to 'give themselves,' as one says, to their work, and the mechanisms permit an instrumentalization and commodification of what is most specifically human about human beings."[22] Under this new spirit of capitalism, the individual comes to resemble a brand and their actions are made available for the accrual of capital.[23]

Indeed, while neoliberalism is anchored to a series of twentieth-century economic policies and political conditions,[24] which arose before the proliferation of new media, it has nonetheless shaped and been exacerbated through those systems.[25] Wendy Chun argues that interfaces, in particular, are what enable subjects to interpret, navigate, and participate in the neoliberalist landscape that Boltanski and Chiapello characterize. As Chun maintains, "Interfaces—as mediators between the visible and invisible, as a means of navigation—have been key to creating 'informed' individuals who can overcome the chaos of global capitalism by mapping their relation to the totality of the global capitalist system."[26] In a subsequent work, Chun builds on these ideas by theorizing how the notion of *habit* determines the nature of individuals' interaction with interfaces.[27] Drawing upon Chun, *Homebodies* suggests that participation in neoliberalist systems occurs foremost in and through the body, indicating the ways in which neoliberalism is grounded in *practice*. I propose that intimacy, in particular, becomes a lynchpin in neoliberalism's twenty-first-century cultural life.[28] The role of social media in propagating a culture of self-branding exacerbates the marketization of the self. For Jeremiah Morelock and Felipe Ziotti Narita, the selfie on social media, in particular, works as an emblem of neoliberalism's work on individuation. Referencing Guy Debord's renowned work, *The Society of the Spectacle*, Morelock and Narita articulate how social media cultivates a "society of the selfie" that "is connected to the pervasive need for online impression management and individual self-investment reinforced by neoliberal logics."[29] In such a society, the home dance video, through the picturing and circulation of one's moving body, personal space, and seemingly interior thoughts, reduces its contents to a "strategy of simplification."[30]

While the circulation of home dance videos on social media is under-girded by a logic of neoliberalism, it also is shaped by the powers of watching in a *post-panoptic surveillance society*. This phrase combines Roy Boyne's notion of post-panopticism and David Lyon's discussion of a surveillance society—both of which capture the sense that surveillance is no longer centralized with governing institutions, but has been distributed into wider networks with commercial, educational, and recreational nodes of disciplining through over/seeing.[31] Historical forms of surveillance, then, diffuse through the fibers of one's everyday world and thus sustain themselves through their ubiquity and subtlety. This diffusion then compounds with the laissez-faire logic of neoliberalism to produce a culture in which commodification intermingles with the disciplining powers of watching in the everyday.

With the gaze already at the crux of intimaesthetics, the online circulation of home dance videos promulgates the tenets of a post-panoptic surveillance society. This society's characteristic diffusion of surveillance occurs not only through the imaging of the quotidian space of the home and the movements of the homebody but also through the subsequent envelopment of that performance into new media's systems of capture, or into what Amy Dobson et al. call "digital intimate publics."[32] The degree to which a user's data is collected by the platform, the search engine, the internet service provider, and the third-party apps, to name a few separate arenas, is typically unknown to the viewer and instead rests with the power of machine-learning algorithms that monitor online behavior to then predict future behavior—a form of the disciplining accomplished through surveillance.[33] *Dataveillance*, as some scholars name this capturing and collection of personal information, is indeed a problematic feature of digital culture.[34] Yet, the fact of its obscurity by the companies that engage in it enables users to continue "[giving] themselves"—to reference Boltanski and Chiapello—to the platform.[35]

Homebodies articulates the tensions between dataveillance and the user's choreographies of body, space, and media to produce what Sarah Banet-Weiser calls a "politics of ambivalence." This concept, which Banet-Weiser uses to describe the commercialization of authenticity in brand culture, captures how "utopian normativity" meets critical subversion and how individual agency meets hegemonic structuring.[36] Intimaesthetics reveals a similar ambivalence in that it references, on the one hand, the labor and agency of the performer who aestheticizes intimacy for public acknowledgment and, on the other hand, the technological denial of security and authority over that performer's digital identity. This dynamic reflects the bait-and-switch logic of new media: platforms seduce users with the promise of currency—often in the form of social, cultural, and financial capital—and then mobilize the data that users provide toward ends that often violate that user's performative intent, their identity, and their sovereignty. Platform control, I argue, cannot be considered without an understanding of the duality inherent in the performer's choreography within new media. Denizens of new media are at once *choreographing themselves* and *being choreographed, acting out* their desires and being *acted upon*—and they often engage in such transactions without being privy to the terms of what is being transacted. An in-depth consideration of the homebody's mechanisms, as each chapter uncovers, draws a direct link between the choreographic particulars of intimaesthetics and the platform's inconspicuous pillaging of intimate data.

When conceptualizing the homebodies and homespaces that appear on platforms like Instagram, it is important to recognize the figures and spaces that *do not appear.* That is to say, the home dance videos that circulate on Instagram, and that I examine in this book, reflect a curated, performative vision of intimacy and domestic life—one that, while rich with criticality, is necessarily limited by what is shown. Consequently, this study can only reveal what is already made visible within the bounds of the platform's visual economy. The homes and bodies that remain off-screen, whether due to economic, social, or cultural exclusions, inherently evade my critical lens, leaving gaps in this account of how intimacy and performance circulate through new media. Nonetheless, the theory of intimaesthetics captures the logic of mediatizing certain spaces, activities, and bodily movements that represent an unmediated existence. The treatment of spatiality and embodiment in *Homebodies* is thus inherently paradoxical—a core tenet of intimaesthetics.

While the analytical framework of *Homebodies* reflects an attention to both the performance of self and danced movement, it does not include a consideration of music. Certainly, music factors into the aesthetic choices of a home dancer and may impact the affective register of its circulation and consumption online. However, the *Homebodies* project largely focuses on visual aesthetics and, in particular, how intimacy is choreographed and flattened into an image before circulating through an online visual economy. Thus, any consideration of the musical components of a home dance production, while interesting in their own right and deserving of scholarly attention, falls outside the scope of this project.

Intimaesthetics has woven itself so seamlessly into our digital experiences that it exists both everywhere and nowhere at once. On image-centric platforms like Instagram, curated glimpses of personal moments flood the feeds of users, yet the rhetoric of those images often escapes critical detection and evades public discourse. This ubiquity without scrutiny renders intimaesthetics almost invisible, even as it quietly shapes the contours of contemporary digital culture. By saturating the screens of users without demanding interrogation, intimaesthetics subtly defines how we perform and perceive intimacy in the age of new media—and that subtlety makes it all the more potent. *Homebodies* defamiliarizes the invisible quality of intimaesthetics by revealing its mechanisms of production, circulation, and consumption. Intimaesthetics, then, might seem to be everywhere, but the mere naming of it reveals how moving bodies both *use media* and are *used by media*.

Researching Intimacy

The theory of intimaesthetics—with its choreographies of body, space, and media and politics of circulation—developed from the study of thousands of home dance videos on Instagram dated between 2010 and 2020. The methodological approach to this study consists of three prongs: the platform selection; the collection of home dance videos; and the choreographic, textual, and paratextual analyses of those videos and the accounts on which they were posted. A discussion of each prong grounds this study in its processes of data collection and analysis and provides further detail on its scope and scale.

Home dance videos circulate on and across a range of new media platforms: YouTube, Facebook, TikTok, X, Tumblr, Snapchat, and Instagram—to name a few. Each platform has its own technical particularities (e.g., feature sets, interface design, algorithms, and privacy settings), as well as its own culture of content production, engagement, and circulation. This book underscores, however, how the technological specificities of a platform are in dialogical relation to its culture of production and consumption. Cultures of production on a given platform are, in other words, the product of and the catalyst for the system's structuring. The research design of this study thus focuses on a particular platform: Instagram. Analyzing content on one platform enables a more nuanced investigation of how the settings, features, interface design, algorithms, and company policies and culture all impact the ways in which media is produced, circulated, and consumed on that platform.

The choice of centering this investigation on Instagram in particular—rather than one of the other platforms mentioned above—is a result of several factors. First, Instagram's foundational logic is the circulation of *images* (both still and moving), as opposed to a combination of text, images, and links for the web (like, e.g., X and Facebook). Instagram, after all, began as a photography platform where users could apply ready-made filters to their photos and then share those photos with friends.[37] The addition of video in 2013 enabled users to expand their techniques, thereby broadening the image's capacity for aestheticizing intimacy.[38] Second, Instagram's approach to the personal profile encourages the marketization of self. While the feed—or the stream of recent content posted by users that an individual is following—is the primary page for accessing content, the anchor of the app is the user's profile. In other words, the feed operates on currency, whereas the profile operates on longevity and latitudinal development. The information offered through the profile allows the user to curate their digital identity over time, facilitating what I call autochoreography, outlined in chapter 2.

While other platforms, namely TikTok, may also revolve around images and offer development of personal brand through the profile, Instagram largely defined this combination of functions well before TikTok entered the market in 2017 (for iOS and Android users), thereby emphasizing Instagram's historical relevance.[39] This point gestures toward the final factor in *Homebodies*'s focus on Instagram: how the development of the platform sits at a pivotal point in the trajectory of social media more broadly. While new media has had a relatively short history, it notoriously consists of rapid developments—both in the perpetual updates to individual platforms and in the speedy transmission of ideas and images—so much so that a short amount of time compacts a profusion of shifts in the cultural and technological landscape of new media.[40] The decade of 2010–20 captures a series of major shifts that occurred in this terrain: the development and implementation of behavior-predicting algorithms, the intensification of commercial advertising in and through everyday media artifacts, the political and commercial leveraging of echo chambers, and the abrupt pivot from in-person to online engagement during the COVID-19 pandemic in 2019/20 (depending on the country), to name a few. Instagram's own development coincides with these wider changes: Instagram launched in 2010, was acquired by a major social media company in 2012 (then Facebook, now Meta), added "sponsored post" advertising in 2013, changed its algorithm from a chronological feed to a "relevant" one in 2016, and became a locus for belonging and home quarantine communication during the early moments of the pandemic. These developments demonstrate how Instagram is entwined with the wider landscape of new media; and they also point to how the platform is an apt and appropriate venue through which to consider the cultural production of intimacy under the command of neoliberalism. The rise of Instagram thus heralds the emergence of other new media platforms, like TikTok, that similarly aestheticize and commodify intimacy.[41]

My use of the term "new media," as opposed to "social media," requires a bit of unpacking in and of itself. New media, appearing in the subtitle of the book, refers to a type of media object (text, image, etc.) that is produced and/or transmitted digitally.[42] I add "in the age of" to describe the historical period wherein this type of media proliferated, the beginning of which some scholars place before the internet, though the life of this type of media is now associated with internet cultures.[43] Considering this technological linking, the age of new media began well before the historical focus of this book. Nonetheless, the period of 2010 to 2020 focuses the discussion of new media to the particular decade when new media became fused with digital culture's co-optation of intimacy.

The term "new media" not only functions as a historical marker in the title of the book but also appears throughout the chapters to reference the objects of analysis. This word choice is deliberate. Even though Instagram is often considered a social media platform, I resist this language in my conceptualization of intimaesthetics. Instead, my use of "new media" captures critical concepts that run through digital culture and seep in and out of social media—concepts like intimacy, privacy, surveillance, personal branding, algorithmic tracking, and the digital archive. Thus, while my analysis is focused on a social media platform, the implications of that analysis resonate more widely and thus require a broader term to reflect broader implications.

The second prong of my method concentrates on locating thousands of media that this study involved: following and scrolling through the profiles of known performers, often "microcelebrities"; locating other performer profiles through the follower counts of known accounts and then scanning those profiles; scraping media that included hashtags like #homedance, #homedancer, #kitchendance, #bedroomdance, and #homepractice; and finding media with those same keywords simply by engaging directly on the platform. A prerequisite for locating these videos was that the users

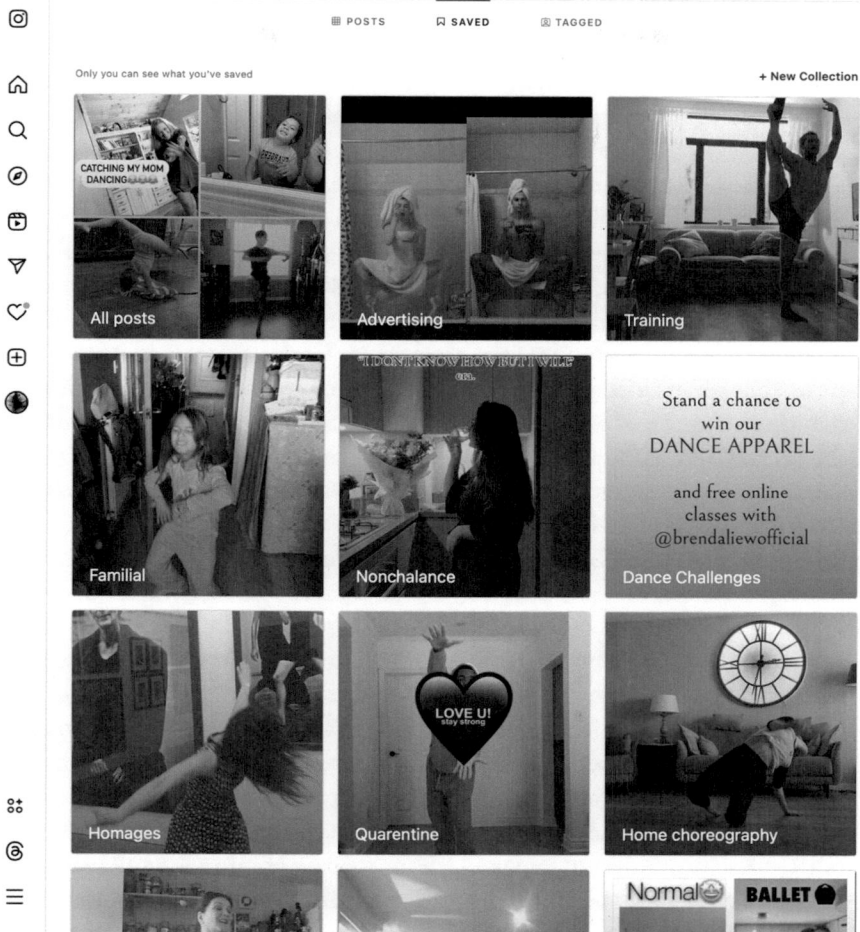

Fig. 1. Screenshot of saved Instagram posts with different collections for various analytical themes

who posted the content would have had to have a public profile. Thus, all the media at the time of its collection was publicly available. Upon finding a home dance video, I would use Instagram's "bookmark" feature (later renamed "collection") to organize the content into a folder—folders like "advertisement" (for when a dancer was marketing some product or service), "family dancing" (for when an individual seemed to be dancing with or for a family member), and "trainings" (for when individuals appeared to be rehearsing some previously learned material) (see fig. 1). This approach to utilizing Instagram's own features in ways that the platform did not intend became a tactical research method. Indeed, Instagram is littered with media objects; however, the platform offers tools that the researcher might leverage toward the critical study of those objects. Such a *within-and-against* approach allowed me to take a critical cross-section of Instagram (i.e., home dance videos that float across user groups, hashtag aggregations, and other boundaries of digital culture) in order to examine the aestheticization of intimacy via that platform.

The tension between the public nature of the videos I examined for this study and the personal, intimate content of those videos underscores my theory of intimaesthetics. Despite this facet of *Homebodies*, I have deliberately chosen to not include the screenshots of the videos I analyze. The posts that serve as case studies in each chapter contain identifying information and personal content—albeit content that may be aestheticized for the purposes of public circulation. Nonetheless, my own reproduction of those images would undercut my critique of Instagram for its cultivation, circulation, and pillaging of intimate data.

For this reason, I have commissioned hand-drawn representations of the digital performances I study. By including artist-created illustrations as opposed to screenshots of the actual posts, I aim to defamiliarize the digital immediacy of the performances under examination, foregrounding the mediated nature of the images while also respecting the personal contexts from which they originate. These renderings provide a critical distance that emphasizes the constructedness of the intimaesthetic image without reproducing the conditions of digital visibility that may further exploit the performers' data. In this way, the drawings serve as interpretive representations, allowing readers to engage with the themes of intimacy and privacy, as revealed through the analyses of those media, without perpetuating the complexities of digital exposure that platforms like Instagram perpetuate. This approach aligns with the broader ethical concerns of my work, which serves to critique the ways in which digital platforms co-opt intimate performances for commercial and corporate gain.

The significance of this study lies in its critical examination of how intimacy is actively constructed and aestheticized within the landscape of new media. By introducing the concept of intimaesthetics, this work unveils the intricate mechanisms through which individuals choreograph their bodies, spaces, and media to produce images that cultivate a sense of closeness and familiarity—all while vying for visibility in a saturated digital environment. This challenges the prevailing assumption of intimacy as an innate, universal human experience, revealing it instead as a dynamic process shaped by cultural, technological, and economic forces.

By focusing on home dance videos on Instagram, the study highlights the interplay between personal agency and platform control, emphasizing how the attention economy incentivizes the sharing of personal moments to capture audience engagement. At the same time, it exposes how performers navigate the tensions of expressing individuality and authenticity while being subject to algorithmic determinations, data collection, and neoliberal commodification. This examination sheds light on the subtle ways in which everyday performances in everyday spaces are appropriated by digital platforms, contributing to a broader understanding of surveillance and the marketization of personal expression in the twenty-first century.

Given these considerations, *Homebodies: Performance and Intimacy in the Age of New Media* is designed to engage readers in the field of performance studies, particularly those with an interest in the intersections of performance and intimacy within a network society. The book will resonate, more specifically, with readers invested in examining how image-centric platforms transform conventional conceptions of performance, pushing intimacy into new aesthetic and transactional realms. The theoretical framework of intimaesthetics will be of particular interest to readers concerned with the broader cultural implications of these performances, particularly in relation to identity, agency, and surveillance within the neoliberal context of Web 2.0. Discourses on dance help to ground these discussions and underscore the value of the dancing body in new media. As an interdisciplinary text, *Homebodies* thus stretches across fields of study to articulate the pervasive aestheticization of intimacy in twenty-first-century digital culture.

Typology of Intimaesthetics

Researching the intricacies of performed intimacy through the study of home dance videos ultimately reveals a typology of intimaesthetics, which structures this book. The fulcrum of this typology is how—despite the range in semiotics of space, sociocultural situation, and economies of circulation—home dance videos on Instagram articulate two critical features: a relationship between the performer and the camera and a relationship between the performer and cameraperson. For the former, the performer either acknowledges the camera or not, thereby using their gaze and facing in different ways. For the latter, the video indicates that either the performer was also the one to set up the camera and record themselves or someone else was in the space recording the action. Both elements become entwined with the semiotics of the video, so much so that the viewer understands the degree of self-production without dwelling on the meaning of the camera movement. Similarly, the viewer may receive the *effect* of the performer's recognition of the camera but might not unpack how the choreographies of body, space, and media cultivate that sensibility. These two relationships of performer-to-camera and performer-to-cameraperson ultimately cleave to form four types of intimaesthetics: one in which the performer does *not* acknowledge the camera and suggests that they did *not* record the video; one in which the performer *does* acknowledge the camera and suggests that they *did* record the video; one in which the performer does *not* acknowledge the camera but suggests they *did* record the video; and, finally, one in which the performer *does* acknowledge the camera but suggests that they did *not* record the video.

Each type of intimaesthetic is constructed through layers of choreography, and then those choreographies open out to particular intricacies of their respective online circulations. The four chapters of this book offer an in-depth investigation of these types of intimaesthetics, respectively: *candid dancing, moving selfie, nonchalant gestures*, and *home concerts*. Chapter 1 focuses on candid dancing, the type of intimaesthetic where the dancer does not acknowledge the camera and seemingly is not the one who recorded the video. This relationship between performer, camera, and cameraperson thus suggests that the person in the frame does not know they are being filmed, much less watched. Through a grounding in theories of the gaze, the analysis of this intimaesthetic reveals the *choreography of abandon*, a concept that describes, on the one hand, the performer's desire to move beyond the capturing forces of the gaze and, on the other hand, the omnipresent gaze that captures the (seemingly) unseen interior performing body. Once online, candid dancing media acquires an affective dimension around the apparent authenticity of its movement, promulgating a softening of surveillance. This chapter thus draws together a performance studies approach to the politics of watching and a media studies approach to surveillance to demonstrate the political intricacies of intimaesthetics in a post-panoptic surveillance society.[44]

Chapter 2 focuses on what I call the moving selfie, wherein the performer acknowledges the camera and makes obvious their role as both subject and producer of the image. Drawing on the wider phenomenon of selfie-ism, this type articulates the performer's work in creating an image that represents their digital identity. Such a process illustrates the homebody's *autochoreography*, or choreography of self. Once uploaded to a platform like Instagram, the image then acquires a new character, as it not only contributes to a personal brand that the performer actively shapes but also is subjected to the rhythms of the algorithm, over which the performer has no agency. In this way, the performer's autochoreography gestures toward the tensions between the user's sovereignty and the platform's power in determining one's digital identity.

Chapter 3 addresses nonchalant gestures, the type of intimaesthetic where the dancer does not acknowledge the camera but makes obvious that they created the production. Similar to candid dancing discussed in chapter 1, the nonchalant gestures type presents a surveillance aesthetic, but one that is part of the dancer's own crafting. Their way of modeling privacy through their nonchalance toward/with the camera reflects their *choreography of oblivion*. In other words, by performing an obliviousness of and for the audience, the performer shapes a narrative of forgottenness: they seemingly forget the camera and, in doing so, create an image of domestic oblivion. Suggesting their own *forgottenness*, *marginality*, and *rogueness*, the performer provides an image of the paradoxes of memory: unseen and seen, forgotten and remembered, absent and present. Then, the online circulation of the image exacerbates those paradoxes, as its circulation folds the performance into systems of memory and enables its engagement with cultural dialogue, but through algorithmic determination.

Chapter 4 focuses on the final type of intimaesthetic, home concerts. Structured through the performer's recognition of the camera, yet with the suggestion of another person's involvement (as the camera operator), home concerts touch on the aestheticization of intimacy through familiarity and familiality. The performer, that is, is conducting themselves *in concert* with someone else in their space. This type of intimaesthetic is fleshed out through an analysis of a specific phenomenon on social media wherein parents create and manage accounts in their children's names—accounts specifically devoted to images of their children. Through their choreographies of body, space, and media, the parent and child jointly contribute to what I describe as *minor choreography*, a coordinated fashioning of a child's public persona. The child's expression of gender, in particular, comes into focus in this chapter. The ambiguity, however, of the parent's role in that expression is integral to this type of intimaesthetic. It ultimately articulates a problematic confusion of roles, responsibilities, and authority over one's image and digital identity. Then, once circulating on Instagram, these images give way to the platform's own minor orchestrations—which includes (1) the inculcation of systems of value that are expressed through the image and (2) the expansion of the platform's marketability of youth audiences and youth culture.

While these chapters articulate the typology of intimaesthetics, as determined by the relational dynamic of performer, camera, and cameraperson, they reflect different phenomena in digital culture to varying degrees. For instance, chapter 2 on the moving selfie represents a wide swath of media online, whereas chapter 1 on the phenomenon of caught dancing reflects a much smaller portion of media. Moreover, each chapter captures a type of intimaesthetic, but I demonstrate that type through case studies that may represent a more niche practice or movement in digital culture. For chapters 1 and 2, the type of intimaesthetic happens to capture an existing practice on social media: *candid dancing* is animated through the hashtag #caughtdancing; and the *moving selfie* corresponds to the broader practice of selfie-ism. For chapters 3 and 4, however, the relationship is a bit looser: *nonchalant gestures*, as a type of intimaesthetic, is demonstrated through media where fans perform homages to public figures, an admittedly more niche practice online. Similarly, *home concerts* is a broad category of intimaesthetics but is exemplified through a trend of parent-managed accounts featuring children. Despite these variations in how the typology of intimaesthetics aligns with practices and phenomena in digital culture, the videos I spotlight nonetheless function to animate and exemplify the typology under discussion.

Though distinct in its relationship between example and intimaesthetic, each chapter highlights existing home dance videos to both substantiate and demonstrate the theoretical arguments of *Homebodies*. These media serve as exemplars of that type and in no way exhaust the field of media that reflects that type of intimaesthetic. As a way to highlight the techniques of practice and to critique the politics of circulation, I delve deep into two examples for each intimaesthetic, following each one from production to circulation and consumption. This choice of depth over breadth challenges Instagram's logic of overabundance and overstimulation. Indeed, Instagram is cluttered with intimaesthetic media, contributing to an uncritical consumption culture. Yet, my practice of zooming in on certain videos from a system of content overload and engaging with that media with careful analysis defies social media's carousel of chaos.

Each of the four chapters follows the same score, structured through parts 1, 2, and 3. Part 1 entails a theoretical grounding of the type of intimaesthetic covered in the chapter, which includes a genealogy, discussion of aesthetics and semiotics of the image, and the naming and description of a particular mode of choreography that constructs the intimaesthetic (respectively, choreography of abandon, autochoreography, choreography of oblivion, and minor choreography). Part 2 explores the production of each intimaesthetic through a choreographic analysis of two home dance videos, each one modeling a different version of the mode of choreography discussed in the chapter. Part 3 delves into the intricacies of the circulation for the respective intimaesthetics. In addition, at the beginning of each chapter is a short video of me dancing in my own home, which serves to model the type of intimaesthetics of focus in that chapter. Like stretching our limbs before a theory jog, these performances allow us to warm up to another intimaesthetic, while also capturing the techniques and approaches of that type. And maybe, *maybe*, we might cultivate a sense of closeness in the process.

ONE

Candid Dancing

An adult man dances alone in the kitchen to the song on the radio. He looks as though he is in the process of putting away groceries. All of a sudden, he picks up two tissue boxes, one in each hand, and expressively gestures upward with his arms.

Does he know we are watching him?

His eyes are closed as he smiles with delight in himself, in the music, and in his Kleenex box promenade.

No, he is completely unaware of an audience. Would he be doing this if he knew we were watching?

Elsewhere, in a different home across the globe, a woman dances to what could very well be her favorite song as she mops the dining room floor. The camera jostles as she performs a moonwalk-esque slide backwards, using the mop to leverage a twist and kick.

Indeed, these dancers do not know we are here: they do not see the person peering in on them from around the corner of their respective spaces, observing their dancing in stealth while recording the action with a camera; and they do not know that their dancing will be the subject of innumerable views online, including our own.

Introduction

Scrolling through one's Instagram feed may reveal glimpses of a subtle, yet poignant phenomenon wherein a person is caught dancing in the home. The scene unfolds as an onlooker in the home discovers the seemingly private dance, grabs a camera, and records the event. The dancer might be lost in thought or activity, not even realizing they are dancing, or they may be merely trying out some new moves. Unbeknownst to them, their movements are the subject of humor and delight to another. The onlooker who catches the dancer, however, is not the sole audience. Instead, the video makes its way online to meet the eyes of innumerable viewers. The vignettes above animate this phenomenon, articulating a gap between the audience's omniscience of the scene and the dancer's experience of introspective embodiment. Their scenes, the subject of greater in-depth analysis later in the chapter, reveal how the seemingly unseen dancing body becomes the subject of both discipline and fetishization. This body, in other words, is inscribed with a contradictory logic of, on the one hand, unauthorized abandon and, on the other hand, the whimsy of unmediated existence.

Candid dancing reflects this process, transforming a mere jig in the kitchen or boogie in the dining room, intended to be unseen by even familiar parties, into an event that can be easily uploaded, time-stamped, circulated through feeds, and viewed by anyone and everyone. This chapter traces this scale-jumping process, from production to circulation to consumption, to unpack how the candid dancing intimaesthetic is particularly fraught with a politics of the gaze. Namely, the candid dancing video demonstrates (1) the choreography of abandon, wherein the performer's embodiment works to transgress the gaze; and (2) a desire on the viewer's end to fetishize and discipline a subject who dares engage in such a choreography. Layers of surveillance are embedded within the scene: from its initial, covert discovery, to its mediatization, to its online circulation. In the process, these media become rhetorical vessels for complex issues surrounding race, gender, sexuality, class, and other facets of identity.

Indeed, the candid dancing body is imbued with a political valence. The issues that this body presents are threaded throughout this chapter, presented in three parts that approach candid dancing through a different lens. Part 1 reveals the theoretical, historical, and aesthetic underpinnings of the candid dancing movement by unpacking its cultural genealogy, defining the concept of the *choreography of abandon*, and articulating the semiotics of the candid dancing body and scene. Part 2 animates the theories discussed in part 1 by offering an in-depth analysis of two candid dancing videos found on Instagram—the same two videos briefly described above. Together, this analysis reveals, for the performer, the appeal of unfastening from the body's patternings and, for the onlooker and viewer, the desire to surveil and discipline the unseen dancing body. Part 3 follows this discussion with a consideration of the online life of candid dancing media, including its *eventicization* and its incorporation into a digital system wherein media objects are categorized, framed, and imbued with affect. Specifically, the ways in which a candid dancing video becomes an *event* through its online circulation underscore the aesthetic, semiotic, and ontological leap it takes from the private, personal, and unseen world to a public, ocular-centric sphere of intimaesthetics. The fact that the dancer is often not involved in the video's upload or considered to be the owner of the post further riddles the online life of the candid dancing video with issues of authorship, ownership, and origin. Once in the space of individual ownership (manifesting through the personal profile), the candid dancing video acquires an entertainment value and its humor begins to mask its operations of surveillance and discipline, which then reiterates the power of those operations. This outcome ultimately reveals the reincorporation of the candid dancer back into the visual economy that they seemingly sought to abandon.

Part 1. Defining Candid Dancing

Candid dancing videos that circulate on new media today have their roots in other streams of cultural practices and products. A genealogy of the candid reveals threads of influence in proverbs about the unseen dancing body (i.e., "dance like nobody's watching"), as well as the notion of the "candid camera." These instances of historical precedent represent some desire either to let loose beyond the reach of the gaze, in the case of the former, or to "catch" an unsuspecting subject, in the case of the latter. While these two instances do not exhaust the breadth of cultural, social, and technological antecedents, they reflect a sliver of history that helps explain the meaning of candid dancing and its life on new media.

Appearing perhaps in some calligraphy font, the phrase *dance like nobody's watching* appears on/in a range of cultural products: blasted on T-shirts and coffee mugs, featured on myriad motivational signs and posters, and even written into the lyrics of songs played on repeat. Neither event nor object, *dance like nobody's watching* lives a social life that is not tethered to any one *thing*, but may be attached to virtually any product or image.

Its wide circulation and broad popularity across the popular imaginary (particularly in English-speaking domains) give this authorless phrase a cliché status. That is to say, it tends not to prompt deeper conversation or evoke additional questions or comments from its audience; rather, it is often used as a one-liner: a singular piece of advice that does not seem to address any particular problem or concern but might cultivate a sense of excitement and whimsy. Of course, this seemingly innocuous piece of advice is fraught with politics surrounding the body, the gaze, and the social mis/perceptions of dance. Before unpacking this political dimension, it is helpful to first consider the textual structure of the phrase.

The grammatical structuring of *dance like nobody's watching*, specifically its status as a command, articulates a moral dimension through its presumed universality. That is, the subject of the phrase is an implied "you": an address to a universal audience. "(You) dance like nobody's watching." The suggestion here is that anyone and everyone who encounters the phrase will understand the plight of being watched while dancing—that to dance is human and the urge to dance alone satisfies a base desire. Following the essentialist logic embedded in the phrase, the gaze sullies whatever authenticity of body and subject may be derived from dancing alone and thereby impedes the dancer's pursuit of some ideal state of uninhibitedness. The *unseen*, in this respect, appears to be tethered to a sense of moral purity found in transcendent interiority, whereas the sphere of the *seen* is subject to external forces that encumber the "natural body" and its divine expression of individuality and agency.[1]

The suggestions of morality articulated through the command status of the phrase are further complicated by the implications of the word *like*. This seemingly minor word draws a comparison between dancing with an audience and dancing without an audience. The suggestions of this element are twofold. On the one hand, the comparison implies that to dance *like* nobody's watching is to dance in the presence of others but to use one's imaginative faculties to *imagine* as if no spectator were present. In this understanding of the phrase, the word *like* emphasizes not only that there is a difference between dancing with others present and dancing alone but also that that difference is sharp enough to be salient to anyone and everyone who encounters the phrase. On the other hand, there exists another, more politically charged reading, which indicates that perhaps there is *no dancing* that is not watched—no dancing that is beyond the reach of the gaze. One can only dance *like* nobody is watching because they cannot dance *when* nobody's watching, as the powers of the gaze are omnipresent. In other words, to pretend no one is watching, as a way of accessing abandon, one must know what it is like to dance alone. However, making such a connection only reinforces the presence and powers of the gaze—both while dancing in the presence of others and while dancing alone. This reading points to the possibility that, even when the dancer might suspect no immediate audience is present, the gaze remains. It remains through the dancer's envisioning of their own movement, through the patternings and habitations of their body, through the imaginary audience they may perceive, and, finally, through the processes of mapping the experiences of "dancing like nobody's watching" back onto their unwatched movements. Indeed, the unseen dancing body, though eager to escape the gaze, has, on many levels, internalized its audience. They may dance *like* nobody's watching, but never without the complex layers of visuality that determine their body and movement.

Shaped by its textual structuring, *dance like nobody's watching* is rife with implications about the powers of the gaze. Seemingly, the phrase is a recommendation for all to release, suspend, or transcend the restrictions that the outsider's gaze and judgment place on one's body and movement.[2] Yet, its invocation tends to reinscribe the powers of the gaze rather than absolve one from them. The irony here is that, in dancing like nobody's watching, one must simultaneously recognize the power of the gaze, imagine themselves moving beyond it, and then perform that imagined state in the presence of viewers—viewers whose visuality represents the very forces that the dancer attempts to evade. By identifying the source of one's duress, they are in fact reaffirming that entity's power.

Through a visual image of the seemingly unseen dancing body, candid dancing manifests many of the same politics that underpin the logic of *dance like nobody's watching*. While the two examples differ in their form, contexts for production, and affective registers, they both evoke a subject that believes themselves to dance beyond the reach of the gaze. Both phenomena work to maintain the purity of the interior dancing body so that the dancer is encouraged to experience some sense of abandon and viewers are delighted to encounter it. Both capture the complex messaging around dancing alone, in private, and without an audience, suggesting a simultaneous delight in unfastening from the gaze and humiliation upon discovery. This simultaneous fetishization and disciplining of the unseen dancing body is central to the phenomenon of candid dancing.

If the phrase *dance like nobody's watching* reflects the appeal of moving beyond the gaze from the *dancer's* perspective, then *candid camera* articulates a fascination with that body from the *viewer's* perspective. Like the semiotic richness of *dance like nobody's watching*, the latter movement represents a host of political and cultural intricacies dealing with the plea-sures of watching the moving body, including the softening of surveil-lance, a voyeuristic interest in the seemingly natural body, and the disguise of humor. A discussion of this cultural phenomenon and its underlying logic, however, requires a review of its namesake: an American television program that began in 1948 and aired for thirty-eight seasons, ultimately ending in 1992.[3]

The show *Candid Camera*, created and hosted by Allen Funt, is based on the premise of pre-orchestrated pranks carried out on unknowing and typically ordinary individuals. A single episode consists of five or six dif-ferent practical jokes or otherwise unusual situations—each devised and orchestrated by Funt and his team. These scenarios typically unfold in everyday spaces: parks, elevators, hotel rooms, markets, sidewalks, zoos, or other types of public and private spaces. Hidden cameras would then capture the action as it unfolds, ultimately ending in a moment of reveal, wherein the subject discovers the camera and crew. At this point, the sub-ject is told, "Smile, you're on Candid Camera," a now iconic catchphrase that, for the subject of the prank, would then clarify the otherwise confus-ing or startling events that had preceded.

The affective sensibility of the show is lighthearted and humorous. Funt even claims of *Candid Camera* that the show can act as "laughter therapy" for the audience.[4] The quality of humor that Funt indicates is reinforced, if not cultivated, in a technical manner by the addition of studio laughter, which may be heard at points intended to be funny: someone discovering a talking mailbox, trying to start a car with no motor, or reach-ing for a wallet attached to a string that moves with every attempt to grab it. The narrator, too, verbally walks the audience through the joke, telling them what to look for as the situation unfolds. These aspects of the show work to ensure laughter from the audience at home, instructing them on how to perceive the otherwise bizarre and confusing situations of the show.

The element of humor that *Candid Camera* constructs works to not only clarify for the audience any confusion around the events but also alle-viate whatever anxieties might arise around the role of the hidden camera. The success of the joke is, after all, contingent upon the subject not recog-nizing the camera and production crew. In other words, the individual be-ing filmed must maintain their *candor* in order for the audience to perceive the scene as humorous. As Stanley Milgram and John Sabini note, this sense of candor allows the audience to relate to the subject of the joke.[5] The audience, that is, can imagine themselves in the scene: being filmed, being watched, and being humiliated. At the same time, the viewer is insulated from the prank, as they are able to sit back and watch the scene unfold. This dual perspective might create a dissonance for the viewer between the ordinary and extraordinary qualities of the show. So, while the joke's unique scenario might seem funny to the viewer, the everydayness of its setting compounds with the apparatus of the hidden camera to send the viewer an unsettling message: "This could be you."

Indeed, humor shapes the mood and reception of the show, yet its subtext articulates the omnipresence of surveillance. However, surveillance also plays into the aesthetics of the show and reveals a certain embrace of the tensions between voyeurism and everydayness. As Fred Nadis writes:

> Funt intentionally gave his footage the feeling of a wiretap or surveillance film. He insisted on a stripped down aesthetic for his show, with apparently only one camera recording a scene to give the audience a surveillance camera perspective. Sequences were concluded and connected with lap dissolves showing Venetian blinds closing on a scene, blacking it out and opening to the next.[6]

Funt combines these audio and visual techniques to aestheticize surveillance. This dimension of the show compounds the obvious role of the hidden camera—without it there would be no show—and the technical construction of humor to effectively soften surveillance. The outcome is twofold: (1) In seeing what the surveillant assemblage sees, the audience becomes part of that assemblage; and (2) in finding the humor in such a scene, the audience becomes conditioned to think differently about what it means to *be watched*. "Maybe surveillance isn't so bad."[7]

Rooted in a twentieth-century geopolitical landscape, *Candid Camera* set in motion a larger and more widespread movement that continues into the twenty-first century. While the show is not solely responsible for aestheticizing surveillance or for popularizing voyeuristic practices, it nonetheless initiated the cultural phenomenon of catching people in some act of apparent authenticity.[8] The phrase "Smile, you're on Candid Camera" became a sticky utterance for anyone holding a camera, capturing some reality of the moment. Perhaps, too, these practices borrowed a surveillance aesthetic and propagated a fascination with looking in on the unknowing body.

Considering the longevity and popular appeal of *Candid Camera*, it is no surprise that surveillance aesthetics and voyeuristic practices continue to thrive in new media. The appearance of these aesthetics and practices in contemporary digital culture speaks to the momentum of Funt's maneuvers with the camera, his orchestrations of/in everyday space, and his instruction in the humor of watching the unaware subject. Indeed, the candid camera is more than just a television program—it is an artistic and social practice and a cultural phenomenon. Its tenets appear in everyday photography, film and television, and design. Jonathan Finn reflects this point when charting the practice of surveillance aesthetics in everyday photography:

> Surveillance is no longer to be conceived as a technology employed by the state in the control of dangerous populations or a tool used by corporations to serve the interests of global capital, but is something that we encounter in advertisements and corporate communication, in video footage for news broadcasts and in our favourite (and least favourite) television programmes and films.[9]

Though Finn does not cite *Candid Camera* in his discussion of how surveillance manifests and how it has changed over time, we might imagine how televisual constructions of candor factor into the gradual shift of surveillance away from government control and toward capitalist enterprise. Ultimately, this shift gestures toward the imbrication of Candid Camera in Web 2.0, including the rise of candid dancing. Surveillance aesthetics appear, for instance, in how the camera operator furtively captures the dancer without being detected, and the softening of surveillance takes effect in the entertainment value that the video accrues online, namely, how viewers come to view the scene as funny. While these matters are discussed in further detail in subsequent sections of the chapter, the connections between the two phenomena are critical to understanding the meaning of candid dancing.

Together, *Candid Camera* and *dance like nobody's watching* demonstrate the powers of the gaze, while also underscoring how notions of candor are inherently embodied. While the phenomena that these objects represent shape an understanding of the candid dancing video, there are also many distinctions that set this new iteration apart from its cultural antecedents. Namely, the production, circulation, and consumption of the candid dancing video are aesthetically and semiotically tethered to the dancing body. This body is imbued with complexities of gender, race, sexuality, class, and ability, and, as such, shapes the meaning of the unseen dancer and whatever apparatus of surveillance capture them. Thus, more so than its cultural influences, the candid dancing video on new media becomes a moving emblem of twenty-first-century systems of power, as it both foregrounds the politics of the dancing body and provides a quintessential picture of contemporary modalities of surveillance. At the same time, the subject attempts to move *beyond* those systems to seek respite from the tolls they bring—to dance somewhere those powers seemingly cannot access. The *choreography of abandon* captures this struggle: the struggle to recognize how one is choreographed, while also working to unfasten from that choreography.

Choreography of Abandon

Upon first glance, the choreography of abandon may seem oxymoronic (*How can abandon be choreographed?*). According to Susan Leigh Foster, choreography articulates "a structuring of deep and enduring cultural values," which manifests foremost through the body.[10] Yet, the notion of bodily abandon alludes to the relinquishment of such a structuring. Capturing the tension between these two positions, the choreography of abandon reflects a cultural attitude toward the body: the appeal of unfastening from the ways in which the body is choreographed, while also gesturing toward the impossibility of that endeavor. In other words, if bodies are always entrenched in systems of value, which appear in and become reiterated through movement, then, seemingly, different ways of moving may offer a respite from the tolls that those systems take on the body. Like the mirage in the desert, the prospect of abandonment offers this illusion but cannot fulfill any complete untethering from the codes and conventions that determine the body. The term is, thus, inherently paradoxical, as one may never undo their own patternings, never strip away their acculturations, never access a purely natural body—as much as they might flitter and twist, waggle and whip, jostle and jive.

The systems from which the body seeks to unfasten are numerous: the impositions of public space; the requirements of sociality; the demands of the market; and, among others, the pressures of one's gender, race, ethnicity, sexuality, and class. Of course, undergirding these streams of activity is the disciplining gaze, which regulates the body in subtle yet effective ways. The mere participation in those systems tends to ingrain obedience in bodies and secure compliance. In this way, these everyday structures of power—articulated through public space, social engagement, and the capitalist marketplace—resemble those enforced through *panopticism.*[11] According to Michel Foucault's outline of this theory, the disciplining gaze does not need to actively enforce anything to render its subject obedient. Instead, the subject's recognition of its presence creates merely the *pos-*

sibility of enforcement and is thus enough to discipline the subject. This trickery results in the self-disciplining, self-censoring, and self-correction of the subject, thereby producing "docile bodies."[12]

While panopticism has influenced a range of disciplines and continues to impact innumerable fields of study, the life of its discourse has developed since Foucault's writing. As surveillance studies scholar David Lyon notes, Foucault's theory aims at a critique of visuality, which Lyon deems to be productive in unpacking the power of watching. Lyon continues that panopticism, with its focus on physical structures and a concentrated source of power, may also be limiting. It does not, for instance, attend to the "growth of mass media and thus the persistence of 'spectacle.'"[13] For Lyon, the power of watching takes effect through a more disaggregated network of control. The subtlety of these more covert mechanisms ultimately ensures their effectiveness.[14] That is, if power is not looming in the face of the subject—as is the panoptic tower in the center of a circular structure—then it may continue to dominate its subjects without them knowing. This manner of docility-through-subtlety reflects the power evident in what Roy Boyne calls "post-panopticism."[15]

The choreography of abandon is grounded in a theoretical space between Foucault and Lyon. Following Foucault, it reflects a recognition of the power inherent in visuality and the subject's internalization of obedience; yet, following Lyon, it also attends to a more decentralized network of power and the role that mass media and digital technologies play in the activation and enforcement of that power. Twenty-first-century mechanisms of power have, after all, evolved from the nineteenth-century examples that Foucault engages. The onslaught of new media and the persistence of neoliberalism have, in particular, ensured that power manifests through social, cultural, and economic systems of activity and that subjects are active in their own subordination via their engagement in those systems. In this landscape lies the perpetual inundation of images, the cultivation of a consumerist allure, and the routinization of identity data collection. However apprehensively, enthusiastically, or otherwise unknowingly, individuals engage in this landscape and, as such, must learn to navigate its rocky terrain of excess and post-panoptic surveillance. Through this activity, like swimming against a water's current, docile bodies become *exhausted bodies*.[16]

As a response to these subtle yet effective operations of power, the choreography of abandon promises to the subject a momentary retreat from the burden of excess and the toll of exhaustion that have come to define contemporary, post-panoptic life. To move seemingly beyond the reach of the gaze, in apparent solitude, is to engage in the choreography of abandon. It allows the individual a sense of solace in such momentary illusions of abandon. Yet, in doing so, the individual does not actually undo much in terms of their corporeal patternings or their relationship to the powers from which they seek to unfasten. In this way, the choreography of abandon is a tactic of, in Susan Sontag's terms, anesthetization. Sontag exclaims, "A capitalist society requires a culture based on images. It needs to furnish vast amounts of images in order to stimulate buying and anesthetize the injuries of class, race, and sex."[17] Abandon adds an additional layer to the process Sontag discusses: By engaging with a culture based on images, one works to anesthetize themselves from the injuries of class, race, and sex—but then, at some point, the very engagement with this culture requires relief as well.

The choreography of abandon claims not only the dancer but also the one who ultimately views the scene. To watch a body that is under the pretense of having no viewer—to see someone who does not want to be seen—is to observe an act that is seemingly not available in public life. The pleasures of this sight are manifold: First, the viewer is linked to the sheer rarity of the event, as if they had an exclusive ticket to a one-time-only show. Second, this sensibility is heightened by the notion that the dancer intends no audience nor is cognizant of one. The sight, then, acquires a lure of forbiddenness. Finally, the viewer's pleasure in watching the candid dancer is further complicated by the ways in which the dancer moves. That is to say, because the candid dancing body moves in ways that it may otherwise not move when in the presence of others, the viewer gets a glimpse of a body taken by its own inhibitions, and in its own habitat. This sensibility of the candid dancing body prompts the viewer to read that body as whimsical, if not erratic. Like footage of a creature in the wild, the sight of the candid dancing body cultivates some sense of an unmediated, unchoreographed existence. At the same time, the viewer might identify with the dancer as a fellow body and fellow subject of the forces that shape that body. From such a removed vantage point, then, the viewer may simultaneously consume the dancing body as an exotic curiosity while also relating to that figure and their attempts to unbind themselves.

Compounded together, these three layers of the viewer's experience underscore both an outside investment in the dancer's choreography and a cool, distant consumption of the image. The result of this process is particularly palpable when the dancing is recorded with a camera and that video is uploaded to new media. On a platform like Instagram, viewership not only is inevitable but also constructs the meaning of the content—a meaning that is linked to the dancer's very attempts to choreograph abandon. Once the dancer's movements are captured on camera and shared online, that is, the significance is determined by the video's display of a body in abandonment. The platform continues to circulate the content, expanding its scale of exposure as it becomes further engulfed in an ocular-centric world under the command of the gaze. Such instances of choreographing abandon thereby underscore its post-panoptic, neoliberal character.

While the choreography of abandon proves itself as much a mechanism of power as it does an illusion of escape for the dancer, it also functions as a lens of analysis for deconstructing representations of candid dancing. The videos that end up circulating on new media platforms reveal both the dancer's efforts to move beyond the gaze and the powers that reincorporate that body into a system of surveillance, discipline, and fetishization. The following section employs this lens to demonstrate how the choreography of abandon unfolds aesthetically in the moment of production, ultimately pointing to its semiotics of gender, sex, race, and class.

Aesthetics and Semiotics of the Candid Dancing Body

A primary meaning-making feature of the candid dancing video is the suggestion of the onlooker's presence and position, both of which are embedded in the aesthetics of the video. This feature is made obvious by the image's shaky frame, which is a result of the handheld approach of the cameraperson. Similar to the phenomenon of *home concerts*, discussed in chapter 4, this obvious factor of the frame immediately indicates to the viewer that the dancer is not the producer of the image. Instead, someone else is both looking in on the scene and recording its activity. Of course, the domestic setting further shapes the meaning of this encounter by suggesting that the cameraperson has a familiar (and possibly also familial) relationship to the dancer. Without seeing the cameraperson in the frame and without knowing either dancer or cameraperson on a personal level—as may be the case on social media—the viewer detects the closeness between the two parties. Whether a sibling, spouse, or roommate, the viewer understands that the candid dancing video is embedded in a wider and more storied history between dancer and cameraperson.

The camera movement not only suggests a separation of and relational dynamics between dancer and cameraperson but also gestures toward the furtive nature of the scene, as the onlooker must act quickly and quietly to effectively catch the dancer before being detected. When the cameraperson initially stumbles upon the scene, there is likely no time to thor-

oughly prepare the device or scene for recording or to record with preci-
sion. The result is a video that is stable enough to discern that the subject
is dancing—and perhaps to even reveal their identity—yet it still quivers
with every subtle movement of the onlooker's hand. This movement cues
to the viewer that (1) the cameraperson did not prepare to record this
moment and (2) the dancer did not realize that the cameraperson was
present. These elements of the candid dancing video—all sourced with
the camera movement—compose the basic structure of its semiotics: that
the event was captured in stealth because the dancer is unaware they are
being filmed.

Alongside the information revealed through the camera movement,
the dancer's directionality is also telling. Whether they may move about in
circularity or remain fixed to a particular facing, perhaps while looking in
the mirror, they are likely not facing the camera, as that would reveal their
audience and likely result in them no longer dancing. Because the dancer's
use of space seems untethered from the camera, their directionality appears happenstance, determined by a task in which they may be engaged.
Either lost in thought while dancing out their imagination or moving their
body while preoccupied with some other task—domestic or otherwise—
the candid dancer *dances-while*: *while* folding laundry, *while* watching television, *while* imagining their own concert performance, *while* eating lunch.
This character of preoccupation means that the dancer's facing is not a
determining factor in their performance but rather a coincidence.[18]

The dancer's seemingly aimless directionality is central to the semiotics of the candid dancing video, as it highlights the disciplining power that
the camera both represents and wields.[19] By *not* recognizing the camera,
the candid dancer suggests that they did not consent to being watched
or recorded. Nonetheless, the onlooker watches and the camera records.
Even more, the video that ultimately appears online reaches countless
others who also watch the dancer without either their express or their
implied consent. While the notion of consent on new media is the subject of discussion in part 3 of this chapter, it is relevant to the discussion
here, as it articulates how the aesthetic components of the dancer's performance—in particular, their gaze, facing, and focus of attention while
dancing—structure their inadvertent deference to the camera. After all, the
subject has no opportunity to surrender to the camera's gaze because they
do not even know a camera is present. Yet, their docility is implied by their
lack of recognition of the camera and their pursuit of abandon. Ultimately,
the dancing unknowingly reinscribes the camera's power to surveil.

The dancer's gaze and their inadvertent docility compound with the movement of the frame and the dancer's orientations in space to suggest a level of introspection that is not readily available in other types of intimaesthetics—and, even more generally, not readily available in presentational dance performance at large.[20] By not connecting with the camera, onlooker, or impending audience, and by dancing while engaged in some other activity or imaginative preoccupation, the dancer, in their movements, comportment, and use of space, indicates that their performance is for no audience but rather for themselves. This reading of introspection is further underscored by the drastic transition—a climax of sorts—that typically takes place in this type of video: the moment of discovery. Often in candid dancing videos, the camera captures not only the subject's dancing but also their *realization* once they understand they are being watched and filmed. In this moment, the dancer typically expresses shock, surprise, embarrassment, or some other sentiment that articulates a departure from their earlier state while dancing. Such a change in the dancer's movement, behavior, and emotional register helps define for the viewer the meaning of the dancing that occurred just before it. The suggestion here is that the actions taking place moments before the discovery are something that *should* elicit embarrassment. Dancing without an audience and in a space not intended for such an activity (as a stage or studio might be), the candid dancer moves beyond the conventions of visible domestic activity. Their performance represents a scene of *mundane deviance*.

The shift observed in the candid dancer not only underscores the deviance of their abandon but also enacts a sudden change in the dancer's own bodily experience. In the sharpest of moments, the dancer is abruptly drawn out of their moment with themselves—at which point, as described above, their gaze is understood to be directed inward—and forced into a different, unintended, and more externally focused mode of looking. As they spot the onlooker with a camera, they must come to terms with the audience they did not know they had and how their dancing may have been perceived by that audience. This rapid, if not forceful, shift in focus, attention, and gaze—from in to out, intra to extra—marks a deceit in the presumed privacy that secured the dancer to move in such a way in the first place. What they understood to be *unseen* was suddenly recast as *seen*, as their closed rehearsal had to be retroactively redefined as a staged performance. As the dancer registers this shift in their reality, they must do so all while continuing to be watched and filmed. So, not only is their seemingly private and personal performance jarred out of itself by the recognition of an audience, but also their reaction to that discovery inadvertently becomes part of their performance.

Of course, the dancer's kinesthetic experience of dancing and then getting caught is difficult to determine but important to consider. Specifically, recognizing the ways in which the dancer's experience might be divergent from that of the onlooker's reveals an intriguing irony in the candid dancing phenomenon: that the experience of introspection, or "looking inward," not only is *determined* by the outsider's eye but also is structured through a collection of aesthetic elements—the frame of the video, the dancer's position and facing in space, the distance between the camera and the subject, the dancer's gaze. Through these components, among others, the candid dancing body stands as an aesthetic emblem of introspection: an outside representation of interiority, regardless of whether the dancer is actually experiencing some state of introspection. It is these qualities of the dancer's performance—in particular, their closed eyes or meandering gaze, their absorption in their improvisatory style of movement, their obvious multitasking, their apparent absorption in those tasks—that shape the outsider's impressions of the moment.

The gap between the performer's experience and the onlooker's reading of their body as "introspective" maps onto a prime tension of the candid dance scene: that between the performer's unseen, private experience of dancing-while and the realm of "ocular hegemony," whereby visuality is wielded to maintain the dominance of the spectator's experience over that of the performer.[21] For the viewer of the candid dancing scene, the dancer is understood to be introspective because they have no visible audience to perform for and, in turn, must be lost in thought and their dancing must be spontaneous and whimsical. Such an appraisal, however, forecloses whatever choreographies—either premeditated or in the moment—may be involved in the dancer's activity, further complicating their sense of agency and consent. The candid dancing body, then, becomes a figure that cannot define itself but is instead determined by the many layers of the gaze that consume it, discipline it, and authorize its reproduction. It is simultaneously desired and ridiculed: desired because it conjures illusions of the natural body and ridiculed because those illusions betray its acculturations and comportments.[22] This semiotic collision of fetishization and discipline results in an image that is affectively unstable. It is both humiliating and humorous, evidence of a blunder and of voyeuristic desire, a warning and an enticement.

Indeed, the candid dancing body is a precarious figure, as it is subject to the powers of the gaze, the weight of its own desires and imaginative wanderings, the fascination and fetishization of the viewer, and the whims of circulation that shape the social life of the video product. While these layers are theoretically complex, they are most palpable through example, as the videos that end up circulating online reveal both the dancer's efforts to move beyond the gaze and the powers that reincorporate that body into a system of surveillance, discipline, and fetishization. The following section affords such attention through an in-depth analysis of two candid dancing videos on Instagram—the same instances introduced at the beginning of the chapter. Consideration of these examples reveals how discipline works to correct the candid dancing body, how surveillance manifests in the most unsuspecting corners of activity, and how efforts to abandon the body's structures of discipline get subsumed into mass circulation.

Part 2. Catching Candor, Imaging Abandon

The work of part 1 was to define candid dancing and lay the theoretical, historical, and aesthetic groundwork of the candid dancing phenomenon. Part 2 animates those ideas through a close analysis of two videos posted to Instagram. Themes and concepts from the previous part move through the candid dancing media artifact: how an impulse to "dance like nobody's watching" disguises operations of discipline and fetishization, how the recording of such a scene reinforces the powers of the gaze, and how the video's social life on new media represents a softening of surveillance. In each of these examples, gender, race, ethnicity, and class mingle in different ways to reveal the complex work of abandon. While these two examples do not exhaust the field of candid dancing or capture the extent of the choreography of abandon, they articulate a range that might be helpful in envisioning the contours of these concepts and the complex mechanics of post-panoptic surveillance. Indeed, countless other instances of candid dancing may be found on Instagram and other image-based platforms, and those instances may capture differing portraits of abandon. The videos here, however, serve as exemplars of the many political, aesthetic, and semiotic threads that run through this type of intimaesthetic.

Catching Intersectional Masculinity

In motion from the outset, the dancer opens and closes his arms as he twirls his wrists in rhythm with the music. The song "Alame Eshgh" by Iranian pop musician Homeyra is playing in the kitchen where he dances. The movement of the man's arms and wrists is accentuated by the rectangular tissue boxes that he holds in his hands. He draws the tissue boxes in toward himself, with an audible tap of the cardboard against his chest, as his gaze shifts left; he then opens his arms outward, as the tissue boxes extend his reach, and his gaze moves to the right. He repeats this gesture several times, adding a slight twirl of his wrists as he expands his arms. Throughout these movements, the dancer's eyes are closed, his chin is lifted toward the light, and his face beams with a wide grin. After just a few seconds, the dancer opens his eyes, still unaware of the camera. He resolutely places the tissue boxes on the kitchen counter and takes two audible breaths, pushing the air out of his lungs as if exhausted by his exertion. He stretches his arms, shoulders, and neck like he just completed an intense workout at the gym. It is at this moment that he glances toward the camera and, upon seeing it, expresses his realization of the turn of events. His countenance changes from contemplative to surprise to alarm as he registers that his dancing has been the subject of entertainment and capture. He laughs in embarrassment. The video ends with the man energetically charging toward the camera, continuing to register the event of being caught dancing.

The caption beneath the video reads "#MyFavouriteHuman #Caught-Dancing #TheEndingIsPriceless 🏃🤮😂." It was posted to a personal profile on January 13, 2018 (see fig. 2).

The circumstances that brought this man to dance in the kitchen—perhaps *his* kitchen—are unknown, and the events that unfolded after he charged toward the camera are also a mystery. However, the thirteen seconds of action captured in this video reveal a candid dancing scene that is imbued with meaning regarding the body, its gender and ethnicity, and its choreography of abandon in a post-panoptic digital age. On an aesthetic level, the man's dancing demonstrates embodied candor, dancing-while, and introspection. On a semiotic level, his movements articulate how candid dancing cultivates a seemingly aberrant masculine figure whose dancing is complicated by the prerevolutionary Iranian pop song playing in the space. Finally, the video reveals the intricacies of contemporary post-panoptic surveillance: how inherently surveillance pervades the home, how bodies already engage in self-surveillance, and how new media exacerbates that surveillance. Of course, these constructions are contingent upon a reading of the video as indeed candid—a reading that occurs so subtly that its components require overview.

Of the many features that articulate the dancer's embodied candor, foremost is his bodily comportment. Throughout the dance, the man faces away from the camera, his body in profile, with his eyes closed. He appears to direct his energy toward some unknowable, absent audience as he opens

Fig. 2. The dancer performing in a kitchen with his tissue box props.
(Meagan Willoughby)

and closes his arms in a presentational manner and lifts his chin toward the light. His smile suggests he is absorbed in the movement experience, either enjoying himself or imagining himself performing in front of an audience—or perhaps both of these possibilities, experienced simultaneously. The repetition of the movement, too, indicates that the dancer is compelled by the moment and is responding to the steady rhythm of the music. While the viewer cannot prove that the dancing is not premeditated or structured by some larger score, the qualities of the dancer's movement, engagement with the music, and bodily facing articulate an impromptu quality, which works to cue the viewer to the candor of the scene.

The dancer's relationship to the camera works in conjunction with his bodily movement and behavior to construct the candidness of the scene. For the entirety of his dancing, the man does not appear to recognize the camera's presence. Instead, his focus is on the music, his movement, and whatever situation he might be imagining. For the viewer, his absorption in the activity presents as an apparent introspective experience for the dancer: a looking inward toward the self rather than a focus outward on an audience. The dancer faces away from the camera throughout the dance, too, which further establishes a loose connection between his experience and the camera's eye. This disconnection then couples with the slight jostling of the frame to indicate that the dancer did not prepare the camera himself, that his dancing is intended for no audience, and that its capturing is happenstance (determined by the operator's timing of stumbling upon the activity). Collectively, the seemingly impromptu qualities of the video suggest the candidness of the dancer's movement. The dance's setting within the home is another feature that invites the viewer to see the dance and the dancing body as candid. Without knowing the dancer or where he lives, the viewer understands that the setting of the video is a kitchen of a residential space. While there is no indication that the space *belongs* to the dancer (that he owns, rents, or otherwise resides in that home), his dancing suggests that he is familiar with and comfortable in that space, as he moves through it with ease and abandon, listens to music he apparently enjoys, and understands his surroundings well enough to incorporate everyday domestic objects he encounters in that space.

The man's incorporation of the props further reiterates the candid sensibility of the video. That is, his decision to dance with the tissue boxes— items that are not typically a fixture of the kitchen (especially not two of them at the same time)—seems too random to be premeditated but familiar enough to make sense out of context. One might imagine, for instance, that while out shopping earlier that day, the man saw a buy-one-get-one-free offer for tissues, so he grabbed two; then, back at home, as he was putting away his items, he became moved by the song playing on the radio and broke out into a dance, mid-task. While this sort of narrative is fictional, it is also *believable*, which speaks to the effective constructions of candor in the video. The props articulate the man's absorption in a state of *dancing-while*: They make clear to the viewer that there is a context surrounding this event and that context represents some slice of authenticity regarding the man's quotidian world. Then, compounded with the dancer's bodily comportment, his relationship to the camera, and the subtle movement of the frame, the ordinary, private, intimate existence is effectively aestheticized.

The candor that is constructed through the man's dancing and his domestic scene is underscored by the moment in which he identifies the presence of the camera operator and ostensibly also their camera. The introspection embedded in the act of dancing with the tissue boxes immediately transforms when the subject registers that he is being watched and filmed. His expression of pleasurable abandon turns to shock and embarrassment just before he charges toward the camera. Through juxtaposition, this shift brings attention to, and even augments, the subject's earlier performance of abandon (see fig. 3).

The reading of the man's dancing as unquestionably candid is linked to the momentary unfastening from his masculinity. First, the man's location in the home—especially in the kitchen of the home—plays on the historic gendered division of labor that often associates women with domestic activity. His setting calls forth this association, as his masculine form moves in opposition to the images that the association conjures (e.g., a woman cooking in the kitchen, a woman doing dishes in the kitchen, and a woman putting away groceries—and perhaps tissue boxes—in the kitchen). Second, the fact that the man is *dancing* summons, and ultimately cuts through, stereotypes that link dance to femininity.[23] The man dancing in the video may or may not be conscious of this association while moving; yet, his sudden cessation of movement, abrupt disregard for the tissue boxes, and prompt stretch of his shoulder muscles as if he were between reps at the gym indicate a shift in his consciousness. As if jolting himself back to the reality of his current state, place, and gender, he corrects his comportment and reinstates his muscle-flexing form, all before being caught by the onlooker with the camera. This manner of apparent self-surveillance and self-censorship reflects the effectiveness of a Foucauldian mode of discipline, as it demonstrates how discipline is internalized and requires no external action. The dancer catches himself, and before even realizing the presence of the onlooker and camera, he corrects his body

Fig. 3. The dancer charging toward the camera after realizing he had been caught dancing. (Meagan Willoughby)

and resumes a more everyday masculine comportment. However, while the presence of the camera *reveals* a layer of surveillance evident in the scene—that is, the man's self-surveillance—the recording of it *creates* new layers of surveillance. This irony reveals the futility of the choreography of abandon. By complicating his masculinity yet ultimately getting caught in the act, the camera reasserts the power of visuality and the disciplining gaze while also indicating how gender is beholden to ocular mechanisms.

The man's momentary abandon and the swift return to gendered decorum are complicated by his race, ethnicity, and nationality. While details of his personal life and identity are not made obvious from the video, the account to which the video was posted appears to be owned by his sister, an Iranian Canadian woman living in Toronto. This information suggests that the politics of the man's candid dancing body emerge through the specific lens of Iranian Canadian culture rather than a universal framework[24] Constructions of gender in Iran have themselves undergone profound changes over the last two centuries. For instance, Afsaneh Najmabadi shows that pre-twentieth-century Iranian society did not adhere to a rigid gender binary, a nuance erased by European spectatorship that marginalized "effeminate masculinities" in the following century.[25] The Iranian Revolution (1978–79) brought about further shifts in gender, especially for women and their roles in public life.[26] The Iranian diaspora that, in part, resulted from this event prompted individuals to orient themselves in new ways toward the values of their homeland—perhaps eschewing, reconfiguring, or maintaining those values.[27]

Without viewers knowing the personal and familial history of the man in the video, the historical constructions of gender in Iran and the Iranian diaspora shape the semiotics of his kitchen dance scene. The fact that he is dancing to a song by Homeyra, an icon of prerevolutionary Iran whose success as a woman and musical artist led to her exile following the establishment of the Islamic State of Iran (1979), further complicates the already intricate layers of identity that give meaning to the man's candid performance. Is he dancing in solidarity with this iconic singer and performer? Is he nostalgic for an earlier Iran, when Homeyra was able to perform in her own country? Or is he perhaps entranced by her majestic voice and melodic tune? The intricacies of these histories and intersecting cultural logics may not be immediately evident in the candid dancing scene, yet they subtly move through the man's body, all while his image speaks to his self-disciplining.

This consideration of one man's seemingly unseen kitchen dance aptly reflects the theoretical underpinnings of candid dancing and articulates the infinitely layered gaze that imbues instances of unexpected spectator-ship. At the same time, the particular example of the tissue box improvisa-tion demonstrates the many investments that the gaze has in the home-body and its relationship to gender, ethnicity, and nationality. This body is the prime object to discipline over and over again. However intricate and situationally rooted relational dynamics may be, the camera and the social media platform work to aestheticize the home dance activity and thereby augment, propel, and propagate its operations of surveillance and discipline. The analysis of the next example reveals additional layers of abandon and its entrapments by the gaze.

Laboring Domesticity

Holding a mop in one hand, she jauntily grooves backward as if doing some version of the moonwalk—not so much gliding like MJ but more bouncing backward to the beat of Hot Chelle Rae's "Tonight, Tonight." With the lyrics "Whoa, oh oh. Come on, oh oh," she shifts her weight from side to side. The person behind the camera laughs, prompting a dog that is also out of frame to bark. Without paying mind to these noises, the woman brings the mop to her body and sings into the end of the stick as if it were a microphone. She points her left hand upward toward the ceiling and, again in the fashion of Michael Jackson, quickly rotates her knees in and out, in and out, in and out, just before throwing her left leg up, articulating at the knee, and twisting to a new direction. Her back is now to the camera.

Though the woman moves through this dining room space, indicated by the large wooden dining table and matching buffet in the background, her oversized blue housekeeping dress remains stiff, as if freshly starched. The large pockets sag with the weight of their contents, anchoring the un-dulations of the fabric. "Tonight tonight, there's a party on the rooftop, top of the world." With her back still facing the camera, the woman grooves to the upbeat rhythm, shifting her weight again from side to side. She contin-ues to twist her knees in and out as she rotates clockwise, now facing to the right. Bobbing her head while emphatically singing, she grabs the head of the mop as if to check its level of absorption. As she lifts her face, she seems to notice the camera and belts out in surprise and humor, "[something inaudible] What the!"

Despite her recognition of the onlooker, the woman continues dancing. She places the mop down, resting it against the wall of the dining room, claps emphatically on beat, and bends over to the bucket while dancing. Turning toward the camera now, she tosses her hand toward the cam-

eraperson in disregard. Just then, as the woman bends back toward the bucket, she turns to the camera and points toward the device. "Heyyyy!" she exclaims, as if realizing that her onlooker is recording her. With that realization, the woman ducks and slides out of sight.

The caption of the video, posted on December 15, 2016, reads "When your favorite song starts playing 😂 🎧 🎵 " (see figs. 4 and 5).

While the abandonment of gender, explored in the first example, presents key characteristics of the candid dancing body and scene, there are other aspects of identity and life conditions from which a dancer might attempt to unfasten. The second example above reveals one of those instances: a woman—ostensibly a housekeeper—is caught dancing by, presumably, a resident of the home she is cleaning.[28] In this situation, the politics of class and race are layered on top of the existing politics of capture. Foremost, however, this video, like that of the previous example, constructs a sense of candor through its depiction of a dancer who is unaware of an audience. As such, it is necessary to first discuss this element before delving into the dancer's choreography of abandon.

Several features of the video contribute to its construction of candor—primary among them is the dancer's untethered relationship to the camera. For the entirety of the dance, the woman's face is obscured from view. From her moonwalk-esque movements at the beginning to her mop play toward the end of the video, the audience mostly sees her back. This element combines with the fact that someone else is recording the video, exhibited by a shaky frame and laughter from behind the camera, to suggest that the dancer is not aware that someone is recording, much less observing, the scene. Finally, the dancer's initial, disregarding hand toss followed by her more embarrassed escape out of the frame suggests that her discovery of the observer preceded her discovery of the camera. This gradual recognition of the observational faculties of the performance underscores the previous *lack* of such a recognition.[29]

The intricacies of the dancer discovering the reality of the scene not only gesture toward the dancer's experience but also reveal information about the relational dynamics between the dancer and cameraperson. Once spotting her audience, for instance, the woman continues dancing as if nothing has changed, suggesting that she does not mind being watched by the onlooker. She even expresses her indifference toward the individual's presence by tossing an arm toward the cameraperson in playful disregard. This reaction is telling of the dancer's level of comfort with—or per-

Fig. 4. The dancer using a mop as a microphone as she dances to Hot Chelle Rae's "Tonight, Tonight" (Meagan Willoughby)

Fig. 5. The dancer pointing at the camera as she realizes she has been caught dancing by the onlooker (Meagan Willoughby. Example of moving selfie)

haps apathy toward—the cameraperson. If the dancer had been surprised by the sudden discovery of an audience, perturbed by the identity of that audience, or embarrassed by her own actions, she may not have continued dancing. She may have stopped in her tracks and resumed her mopping. Not only does she respond, however, by continuing the dance in a calm and steady manner, but she also casually rebukes her audience. Here, the dancer refuses to correct her dancing and denies the onlooker the satisfaction of her humiliation, thereby subverting any attempt at surveillance. In other words, the disciplining gaze that would typically have manifested in such a scene does not elicitly discipline the subject here. The woman, instead, refuses to submit to its power.

The dynamics between the dancer and cameraperson are especially provocative considering the occupational status of the dancer. Her attire is a primary indicator of her role as housekeeper. The oversized, almost baggy, piece of clothing—maybe a dress, maybe a jacket—resembles a uniform, with its light blue, scrubs-like hue. It appears that this article of clothing is worn on top of a more casual outfit, perhaps to be draped over one's day-to-day attire and removed at the end of a shift. Alongside her attire's aesthetics, the way in which the woman wears the clothing is also indicative of her occupational status. The large pockets appear to be holding objects, presumably items that the woman needs or collects as she goes from room to room: tools to make small repairs, keys to lock and unlock certain doors, items that need to be relocated. Her hair, which is pulled back into a tight, low bun—ostensibly intended to stay out of her face while she works—rounds out this reading of the housekeeper.

The fact that someone else is in the space watching her contributes to the larger meaning of this woman's occupation, as it tends to suggest a relation of employer-employee, to reinforce the hierarchy therein, and to enhance the power dynamic *already* available in the video. This reading of the relation between dancer and cameraperson is further shaped by the apparent identity of the woman who recorded the video—a teenage girl of Portuguese descent who lived in South Africa at the time of posting the video, according to the personal profile in which the video appears. We may also discern from this information that, because the video appears on this individual's personal profile and because we hear girlish laughter in the video, the person who posted the video is also the one who recorded it: Bianca, we will call her. Perhaps this young woman is the homeowner's daughter. Perhaps the dancer was involved in caretaking for the girl—a nanny of sorts. Regardless of their exact relation, the age difference between Bianca and the dancer, who appears to be middle-aged, might explain the dancer's initial disregard of Bianca's presence. On the one hand, Bianca holds power over the dancer, not just in her wielding of the camera but also in her relationship to the dancer's employer, and could therefore hold sway over the future of the dancer's employment; yet, on the other hand, the dancer may view Bianca as "just a kid"—someone who may often get in the way of her duties and yet someone with whom she could also play and joke while working.

The suggested relationship between the dancer and cameraperson gestures toward complex politics of class and race, particularly in terms of the semiotics of the dancer's status as a Black housekeeper. Of course, the political and economic nuances of hired domestic labor are contingent upon the context of a given place and situation. The evident location of this video—Pretoria, South Africa—points toward how the woman's dance acquires a meaning that is linked to the cultural, political, and economic milieu of that place. Ena Janson argues, for instance, that domestic work in South Africa not only is "ubiquitous" but also reflects an important economic and social institution for the country. In particular, this line of work represents a close but distant dynamic that is entrenched in complex race relations.[30] Narratives of domestic workers being "part of the family" during apartheid dominate public memory in South Africa.[31] Tamara Shefer draws on the work of Shireen Ally to describe how these narratives of white employers were tinged with contradictory sentiments of love and guilt toward their often Black nannies and housekeepers, yet how such narratives ultimately articulate the reproduction of white privilege.[32] The "part of the family" myth and its dialectic of intimacy and distance did not subside in 1994 with the end of apartheid but continue into twenty-first-century South Africa. As Janson asserts, "Domestic workers continue to be the most important contact figures in South Africa between white and Black, urban and rural, and between the wealthy and the poor."[33]

The complex dynamic of intimacy and distance found in domestic work in South Africa amplifies the existing intimaesthetics of the scene. Domestic work is, as scholars like Janson, Ally, and Shefer argue, inherently intimate. Workers come into the home of their employers and end up developing a deep familiarity with—and often a compassion for—the individuals who live in that home. Bonds tend to form especially between domestic workers and the children of the home.[34] Intimacy, then, becomes inextricably linked to both labor politics and race relations. The woman's dancing-while-cleaning performance animates these tensions. The dancer's blithe but jovial regard for Bianca upon discovery articulates a close relationship and intimate connection between housekeeper and child-employer. Yet, Bianca's use of the camera and its capacities to surveil the dancer-worker, and then subsequently her decision to post the video online for added humor/humiliation, underscores the violence of that relationship. It is both playful and disciplinary, affectionate and oppressive, intimate and antagonistic.

The intimaesthetics of the housekeeper's dance are thus twofold. First, her way of dancing-while-cleaning illustrates her maneuvers within the dialectics of her occupation. Perhaps she needed a respite from the impacts of her work: a moment to relieve the physical and emotional tolls of its simultaneous intimacy and antagonism. This choreography of abandon, however, became futile the moment she was spotted by Bianca, hence the second layer of intimaesthetics. The role of the camera fractures the dancer's choreography of abandon, while also capturing the contradictory nature of her relationship with Bianca.

As indicated above, instances of the choreography of abandon, like those revealed through the two videos discussed in this section, become transformed once uploaded to a new media platform. That is to say, not only does the initial recording of the scene enact a politics of watching and activate various streams of the disciplining gaze, but also the circulation of that recording on an app like Instagram exacerbates the failures and futility of the choreography of abandon. The expanded audience, the algorithmic determination, and the possibility of accruing social capital all initiate a new life for the candid dancing video as it enters a network. This leap also opens the video up to evaluation and commentary through the comment section of the post—a feature that may shape the affective dimensions of the scene, as well as its meaning in digital culture. The next section addresses the social life of the candid dancing video through a discussion of, first, its eventicization and, second, its cultivation of humor. These discussions stress the pervasiveness of post-panoptic surveillance and the futility of one's attempts to unfasten from the gaze.

Part 3. Circulating Candor

Candid dance videos on new media are somewhat commonplace—not trite or boring but quotidian in an extraordinary way. Viewers tend to enjoy encountering such videos, just as they might also appreciate videos of cats chasing laser pointers, for example. Yet, also like cat videos, candid dancing media typically do not prompt much dialogue, but they do tend to gain enough algorithmic traction to reach wide networks of friends and families and offer delight in viewership. While commonplace, the uploading of a candid dancing video nonetheless produces a rupture in the dancer's privacy, in their sense of ownership over their dance, and in their project of choreographing abandon. This rupture coincides with an exacerbation of the power dynamics already at play in the production of the video by drawing the dancing body further into the realm of surveillance and amplifying the disciplining forces of the gaze. Part 3 unpacks these processes—both the rupture that occurs and the amplifications of power—by focusing on two dimensions of the video's circulation: eventicization and the cultivation of humor. The two cases of candid dancing discussed above will continue to exemplify the politics and poetics of this type of intimaesthetic, as applied to its online life.

As previously indicated, the process of uploading a candid dancing video onto new media changes the meaning of the dance by emphasizing its visual qualities and making it available for consumption in the public sphere. Ultimately, this process formalizes the dance so that it may swiftly move through its new digital environs for others to view, evaluate, and enjoy. This formalization, or *eventicization*, captures the ontological leap as the dance crosses into a new paradigm of existence and concretizes the ruptures in the dancer's movement experience. This process is preliminary to all the other amplifications of the discipline and surveillance that occur in the space of new media, as it reflects the move toward a mass, often anonymous viewership that is worlds away from the dancer's sense of authority over their movement, scene, and image. Considering these fundamental qualities of eventicization, it is necessary to discuss this process in greater depth before addressing how new media riddles the candid dancing figure and image with a politics of ownership and the deceit of playfulness.

"Eventicization," a term used in scholarly discourses ranging from education to media studies to tourism studies, refers to the establishment of a linguistic and semiotic continuity around something that is otherwise in a constant state of flux.[35] While the process of making a dance experience more stable begins with the recording of it, it is the placement of the video online that ultimately establishes its record in a systematic way and amplifies its qualities as an *event*. The philosophical discourse on the event, after all, determines the concept through its encounter with its reader/viewer via systems of codes and conventions.[36] According to this logic, cultural artifacts like videos may be understood as events as they encounter the social sphere and reach an audience—or, perhaps more accurately, as they land in a place where audiencing happens.[37] Much like how a brick-and-mortar venue functions to eventicize an in-person, synchronous dance performance, a new media platform works to eventicize a particular private dance experience.[38] Though markedly distinct from one another, particularly in their occupations of space and time, both cases reflect the establishment of fixedness around a dance so that others may consume it as an object of their attention and as a text that gains meaning through exposure.

Applying this concept to the uploading and circulation of candid dancing videos online underscores how, through its public dissemination, the formerly unseen, unknown experience of one dancing in the privacy of their home fundamentally shifts its semiotic register. Specifically, the ways in which this image was created without the knowledge or permission of the dancer exacerbate the shift from some private, in-person dance to video representation and then to new media object. Several indications of a candid dancing video online point toward its eventicization: its time stamp, its place on the personal profile, and its comment section. These three features, intrinsic to new media products across platforms, allow a cultural product to be categorized, labeled, explained, and critiqued—a process that highlights the dancer's continued lack of authority over the video. Of course, each of these features operates distinctively and causes the product to be eventicized in a different way.

The time stamp is the most seemingly innocuous of these features, as it appears through an objective, systematic process, created by coding scripts that link specific metadata to a digital artifact. Each piece of media that is posted to a platform is thus stamped with the moment of its upload. Such a feature is so ubiquitous across new media that it often goes unnoticed and underanalyzed. That is to say, because the time stamp borrows a logic of recordkeeping that is predigital, its place in the digital landscape may seem unremarkable to users who see it in association with the content they produce and consume. This feature of media objecthood is a medium unto itself, falling into a category that John Durham Peters names "logistical media," which, because they "establish the zero points of organization," often "seem neutral or given—something that gives them extraordinary power."[39] Like the clocks and calendars that Peters discusses, the social media time stamp transforms how history is constructed and cultural memory is marked.[40] It is this subtle but powerful dimension of the time stamp that allows social media platforms to eventicize an everyday moment so that it may then be engulfed in a world of enterprise, commerce, and taxonomy—all of which play into the hands of neoliberal capitalism.[41]

Of course, the mechanisms of this process differ depending on the platform. On Instagram, at the time of writing, the time stamp initially displays as the number of hours that have elapsed since the content was posted, and then once it reaches one week after its upload, it begins showing the precise date of the post. Such an approach reinforces a value system that privileges newness and nowness, since the algorithms that Instagram uses to filter and sort media give preference to recency.[42] Most specifically to Instagram, the elapsed time approach, which highlights the original time of upload, functions as a timer on the currency of such an image, ticking down into seeming obsolescence as the post disappears from the feeds of followers.[43] While this method of sorting content—called relevance sorting—is the subject of greater discussion in chapter 2, its place here demonstrates the process by which a seemingly unseen private dance is not only broadcast to the world but also sorted by some notion of *when* it occurred. Thus, for candid dance videos, in particular, the time stamp emphasizes the spatiotemporal leap that occurs between a dance experience that was not intended to have an audience or to be marked in time or history to a dance event that is framed with a date, placed among other time-stamped events, and given value according to its currentness or lack thereof.

In discussing Instagram's emphasis on the original time of upload, it is important to note the broader value that a range of new media platforms place on *origin*. The notion of the "original post"—or, more colloquially, the OP, an acronym used across new media platforms—allows users to maintain a reference to an original artifact, especially as images, concepts, and memes are both transmitted and transformed with great rapidity (as is the case with a meme that jumps platforms and constantly changes in meaning depending on the context in which it is applied). Unsurprisingly, time stamps are integral to the process of tracing an image or idea back to its digital origin, as it allows easy comparison among media to reveal which is the reference, or citation, and which is the original.[44] This culture of tracing and determining origins, however, does not always map so well onto performance, as enacted performance dates/times might differ from posted dates/times. That is, just because a dance video comes to have a date and time attached to it on Instagram, for instance, such data does not always approximate the actual moment in time when the dance/recording took place. However, unless it is otherwise noted in the caption or referenced through objects in the frame, a viewer will typically presume that the performance is recent. Instagram's emphasis on currency ensures this reading, as it is constantly pushing newer posts into the feeds of users—a systematized modality of recency bias. Such a system, then, highlights the chasm that eventicization creates: one between the dancer's movement experience and the point at which that experience enters a representational economy under the command of algorithms.

The examples discussed in this chapter gesture toward the implications of the time stamp when it comes to the eventicization of a candid dance scene. Both cases, for instance, suggest that the time of posting the video is relatively close to the time of its recording—mostly because there is no evidence to suggest otherwise—and thus viewers read the scene through a lens of recency. The captions for each video focus on the humor of the scene rather than noting its place in time or describing the content with a sense of retrospection or nostalgia. Comments on the video also omit time or history and instead capture the playful sensibility of the respective dance. The videos thus represent the presumption of recency that is typical in new media spaces. Ultimately, by emphasizing the media's temporal positioning—even if that positioning does not reflect the reality of when the dance occurred—this sense of recency underscores the purpose and value of the time stamp as a form of logical media.

Even after the candid dance videos dissipate from the feeds of Instagram users, their place on the personal profiles of the individuals who posted them continues to eventicize the dancing. That is, when considering the content within the personal profile of each individual, the videos become part of that individual's personal narrative. For instance, the video that Bianca posted of her apparent housekeeper is situated after images of her graduating from high school and before posts of her at college. This progression of images combines with the linearity and chronology afforded by the time stamp to produce a narrative about that individual's life. We might imagine, for example, how a high school girl feels a kinship with her family's housekeeper before leaving for college or how she and her high school friends might mock the housekeeper, thereby reinforcing the power they may have over her. Similarly, the video of the man dancing in the kitchen might capture a time when he and his sister were roommates—a time that they both look back on fondly. While these narratives are flexible and ultimately depend on the level of familiarity a viewer would have with the original poster, they suggest how each candid dancing event functions within a larger life narrative, as exhibited through the Instagram personal profile. They also point to the ways in which time stamps function not only to eventicize a dance but also to situate that dance event within wider systems of both recency (in terms of the news feed) and linearity (in terms of the personal profile chronology).

The consideration of the time stamp's role on the personal profile reveals a separate issue regarding a perceived sense of ownership of a piece of media that a user uploads. The culture of new media has instilled in its users a cross-platform sensibility that an original post is *owned* by the person who uploaded the content. An original post, which differs from a repost, an obvious reproduction or citation, articulates first of all the presumption that media may be owned in the first place, as if it were any other commodity that may be bought and sold. While media has, to some extent, been historically imbricated in systems of consumerism, the advent of the internet and its promise of open sourcing, peer production, and open collaboration offered the possibility of a new model of authorship.[45] However, the rise of social media, with its incorporation into venture capitalist enterprise and its emphasis on sole authorship through personal profiles for individuals, has not realized the radically collaborative potential of the internet—or at least not in the space of social media platforms like Instagram. Instead, individuals produce and upload their own media, and even though this content may be imbricated in a culture of participation, that content itself is ultimately viewed as belonging to the individual rather than some collective.[46]

Though a post or profile seldom makes explicit mention of ownership, viewers nonetheless make presumptions based on the semiotics of the media. For instance, the profiles of Bianca and the candid dancer's sister do not explicitly say anywhere on them that either individual owns the content they post or that either individual was the person to record the respective videos. Yet, the content on both profiles is received in such a way, as each piece of media is presumed to be authored, and therefore owned, by those individuals. In both cases, the camera movement and first-person voice in the caption support such a reading by connecting the roles of camera operator, poster of content, and author of media. These instances epitomize a general conflation between creator, poster, and author of content that may be seen across other new media platforms. Of course, the implications of this connection are more political than they might initially suggest.

The conflation of poster and owner reveals two important implications related to the phenomenon of performance on new media. First, the perceived sense of ownership of a piece of media obscures the roles of others who may have been involved or others who may be featured in that media. The character of a personal account on Instagram as a page for a sole individual, that is, forecloses the possibility of collaboration that may otherwise characterize the work. In this way, new media platforms like Instagram tend to work against the logic of peer production and open collaboration, while also denying the work and identity of others who may have been involved in the production. While this set of presumptions impacts a number of genres of art in different ways, the implications in the case of dance and performance are quite poignant. When collaboration and cooperation are as integral to a genre as they are to performance, it becomes problematic when such information about a work is obscured, omitted, or primed for misinterpretation. The new media platforms that house and circulate self-produced media as individual by default are responsible, then, for promulgating a system in which these ambiguities flourish.

Second, while collaboration is indeed often ignored or misrepresented in new media, the candid dancing video reflects additional, and arguably more troubling, instances wherein individuals are incorporated into a production without their knowledge, authorization, or consent. In such instances, the unknowing subjects are not aware of the production in the first place, much less the role of any perceived or potential collaboration. Then, once the cameraperson decides to place the video online, the dancer becomes even further removed from their own image, as it is then subject to the commands of algorithms, the judgment of peers, and the decisions of the person who "owns" the media. Upon entering this sphere, the candid dancing body is no longer the object of attention for just one person and is no longer situated in the comforts of the domestic setting but may be witnessed by innumerable viewers. Considering how the individual who posted the video is understood to be the video's owner, the dancer may never have the opportunity to command their own audience or to determine the size and scale of their viewership. An unseen dance in the kitchen may, for instance, come to garner thousands of views, many of them likely by people whom the dancer does not even know. This expansion in viewership—one that was not intended by the dancer in the first place—exacerbates the surveillance present at the initial recording. It enables countless users on new media to get a glimpse into the intimate setting of the dancer, thereby allowing a mass audience to revel in the inhibitions and unknowingness of the candid dancing body.

The dance's new environment means not only that more people come to view the candid dancing event but also that it is opened up to commentary, critique, and the possibility of accruing social capital—another aspect of the dance's eventicization. Specifically, the expansion in viewership of the candid dancing video largely works to construct its affective character and social life. While a video may be perceived as funny *before* it was placed online, the nature of the public post transforms the video's affective potential into publicly recognized humor. Candid dancing videos, through their circulation on platforms like Instagram, tend to elicit reactions of laughter and delight. The audience's engagement with the post further determines and reinforces this dimension of the video. Of course, the person who posted the video ultimately initiates the framing so that the affective qualities may be understood in a particular way. This production includes, but is not limited to, the author-producer's involvement in the scene, as well as their framing of the media through captions. The two examples discussed in part 2 demonstrate this cultivation of humor. For the sister of candid dancer, the caption describing the man as their "favourite human," followed by a cry-laughter emoji, articulates the lighthearted and playful qualities of the scene. Understanding the description of the candid dancer alongside the emoji congeals the production of humor. For Bianca's video, the laughter of the person behind the camera quintessentially illustrates her affective response to the scene. To hear Bianca's audible laughter over the image of the housekeeper dancing-while-cleaning expresses the humor of the scene—an expression that is especially remarkable in a digital culture where the term *LOL*, or *laugh out loud*, does not guarantee that an individual is actually laughing out loud in their offline environment. Thus, regardless of whether either author-producer actually thought their respective scenes were funny, their production of humor becomes embedded in their respective posts.

Of course, these reactions not only reflect the affective cultivations of their producers but also instruct the audience to read the video as humorous. While a viewer might certainly find the scenes funny without hearing laughter or reading the caption, those expressions both *cue* the audience to and *affirm* the humorous qualities of the media: as if to say, "It's okay, you may laugh at this scene. It *is* funny." Viewers then respond by watching the video multiple times, sharing it with others, and expressing their impressions in the form of a comment. In each of the videos, viewers posted comments that articulate laughter through *haha*s, *LOL*s, and 😂's. Together with the author-producer's affective groundwork, these responses reflect how the candid dancing videos are determined as humorous through their consumption just as much as their production.

Indeed, the humor constructed through a piece of media may work to entertain the viewers who encounter it; however, the humor of the candid dancing video functions to disguise the layers of surveillance and discipline, as well as the lack of consent, that appear in or through the media. That is to say, the entertainment value of the candid dancing video works to distract the viewer from the underlying politics of the content: primarily, its blatant surveillance, its disciplining of the unseen dancing body, and its denial of the dancer's consent. If users do not detect such problematics of the candid dancing post, then they may not contest the issues therein, allowing those issues to persist, if not thrive, on their platform. This social life of candid dancing ultimately contributes to a softening of surveillance and a masking of covert modes of discipling gender, ethnicity, class, race, and many other aspects of identity. In the case of the examples discussed in part 2, the cultivation of humor for both posts—evident in the captions, videos, and comments—conceals the blatant surveillance of the camera-person, the betrayals of privacy that occurred in the recording of someone without that person's knowledge, the presumed ownership of that recording, and the uploading of the image online, presumably without the consent of the subject of that image. Then, once online, viewers continue to look in on the unknowing dancing body, continue to evaluate its movements, and, by laughing at it, continue to discipline that figure. Much like public humiliation strategies, the candid dancer may then be discouraged from such activity in the future. And regardless of whether the viewer recognizes it, they too may be inadvertently disciplined through this manner of humiliation. In this sense, *humor* and *humiliation* become imbricated techniques to discourage individuals from moving beyond the gaze.

The ways in which a candid dancing video becomes a humorous event through its new media circulation underscore the futility of one's choreography of abandon. Whether they are working to shake off the injuries of gender, ethnicity, race, class, or some other aspect of identity, the candid dancer's attempts to suspend the power of the gaze by moving beyond the domain of the public not only fall short but also exacerbate the conditions the dancer initially attempts to evade. The eventicization of this supposedly unseen dance takes shape through its upload to platforms like Instagram, in particular, through the platform's time stamp, personal profile, and comment section. In its new online environment, the image of the candid dancer is subjected to a simultaneous augmentation of viewership and disguise of the powers that that viewership represents. Surveillance and discipline become enhanced through the circulation of that image and its new status as an event, primed for consumption, critique, and entertainment.[47] The once private, once unseen, once singular experience of dancing-while gets subsumed into a world of just the opposite, regardless of the interests of the dancer themselves. Indeed, the camera captures the dancer; the platform captures the dancer; and the innumerable viewers on the other side of the screen capture the dancer. At that point, they may no longer capture themselves, it would seem.

Conclusion

An in-depth analysis of the candid dancing phenomenon on Instagram reveals how the powers of the gaze prevail even in the most seemingly private spaces of the unseen, as is the case with experiences of dancing-while that are set within and enabled through the domestic setting. The onlooker's presence and the camera's recording of this scene initiate the mechanisms of the gaze. However, the act of uploading the video online launches the once private, once ordinary dance experience into a process of eventicization, wherein the dance is time-stamped, narrativized, and commented upon so that it might more easily become a subject to be over-seen, disciplined, and corrected—to the ultimate detriment of whatever agency the dancer thought themselves to possess in the first place. The two examples discussed in part 2 indicate this loss and reveal the double bind embedded in the choreography of abandon. The candid dancing phenom-enon, in other words, indicates at once the dancer's desires to undo the body's social patternings, like those that occur through choreographies of gender, race, and class, and the omnipresent mechanisms of the gaze that surveil and discipline the errant body that *attempts* such a choreography. Humor functions here as a mechanism of power that obscures the dancer's abandonment by making light of the event and thus concealing their lack of authority.

While the issues revealed through an analysis of the candid dancing phe-nomenon may seem specific to a particular encounter in the home dance environment, it serves as a quintessential portrait of new media's extension of the quotidian powers of the gaze that command its subjects. That is to say, the facts of being caught dancing in the home, having the mediatized representation of that dance circulate on platforms like Instagram, and then not having authority over that image collectively represent the conditions of a network society under the command of post-panoptic surveillance. The phenomenon also provides a compelling snapshot of the predicament of data collection, wherein users do not own their own data, nor are they aware of what data is being collected about them. Being watched and re-corded as you dance-while folding laundry in your living room, for instance, articulates the subtlety with which information is collected about the body in online spaces. Like the candid dancing subject, new media denizens do not realize the powers that watch, track, and document their movements; the extent to which they are being watched; and what is being seen and known about them. In this manner, the candid dancing phenomenon func-tions as a metaphor for the bait-and-switch logic of subjectivity in a network society: specifically, the inadvertent supply of intimate data to new media systems at the expense of the intimacy itself.

The situation of candid dancing in the *domestic environment* especially underscores the degree to which the post-panoptic gaze permeates all corners of human activity. With its rhetoric of privacy and quotidian activity, the home elicits the dancer's choreography of abandon. Yet, its subsequent imaging, eventicization, and online circulation simultaneously rupture and uphold the home's apparent privacy. Through this paradox of candid dancing, the domestic environment transforms into a space primed not only for intimaesthetics but also for continued surveillance. Chapter 1 highlights this precarity of the home, particularly at a moment when the domestication of technology intensifies. The rapid growth in home devices that see and listen to its inhabitants—doorbell cameras; home "assistants" like Alexa, Siri, and Google; smart thermostats—highlights the need for home dancers to nuance their relationship to the camera and the systems to which the camera connects. Indeed, surveillance in the home and in contemporary life is here to stay. The ways in which performers negotiate its power over the body are to be determined.

While chapter 1 attends to the capturing of the *unknowing* dancing body in the home and its complications with twenty-first-century *privacy*, chapter 2 considers the *knowing* dancing body in the home and its experiences with twenty-first-century *publicity*. The next chapter, then, addresses selfie-ism and cultivations of personhood through self-produced home dance videos on Instagram. The dancer's recognition of the camera—an opportunity that the candid dancer is not afforded—works in conjunction with the space of the home and the dancer's movements to yield a different type of intimaesthetic. Here, intimacy is aestheticized not through the voyeuristic appeal to the interior candid body but through the productions of self—through one's *autochoreography*. The unknowing dancer then becomes not only a knowing subject but a knowing subject with a brand.

TWO

Moving Selfies

Their favorite Fleetwood Mac song is booming from the speakers in their room. Finding their groove, Mar approaches their camera, presses record, and backs away to center themselves in the frame. Occasionally stealing glances at the device, perhaps looking at their video in the making, they follow the rhythm of Stevie Nicks's melody.

Who is this dance for? If it is for themselves, why post it online?

As they sway to the chorus, they may wonder if this take is good enough, interesting enough, captivating enough for their followers. They keep going, thinking they can always trim to find the best part.

How many takes did the video require? Why did this segment of this dance get posted?

Far from Mar, in a different home in a different country, Donté prepares his home dance scene. He knows that he will need to add the music, flying emojis, and text during postproduction, but he choreographs the movements to serve as the foundation for his message. His energy is bounding.

Is the video a reflection of Donté, or is it a reflection of the personal brand he has cultivated? Maybe they are one and the same, maybe not.

Introduction

Situated in their homes, prepared to move, and ready to record that movement, new media users turn toward their cameras to capture an image of
themselves. Yes, a selfie. But not just any selfie, a *moving* selfie—an image
that exhibits the dynamism of one's joints against the stillness of one's surroundings, and at times in coordination with a musical track. This type of
intimaesthetic, the *moving selfie*, reflects a particular relationship between
the performer and the camera: one in which the performer exhibits a recognition of the recording device, thereby indicating the constructedness
of the image, while also building a direct connection with the viewer. The
moving selfie exacerbates the tension between the constructedness of the
image and the performer's cultivation of intimacy through the moving
body, autobiographical setting, and closeness of the camera. Exhibited
by dancers like Mar and Donté, techniques of the moving selfie rely on
the viewer's understanding that the subject of the image is also its creator.
This chapter approaches the selfie through this fundamental component
of image production, employing a broad framing of selfie-ism as a genre
of self-capture that encompasses both photographic and video formats.

Couching this mode of intimaesthetic within the wider movement
of selfie-ism enables an understanding of the mechanisms by which one
might choreograph the self in and for new media. Notions of the self,
for obvious reasons, are integral to this framing. The selfie's etymology
alone illustrates this connection, as does the selfie's impetus to frame and
capture a stable image of the individual at a particular point in time. In
an effort to unpack these choreographies of self, this chapter proposes
the concept of *autochoreography*. While this term conjoins the Latin *auto*,
meaning "self," with the notion of choreography, it also is a play on the
notion of autobiography, a writing *by* and *about* oneself. Through its focus
on self-production, autochoreography identifies how performers engage
a series of techniques to create an image that reflects (and projects) their
personhood. So, while the choreography of abandon in chapter 1 identifies
how performers attempt to *undo* the body, autochoreography articulates
how they might craft their body and space so that the resulting image is a
reflection of themselves. Part 1 of this chapter frames autochoreography
through a review of selfie-ism and a discussion of the moving selfie. Foundational to this analysis is how these two terms relate to one another. While
the moving selfie refers solely to an image-based product, the notion of
autochoreography stretches across both process and product to illuminate the mechanisms by which the performer creates their self-expression,

crafts their media, and frames that product as a representation of the self in new media. "Moving selfie," then, describes the *what* (the product), and "autochoreography" describes the *how* (the process). Autochoreography also, as described below, extends to the platform itself to articulate how the shaping of one's public persona requires attention not only to the production of an image but also to its circulation and consumption.

Following the theoretical framework for the moving selfie and autochoreography, part 2 mobilizes these concepts through an analysis of examples on Instagram. Dancers Mar and Donté provide the material through which this analysis takes shape. While Mar and Donté each employ different techniques in their autochoreographies, they both utilize their gaze, attire, domestic environment, and postproduction layers to build an intimaesthetic where the viewer may sense and engage with the performer's persona. Theses aesthetics and semiotics of the image open out to wider implications on new media. Revealing such implications, part 3 focuses on the nuances of circulation that play into the social life of the moving selfie on Instagram, specifically through the social and economic dimensions of the video's paratextual elements online: the social media feed, the personal profile, and the use of both hashtags and mentions. Ultimately, this discussion suggests how the media that dancers produce and upload to a platform are subject to the whims of algorithms and to the subtle—and sometimes not so subtle—operations of neoliberal capitalism.

Part 1. Defining the Moving Selfie

Anatomy of the Selfie

Linked to the rise of new media, the notion of the selfie did not appear in the *Oxford English Dictionary* until 2013, at which point the term became defined as "a photograph that one has taken of oneself, typically one taken with a smartphone or webcam and shared via social media." Suggested in this definition is how the selfie becomes, first, couched within the medium of photography and, second, defined in relation to social media. The still, photographic image taken *by* oneself and *of* oneself indeed dominates the public imagination surrounding what the selfie is in contemporary digital culture.[1] This framing of the selfie, however, limits it conceptually, particularly when considering instances of performance. The still image, that is, does not inherently capture the dynamics of movement and thus disqualifies movement practices as a powerful semiotic and expressive device in selfie productions.[2] However, a disregard for the reference to photography in the definition of the selfie emphasizes its manner of production: that it is ultimately an image "one has taken of oneself."[3] When focused on this critical element, the selfie becomes colored by its aesthetic and semiotic character rather than its medium. For instance, the meaning of a self-captured image relies on how the subject frames themselves, their preparation of the device, their comportment in the frame, their relationship to their environment, and other critical details that a viewer might read in the image. In this case, from a semiotic standpoint, the medium of the image is secondary to the ways in which the individual embodies the role of both subject and producer.[4]

Relocating the selfie as a relationship-based image rather than a medium-based one not only makes the image more available to a critical discourse about its production and consumption but also emphasizes its generic qualities. The selfie as a genre may be understood through an array of image-based products—including photographic stills, videos, and Graphic Interchange Format (GIF) images—that all share a similar ethos and are shaped by the social, economic, and political intricacies of new media.[5] Mobilizing this framing allows for a productive reading of selfie culture: from the production of the selfie image to its circulation and consumption online.

Of course, the notion of the moving selfie is more than merely a video of oneself, by oneself. When such a production is uploaded and disseminated through new media platforms, it acquires a presentational quality and a narrative dimension—both of which are directed toward an audience and both of which have a socially oriented character. At the same time, the image retains its seemingly private, personal, and individual quality, articulating the paradoxical nature of the moving selfie. This stretching between worlds not only reflects a characteristic of intimaesthetics but also points to an integral component of a moving selfie in particular: the choreographic presentation of one's life and self—or, its autochoreography.

The notion of autochoreography captures efforts to frame and image oneself through the mechanisms of body, space, and media so that the resulting image may be publicly circulated and consumed. In such an image, the performer positions themselves at the center of the production—at times, quite literally—and highlights their pre/occupations, attributes, and personal history. By centering the body and emphasizing its orchestrations of movement, space, and media, autochoreography reflects the mechanism by which individuals create their self-expressions for new media circulation and consumption. Whether it be a performance of elation, an act of confession, an expression of mourning, or a proclamation of boredom, the moving body shapes the performance so that the resulting video is a reflection of the performer at a particular moment in time.

Autochoreography attends to the gaps left by other genres of self-capture while also cultivating something completely distinct. The moving selfie, for instance, draws on a similar impetus to capture the self as seen in self-portraiture and autobiography, two forms of expression with deep histories that predate social media. Like the moving selfie, self-portraiture and autobiography capture the self in some tangible way to be experienced by others, create a record of oneself for posterity, and rely on a "pact" between the creator and audience.[6] In other ways, however, the moving selfie diverges from these pre-internet antecedents. First, the moving selfie accrues value differently than self-portraiture and autobiography. While the abundance of selfies online, and the ease with which they may be deleted, marks the form as relatively dispensable, they possess what Crystal Abidin calls a "subversive frivolity," or a generative power sourced in their discursive marginality. Second, the moving selfie has a particular orientation toward history.[7] The selfie, according to Brian Droitcour, is not a "flat monument" that elevates the subject beyond the ordinary and into the extraordinary and the historical, as other modes of self-capture might do. Similarly, a work of autobiography is developed through the reconstruction of memories and is thus inscribed in the past, yet with a thrust toward posterity. A selfie, unlike both self-portraiture and autobiography, inscribes its creator in a "networked present."[8]

While both Abidin's and Droitcour's respective positions are directed toward the photographic selfie, they might just as easily apply to the moving selfie. Composed like an intimate diary but distributed like a pamphlet, the moving selfie is embedded in the mundane, mobilized by the ubiquitous, and distributed to the masses. It may be reproduced, played back, discarded, or restaged. In creating this production, the performer does not present a monument that will stand the test of time and immortalize them in history. Instead, their expressions are subversively dynamic and of the present, in a way that emphasizes the vitality of the body in that moment.

Autochoreography

Undergirding the theory of autochoreography is the notion that the moving selfie must be read as an obvious self-capturing. In other words, the viewer must understand that the subject of the image is also the author.[9]

Three approaches to capturing a selfie are particularly relevant to the aesthetics and semiotics of such an image: a point-of-view (POV) style, a forward-facing style, and a static-frame style.

Of the various ways that one might capture a selfie, the most obvious occurs when the subject holds the camera and uses a mirror to capture their image. The viewer, in this instance, does not question that the subject is also the camera operator, since that dual operation is made explicit by the mirror's reflection. The subject sees what the camera sees and therefore what the viewer sees: a scene that cues the viewer to its own making—or, a self-reflexive scene captured in the POV style of camerawork. This approach not only clearly communicates that the image is indeed a selfie but also produces a visual manifestation of the subject-operator's kinesthetic experience. With video, the movements of the subject-operator are transferred to the viewer via the camera so that viewers are able to *sense* the shakiness of the frame. The result is a "haptic image," to borrow Laura Marks's term, which works to draw the viewer further into the scene and augment their experience of the image.[10]

In the case of the POV style of the moving selfie, the combination of the handheld recording method and the use of the mirror is especially profound, as it charges the video with a critical semiotics. This approach engages the powers of the mirror to actively work against several conceptions around the dancing body—namely, the dancer's fraught relationship with the mirror, the dancer's historical struggle to be the one to capture their own image, and the viewer's desire to experience a visually stable rendering of the dancer's body.[11] Each of these components entails its own complex discourse, yet they are all foregrounded by the mirror and its capacity to reveal the dancer, their camera, and their use of the POV style. This maneuver remixes the objectifying logic of mirrors, while also revealing the process of mediatization. For this reason, the mirror is both the conceptual and the practical lynchpin of this approach.

Similar to the POV manner of capturing a selfie, the forward-facing style also demonstrates self-reflexivity. This image occurs when the subject uses a device with a camera on the screen side to capture an image of themselves. In order to do this, they hold the camera up to face them, often stretching their arm out to expand the frame. The forward-facing camera allows them to preview the image as they capture it. Often, this approach results in an image where the subject's arm is in the frame, thus revealing the making of the production by visibilizing the physical connection between their own body and the camera. The arm's-length distance then becomes embedded in the grammar of the image, enabling the viewer to understand the subject to also be the camera operator.

While the previous two approaches cue viewers to a work's obvious self-capturing, other images on new media less explicitly indicate their status as a selfie. The static-frame style, where the individual positions the camera and then moves into the frame, is one such technique. In this case, the subject does not hold the camera, which eliminates a primary cue for the viewer to understand the subject as also the operator. However, unlike the POV and forward-facing approaches, the static-frame approach enables the individual to go hands-free while recording, expanding their possibilities of movement. For instance, they may prop up the camera on a desk in their bedroom, press record, back into the frame, and conduct their performance. Once they have recorded their video, they may then take advantage of the built-in editor on platforms like Instagram to quickly trim moments at the beginning and end where they press the record button. The resulting product in such a case further disguises the elements of the self-capture, as it no longer indicates the dancer as the camera operator.

For the individual who creates a moving selfie, the static-frame approach is especially advantageous because it allows them to move their limbs with relatively little inhibition, compared to them holding the camera while moving. Thus, while any of the three methods of self-capturing is available to the dancer, it is this final technique that allows home dancers to most effectively perform, as they would in any other space. For this reason, the forward-facing approach is of greater focus in this chapter.

Indeed, the static-frame approach to creating a moving selfie is the primary technique among home dance selfies, as well as moving selfies in general, on Instagram. Because this approach tends to disguise its status as a selfie by obscuring the performer's relationship to the camera, however, the viewer may pick up on other cues regarding the selfie status of the production: the setting, the gaze, and the media. The setting, first, is integral to the performer's autochoreography, as it communicates information regarding their personal history, preoccupations, and personality. For home dance videos in particular, the domestic environment that surrounds the dancer is imbued with a personal character that contributes to their autochoreography. The location for recording, for instance, is something the dancer must decide—and that decision contributes to the "self" they are working to construct and express through their production. A kitchen performance conveys a different message from a bedroom dance or from a bathroom production. Then, within those rooms, the dancer decides

Fig. 6. Home dancer Donté rearranging furniture to prop up his camera. Drawing created from a CTV News story. (Meagan Willoughby)

Fig. 7. Home dancer Donté performing in front of his laptop camera. Drawing created from a CTV News story. (Megan Willoughby)

how to orchestrate the lighting and the objects populating the space. The books situated on the shelves, the knickknacks resting on the coffee table, the art hung on the walls, and the decor adorning the space all capture the dancer's persona and suggest their storied history and individual style. The viewer might not understand the history behind those objects, but their mere presence connotes a character of familiarity and imbues the scene with untold personal histories.[12] Viewers thus read the home dance video through a filter of the dancer's domestic surroundings, as well as a broad understanding of domestic life. At the most fundamental level, this reading is contingent upon where the dancer places the camera when creating their moving selfie.

While the preparation of the dancer's surrounding space is not typically visible in the video, one might imagine the ways in which they have choreographed the scene. "This painting goes *here*, these dirty clothes *don't* go there, this book and that book should be visible in frame, those dishes should *not* be visible." They might do this work in everyday circumstances—perhaps in anticipation of having friends over—but they might also tweak the space before creating their video. "This vase of flowers should be in the frame, maybe on the table behind me." Regardless of when and to what extent the dancer does this work, their preparations of the space contribute to the autochoreography of their moving selfie. They curate their surroundings to be seen by others, specifically with the knowledge that their domestic space is a reflection of the self—or, rather, a reflection of their *choreography* of the self.

The semiotics of the performer's gaze, second, articulates that the image is a self-capture. For the moving selfie, a look toward the camera indicates that the dancer acknowledges the camera's presence and, as implied by their continued movement, agrees to its recording of them. This look, combined with the dancer's solitary figure and the static frame, functions as a signature of sorts—not only one that indicates authorship but also one that is linked to a particular time and place.[13] For the home dancer, their signature further constructs their autochoreography, as it tethers their image and their performance to the domestic setting, as well as to the everyday activities and in-the-moment temporalities of such a setting.

Along with indications of authorship, the dancer also utilizes the gaze to establish a connection with the camera and, by extension, the viewer. That is to say, the moving selfie makes clear—through the static frame, the solo dancing body, and the relationship between dancer and camera—that there is no one else behind the camera with which the dancer might make eye contact. Instead, their sight line lands on the recording apparatus.

Such a recognition of the camera then tends to function as a *direct address*: a performance device used to cultivate a relationship with an audience.[14] In this seeming correspondence, the dancer, by initiating a direct address, acts as a *speaker* who expresses something about themselves with the intention that that something will be received and understood by another party (see fig. 8). The viewer on the other end of that expression, by recognizing the address, not only sees the speaker as author of the expression but also *responds* by giving their attention to the performance—which, on platforms like Instagram, manifests in the form of a view count. This quantification of viewership works to legitimize the self-expression as an effective production of the self. The author has a reader, the choreographer has an audience, and therefore the moving selfie *lands*, so to speak. In this way, the dancer's direct address activates their autochoreography, establishes their authorship, and suggests their readership.

Of course, the performer's autochoreography is shaped by more than merely the landing of the selfie via the direct address. Movement style and sequence, coordination with music or ambient sound, bodily comportment, and spatial orientation all help to establish a sensibility regarding the dancer's expression. Facial expression, too, conveys a depth of information. For instance, a wry glance over one's shoulder toward the camera has a different sensibility than a direct, deadpan stare toward the lens. Smiles communicate a different message from frowns. The dancer's autochoreography, then, involves what Sherril Dodds calls "facial choreography," or a crafting of facial expressions, which, as Dodds argues, is enhanced through the capabilities of the camera and postproduction editing.[15] These elements of the dancing body are then compounded with the choreographies of the frame to further shape the dancer's autochoreography. For example, the dancer might remain in the center of the frame, thereby limiting their movement to a few square feet of space, as a way to maintain the viewer's attention on their figure. Similarly, they might move toward the camera and thus engage a more close-up framing to create a viewpoint that is otherwise achieved through intimate encounter. They might alternatively dim the lighting or choose to be backlit to disguise their face and setting altogether (see fig. 9). Such activations of body and space contribute to the performer's expression and help to cultivate their narrative of self.

Though the semiotics of the home and the body suggest a wealth of information regarding the performer and their self-expression, the media that is ultimately uploaded to the internet is just as integral in constructing their autochoreography. Edits to the video, filters that enhance or disguise certain aspects of the scene, and music that is added after the recording

Fig. 8. A home dancer performing a direct address to the viewer, indicating her knowledge of the camera and suggesting her authorship of the production (Meagan Willoughby)

Fig. 9. A home dancer performing in a backlit room, thereby disguising their face, dress, and space. (Meagan Willoughby)

has taken place all contribute to the meaning of the selfie. The caption accompanying the image also adds detail to the video, thereby further enhancing—or perhaps explaining—the performance. In Barthes's terms, the caption may function to "anchor" the video by offering a linguistic frame through which the viewer might read the dancer's performance.[16] However, in the case of autochoreography on new media, the dancer's performance is an extension of themselves. In other words, the dance is *of* the performer, *about* the performer, and *by* the performer. Thus, the caption is anchored not just to the image but also to the dancer in the image. It captures, explains, and frames the dancer's preoccupation in that moment. This anchoring of the caption demonstrates how the dancer and their autochoreographic product are contiguous entities, despite the constructedness of the image. The dancer performs themselves in everyday life just as their moving selfie performs *for them* on new media.

As expounded above, one's autochoreography consists of many techniques and styles that are channeled through their body, space, and media. These techniques are all beholden to the ways in which the performer establishes themselves both as subject and operator of the camera. The resulting image might not offer a glimpse into the making of the image, as many elements are cut, clipped, and eclipsed from view, yet a lens of autochoreography grants a greater understanding of the mechanisms by which the performer constructs their selfie. This theoretical framework is most clearly pictured in examples of media available online. Part 2 thus approaches the productions of two creators of moving selfies on Instagram: Mar and Donté.

Part 2. Choreographing the Moving Selfie

While the landscape of moving selfies on Instagram is vast, Mar and Donté represent that field and what can be achieved in it by way of their expertise in selfie creation. Both of these dancers have honed their craft of selfie production and are seasoned practitioners of depicting their domestic selves for an online audience. The Instagram profile of each dancer demonstrates this virtuosity through the sheer number of moving selfies they have posted. Mar, for example, has a total of 230 posts (at the time of writing), about two-thirds of which are self-captured home dance videos; Donté has 821 posts (also at the time of writing), about half of which are self-captured home dance videos. These collections, which do not include the undoubtedly innumerable outtakes involved in creating their online media, indicate a frequency of production that marks both Mar and Donté as exemplary in their technique and understanding of the moving selfie form.

Though these dancers reflect an exceptional virtuosity of the selfie form, they approach their productions with a difference of style, as each engages a distinct mode of autochoreography. Mar employs an approach wherein they expose themselves and their domestic world to forge an intimate connection with the viewer. Donté, on the other hand, constructs his selfie through added layers of media and little personal information, enabling him to maintain a distance from the viewer. These approaches, though they do not exhaust the ways in which home dancers choreograph their personae for online audiences, reflect a range of stylistic orientations representative of the field of moving selfies at large.

It is worth noting that, in addition to their virtuosic yet divergent approaches to autochoreography, Mar and Donté also perform differing identities and therefore represent and appeal to different populations of users. As of this writing, Mar is a thirtysomething, white, gender-queer American whose new media journey marks their transition; Donté is a twentysomething Black, gay, Canadian man.[17] The respective identities of these two dancers inherently inform their autochoreographies; thus, any discussion of how they choreograph themselves for an online audience carries with it an understanding of their individual intersections of race, gender, sexuality, class, age, and nationality. This notion of identity through autochoreography is embedded in the following analyses, wherein Mar exercises "techniques of exposure" and Donté employs "techniques of buffering."

Mar's Exposure

Clad in a sports bra and a pair of high-waisted briefs, which together reveal the illustrative tattoos on their thighs and all down the length of their arms, Mar stands in what appears to be their living room. Eyes closed and forward facing, they dance as if they were home alone, with no one watching, while Fleetwood Mac's "Think of Me" blares in the background. To the sound of Stevie Nicks singing, "I don't hold you down," Mar contemplatively bops in place and pumps their arms as their gaze lifts from the ground toward the ceiling. With the subtle undulation of the torso, Mar rolls their arms in an alternating wavelike pattern. At first, their expression is stoic, if not grave—but as they move, they gradually reveal a slight grin. To the lyrics "Maybe that's why you're around," Mar's smile grows wider and more radiant as they softly shimmy their shoulders with their arms out, closing their eyes and lifting their head until it drops back. Gradually, while still in movement, Mar turns their gaze back into themselves, now with a bit more levity.

Below this video is a caption that reads, "just here to report that if this sober addict can survive VENUS RX [retrograde] without drinking by listening to the same fleetwood mac song on repeat YOU CAN TOO 🦋 WE'RE ALMOST THERE" (see fig 10).

Fig. 10. Mar dancing to Fleetwood Mac. (Meagan Willoughby)

At only eight seconds long, Mar's home dance video ends with a return to the beginning, looping repeatedly until the viewer decides to move on. But something about this home dance video, as short and seemingly mundane as it may be, prompts viewers to continue watching: to pause their undoubtedly rapid scrolling habits on Instagram and pay their attention to this singular dancing figure, Mar, grooving to Fleetwood Mac in their presumed living room, wearing only their undergarments. With over 24,000 views at the time of writing, the video has indeed gained algorithmic traction since May 2017, when it was posted to Mar's Instagram account—an account that houses a collection of videos that together demonstrate what they call their "personal practice": the title of their account.[18]

Appropriately named, Mar's account includes hundreds of "personal" media capturing them dancing alone at home and often engrossed in mundane moments of domestic life. Whether playfully grooving to a pop song while washing the dishes or just taking a contemplative midday dance break, Mar posts content that cultivates a sense of intimacy. More than merely personal, their choreographies of body, space, and media result in many moving selfies that provide a snapshot of their everyday life and a narrative of the world in which they live—a narrative of themselves manifesting as an image. In watching one of their videos, like the one described above, the viewer may gain a sense of Mar's personality, activity in that moment, preoccupations, and stylistic inclinations. Then, on a broader scale, one might also glimpse aspects of their identity, such as their socioeconomic status, level of education, gender identification, sexuality, and personal history. This particular selfie, as an exemplar of their larger collection, reflects these elements of Mar's world and demonstrates the work of autochoreography that is characteristic of moving selfies.

Mar's work of creating this moving selfie is achieved through a number of mechanisms. Specifically, through both the video and the caption explaining it, Mar choreographs a portrait of themselves that demonstrates what we might call *techniques of exposure*: baring the homebody, revealing personal information about themselves, situating themselves in their home, harnessing a confessional gaze, and utilizing a stripped-down video aesthetic. These techniques, though not totally exhaustive of their autochoreography, make up the force by which Mar manifests an image of themselves toward public acknowledgment, exposure, and documentation—both generally and at that moment in time.

Mar's homebody is central among their techniques—quite literally. Their figure is in the foreground of the image and centered within the frame, reflecting how they have positioned themselves as the focal point of the video. This positioning, in part, contributes to how the viewer understands that Mar, framed as the subject of the video, is also the producer of that video. Mar's countenance and gaze reaffirm this impression, as these components work to both demonstrate a self-centralizing aesthetic and establish a connection with the viewer. Beginning with a stoic contemplation, Mar performs their opening movements with a sense of introspection. The viewer can almost see them ponder the day's thoughts while they move. Then, they shed this expression as they maintain eye contact with the camera. The gradual development of their smile—from subtle smirk to sly grin to beaming smile—works to transform their exhibition of pensive interiority into a more outward expression of delight. This transformation accomplishes a couple of important outcomes regarding Mar's autochoreography. First, the smile aimed directly at the camera demonstrates not only a recognition of the viewer but also an attempt to cultivate a sense of closeness with that viewer. This shift from introversion ("turning in") to extroversion ("turning out") exhibits the dual performance of a diary-like self-reflection and an audience-addressing presentation—a movement that folds the interior out to the exterior, exposing the self to the other. Alongside this technique is the transformation of Mar's countenance from contemplative to cheerful, which suggests that they come around to acknowledging the viewer as they perform their interior self. That is to say, the introspective gaze that melts into a recognition in and delight with the viewer articulates a sense of trust on Mar's part that someone is witnessing their homebody and, in turn, that that viewer-witness will respect and nurture their personal practice.

This careful connection forged by Mar's moment to themselves and followed by a trusting nod to the viewer articulates their autochoreography through movement. Of course, this work is complemented by other techniques of exposure, including their attire and caption. Notable among these is Mar's decision to wear high-waisted cotton briefs and a sports-bra-esque top—clothing that reveals their bodily form. This attire enables the viewer to glimpse the dancer's thigh tattoos and to see their bare torso. Despite this exposure of their bodily form, Mar's clothing is distinct from other, more explicitly sexualized garments that reveal the body. In other words, they are not wearing lace or lingerie or any other kind of accoutrement that may be found, for instance, on the shelves of Victoria's Secret. Instead, their dress is rather nondescript and reflects a utilitarian sensibility. In choosing a sports bra and briefs, perhaps Mar had aimed to ensure both mobility and comfort, so that they may dance without limitations to their movement. This attire articulates a style that one might associate with activity around the house, particularly on a warm day. Indeed, it is "homey" in character, but it also is private. It *exposes* a homebody that may otherwise not be seen in public.

Through their choice in attire, Mar not only reveals their bodily form but also works to expose a true or authentic version of themselves—not one that borrows from the airbrushed aesthetic of beauty magazines but a "real" image of their body and self. They pull back the curtain on their home, body, and psyche to share with the world a multifaceted sense of their own interiority. Of course, this aesthetic sensibility is just as choreographed as any other image of the body. Mar chose to wear these clothes, to record themselves dancing, and to post that dance to the internet for mass viewership. Their dancing body is framed in a way that they find suitable to their message—all to construct an image of themselves. Of course, Mar may not recognize that they are making these decisions, as such aesthetic choices often operate subtly for the artist. Even as they go through the motions of their autochoreography, each movement, however conscious, is a result of the ways in which their private, personal, individual body is very much a public, social, collective body. However real or raw it may seem, Mar's homebody is indeed cultural.

Through Mar's moving selfie, the viewer may get a sense of some *real* Mar, despite the fact that such a notion of real results from a host of efforts and aesthetic decisions that articulate Mar's autochoreography. It is important to note in this regard that while Mar exposes themselves in a way that does not adhere to airbrushed ideals of beauty, they are nonetheless dealing in what Catherine Hakim calls "erotic capital."[19] The raw and vulnerable homebody that Mar constructs taps into the voyeuristic desires of the viewer and enables Mar to accrue likes, views, comments, and followers. Thus, as discussed in part 3, Mar is able to effectively convert their erotic capital into other forms of capital.

The effect of Mar's attire and gaze is also amplified by their caption on the post. By sharing a deeply personal struggle with addiction to thousands of viewers, Mar performs an act of trust. An addiction is not just any piece of information about a person. It is not like disclosing a hobby, a favorite film, or a preferred method of brewing coffee. Rather, the sharing of such personal information is typically undergirded by confidentiality, which would therefore require an act of *confiding* in someone. In making this disclosure public, Mar signals a relationship of trust with their audience. Choreographically, this maneuver becomes an offering of interiority, fostering a sense of closeness.

Along with her sharing of personal details, Mar calls for togetherness in the post, which further cultivates a sense of closeness with the viewer. By convincing the audience that if Mar can endure the Venus retrograde so can they, Mar inspires a collective motivation. Their final expression of "we're almost there" exemplifies this communal spirit. The language here is also telling of such a call, as Mar employs not the *singular* first-person "I" but the *plural* first-person "we." This subtle use of the plural first-person voice functions to further cultivate a connection with the viewer. Through this phrasing, Mar suggests that overcoming the Venus retrograde is easier when we recognize how it affects everyone—it is as if they are saying, "I'm the one dancing, but we're all in this thing together." Such an implication of relational belonging emphasizes that Mar's choreographies are not just *in* the public but also *for* and *with* the public. Indeed, while Mar choreographs a multifaceted sense of interiority, they are quite explicitly engaging in public dialogue with their followers.

Though Mar's video is short in duration, it does not lack in its layers of autochoreography. Mar leverages their domestic situation, with its semiotics of interiority, to offer an image of their own psychological state. In their caption, too, they pull back the layers of their persona to reveal intimate details of their life with the viewer, thereby building a rapport with the audience. Both their attire and their caption extend this logic. These facets constitute Mar's techniques of exposure so that they can choreograph an image that expresses their personhood—a product of their autochoreography.

Donté's Bufferings

While Mar approaches their autochoreography through techniques of exposure, Donté approaches his through *techniques of buffering*. In tech speak, "buffering" connotes the period of pause while a video loads for the end user. For Donté's autochoreography, however, this term refers to the ways in which his selfie creates an aesthetic and conceptual "padding" between himself and the viewer. Specifically, Donté creates buffers between himself and his space, himself and the media, and himself and the viewers, resulting in a moving selfie that evades personal capture. So, while Donté's videos reach out to viewers with inspiration, support, and good humor, he does not reveal much personal information about himself. Instead, he incorporates novel media elements that, on the one hand, attract a mass following and, on the other hand, allow him to maintain a distance between his personal identity and the viewing public. Donté's case demonstrates how autochoreography is not always about exposing oneself, airing vulnerabilities, or constructing an "authentic" representation—or at least not in a way that is packaged so concisely into one post (as is the case with Mar's example). Techniques of buffering instead enable Donté to produce an image of himself without fully exposing the details of his personal affairs. An analysis of one particular home dance video that Donté posted on January 11, 2019, will articulate this approach.

Donté stands centered in the frame with his back to the camera, facing a bare white wall and closed door—a space that appears to be a corridor between rooms. To the snapping beat of Victoria Monét's "New Love," he turns to look over his left shoulder, striking his right arm. With this strike appears the word "YOU" just below his hand. He repeats this gesture to the other side as the word "ARE" appears just before he spins to the front, making eye contact with the camera. Then, in rapid succession, Donté strikes his arm toward the ground as the word "KILLING" appears and then up toward the ceiling with the word "IT." Together, this phrase "YOU ARE KILLING IT"—arranged around his body in a compass-like configuration—spins out of view as Donté swings his right arm in a revolution matching the movement of the text. With the swipe of his right arm, we see a green heart emoji appear and move with Donté's gestures before disappearing; a blue heart emoji then appears with the swipe of the right arm and follows Donté's tight spin and also disappears. He twirls both arms above his head as the words "KEEP ON GOING" also revolve in space. The text vanishes as Donté claps his hands on beat.

Donté continues to bop and strike in coordination with both the music and the messages that dance across the screen. The lyrics begin, "On the day I met you, mentally undressed you," as Donté jauntily grooves to the poppy beat. With a kick-step-kick and emphatic point to the right, we see the words "YOU DON'T NEED TO RUSH" appear—text that slides off-screen with a pop of Donté's hip. Then, with a spin of the right forearm, we see "PACE URSELF" also spin into view. As Donté unfolds both arms to the front right, the word "SHIT" pops into view, a clap to the front left reveals the word "TAKES," and a rhythmic sway of the hips prompts the appearance of "TIME," along with an emoji of a clock and a large red exclamation point, one at each hand. The viewer now sees the complete message: "SHIT TAKES TIME."

Donté is in an open and empty space: there is no furniture or fixtures, no decor on the walls, no laundry on the floor—no sign of his living condition. We do see a wide opening to a room with a painted wall to his right, leading to perhaps a living room of sorts. And to his left is a stairwell, possibly descending to a first floor or basement. Despite the lack of adornment, the space nonetheless reads as domestic, with a quintessentially residential six-panel interior door behind him and walls that are trimmed in the style of a modern home. The space is well lit but with no sign of natural light. The recessed lighting above his figure casts a shadow on Donté's face, obscuring his features and expression but highlighting his colorful attire: an oversized lime green shirt that drifts with every movement, pink athletic pants, and matching pink sneakers that screech against the glossy hardwood floors as he moves.

Words and emojis continue to dance with Donté's figure: a kick-step-kick introduces the words "WE ARE ALL ON OUR OWN UNIQUE JOUR-NEY"; a bolt of the arm toward the ceiling throws an emoji of a pink heart with a yellow bow around it; a turn and point toward the camera blasts the word "YOU" across the screen (but in place of the letter "O" is an emoji of a hand pointing toward the viewer), followed by the text "BRING SOME-THING SO DIFFERENT TO THE TABLE"; a sparkle emoji flies in and out of view; a booty-popping Donté shares the screen with the words "DON'T COMPARE YOURSELF TO OTHERS ON HERE!!" And then exploding across the screen with star emojis is the message "YOU ARE HERE FOR A REASON."

The video ends with Donté in a wide stance with his right arm lifted, as if he is grasping an emoji of a champagne bottle. He circles his left arm over his head toward the bottle and then immediately rebounds as if to pop open the champagne. An image of a rainbow flies from the bottle and out of the frame as the words "CELEBRATE HOW FAR YOU'VE COME UR DOIN GREAT" appear. Below the video is a caption that reads: "#YOUareHereForAReason. Bound to do incredible things. Keep your head up and take it steady. #KeepKillingIt ✨🥰☀️ #happyfriday 🎵: @victoriamonet" (see fig. 11).

Together, the video and caption of this post reflect Donté's public persona without divulging information about himself, exposing his body, or revealing any details of his domestic setting. While this positioning of the self might seem at odds with the notion of intimaesthetics, it nonetheless illustrates how a dancer might withhold, and even strategically leverage, personal information toward a sense of camaraderie with the viewer. This is especially true of the phenomenon of candid dancing discussed in chapter 1, wherein the dancer is not even aware that their dancing is part of a production. Even with the moving selfie, wherein the dancer is aware of the camera, they may deliberately resist exposing themselves. Yet, despite the lack of personal information, Donté's approach does not suggest an absence of meaning; rather, it is quite the opposite. Embedded in the videos of scant information and little personal exposure are other, more subtle qualities. In Donté's case, techniques of buffering enable him to convey

Fig. 11. Donté's moving selfie. (Meagan Willoughby)

an abstract public image of himself while protecting himself from personal injury that may accompany public exposure. These techniques, which may be gleaned in the video described above, include his use of space—both in terms of his surrounding physical space and the mediatized space of the video he produces—his eye-catching attire, and his warm yet distanced relationship to the viewer. Before discussing these techniques, however, it is important to first address Donté's relationship to the camera and the image produced: a key feature of his moving selfie.

Donté's autochoreography is grounded in his body and its relationship to the recording device. Though the viewer does not have a behind-the-scenes knowledge of how this video was created, the semiotics of the image indicate its self-capture. This information is expressed in, first, the still, mid-height frame that indicates that the device was propped up on some fixture, as if Donté had strategically positioned the camera before pressing the record button. Second, the way that the video both starts and ends with movement, so that the dance recycles itself time and time again, suggests that parts were trimmed at the beginning and end. While the viewer does not see Donté press the record button, this role is suggested through his constant and direct eye contact with the camera, as well as the appearance of the selfie on his personal, self-named Instagram account. This suggested authorship extends to the text and emojis that appear throughout the video as well. When the viewer reads the words "We are all on our own unique journey," they understand the speaker to be Donté, as indicated by the use of the first-person voice (i.e., the use of "we")—as with Mar's post. This reading of Donté as both the author and performer constitutes the selfie logic of his performance.

Donté's unquestionable authorship of the post grounds his techniques of buffering, which may be understood through a lens of his body, space, and media. While the text and emojis are arguably the most prominent features in Donté's moving selfie, his body and use of space are most germane to this notion of buffering. When considering the layer of body and space, it must be noted that the eye-catching vibrancy of Donté's clothes sits in stark contrast to the bleakness of his space. Indeed, the lime green shirt, pink pants, and pink sneakers that Donté wears attract the viewer's attention, especially against the white background of his homespace—which, also worth noting, lacks furniture, adornments, or evidence of his living condition. This attire and setting allow Donté's movements to "pop," highlighting his buoyancy and lighthearted energy. Such visual dominance of Donté's dancing body in his surrounding space also stands in contrast to the semiotics of his facial expressions. The recessed lighting above him creates a shadow over his face so that the viewer cannot discern Donté's facial features for much of the dance. Certain head positions do make it possible to glimpse his face, as when he tilts his head up toward the light. However, even in those moments, his face still appears expressionless. While a stoic countenance is common in modern, postmodern, and contemporary dance, it functions here as a juxtaposition to the mood Donté creates otherwise—that is, through his bright attire and the energy of his movement. These elements, when choreographed in a vacant, visibly sterile space and with a top-lit stoic face, reflect Donté's autochoreography.

Through his attire, space, and movement, Donté cultivates his public persona as a young Black dancer who has a zeal for life, is good humored, has a positive outlook, and seeks to motivate others to have a similar outlook, all without providing detail about his interior thoughts, personal history, or domestic life. His space is nearly evacuated of clues to his life, character, or intimate world. Then, in terms of his body, he adorns himself in colorful, oversized clothing that upstages his domestic space and obscures the details of his form. Through these techniques of buffering, Donté keeps his personal world at a distance, in terms of both body and space. The effect is that the viewers *feel* like they know Donté, without knowing much about him at all.

Of course, the techniques that occur at the levels of Donté's dancing body and domestic space are compounded by those cultivated by the text and emojis that appear in the video. This element of the dance is integral to the semiotics of the post, as it constructs multiple layers of his buffering. First, the text and emojis that the viewer sees are enabled through the physical space that Donté has created while capturing his selfie. Donté not only stands far enough away from the camera so that his entire figure, from head to toe, is made visible but also creates an added margin of space for his postproduction additions (i.e., the text and emojis that appear in the product). This use of space suggests that Donté is cognizant of how his body is being imaged while dancing, perhaps because he is watching his body on-screen while recording and is thus able to process his spacing (and his dancing) in real time, adjusting his movements and orientations as needed—a common practice in home dance video production. The effect, however, is a doubled sense of one's own spatiality: an understanding of one's body in their immediate environment and also in the mediatized image.

Alongside the buffering of domestic and digital space that Donté enacts is a more conceptual buffering, which results in a personal distance between himself and his audience. While the content of his home dance videos illustrates compassion toward his audience, Donté does not "give himself" to the viewer. Like the buffers created through his dancing body and domestic space, Donté's motivational text focuses on the viewer rather than on Donté. At many points throughout this dance, Donté's text uses the second-person voice: "You are killing it," "You don't need to rush," "You are here for a reason." At one point, his movements even personify the textual direct address by pointing to the camera and thus to the viewer. This movement is coordinated with a large "YOU" (with the "O" being an emoji of a finger pointing out) that grows across the screen. The caption of the post, too, addresses the viewer directly to reiterate the messages embedded in the video. While these variations of the second-person voice might serve as some self-affirmation for Donté, their semiotic function as a direct address clarifies his audience, draws the viewer into his dance, and captivates them with the performance—all without Donté having to describe himself, his positionality, his preoccupations, his personal history, or any other pieces of information about himself (a technique that might manifest through the first-person voice). The text and emojis that are literally layered over the image of his dancing body, then, work as a protective layer: they forge an intimate connection with the viewer so that Donté might preserve himself and his own sense of interiority.

It must be noted that, though Donté dispenses motivation and elicits inspiration through his video, he speaks to an audience he does not know. At the time of writing, Donté's video has well over one million views. While he may personally know some of the individuals included in that count, the video undoubtedly reaches far beyond his personal circles of friends and family. Even if he wanted to ascertain who of those in his circles watched the video, he has little to no technological recourse to do so; he only has the rolling count of anonymous views to gauge the reach of his dance. Because Donté's audience is largely abstract, the second-person "you" is effective, as it applies a universality to his message and eschews any specificity of a direct address. This sense of universality that Donté constructs plays well with the neoliberal ethos of Instagram. The evacuation of the home's character, the lack of personal information made available, the general content of the messaging, and the vagueness of his audience together open Donté's video out to mass appeal—a subject of greater discussion in part 3.

Donté's approach to buffering stands in contrast to Mar's techniques of exposure. Mar uses their movement and gaze, relationship to the camera, situation among personal domestic adornments, and stripped-down attire to pull back the curtain, so to speak, on their intimate world. They then reiterate this aesthetic through the caption on the image. The result is a moving selfie that cultivates closeness with the viewer because of the vulnerability they offer. For Donté, the stark contrast of his body against the bare background of his home allows him to create a moving selfie that emphasizes his message of hope and motivation. However, Donté's dancing and messaging work to obscure himself and his life while paradoxically building a seemingly personal connection with his audience. In both of their autochoreographies, intimacy is aestheticized; however, the mode of that aesthetic and the techniques used to craft it are worlds apart.

For both Mar and Donté, identity is intricately woven through their respective autochoreographies. While facets of their race, gender, sexuality, and class may be evident in the singular videos analyzed above, such integral aspects of their autochoreographies appear in a more incremental fashion for each performer. For instance, Mar's initial identification in one post as a "soft butch lesbian" gives way in later posts to their nonbinary status, alongside details of their "top surgery" (double mastectomy) and use of they/them pronouns. Similarly, Donté does not initially refer much to his sexuality or discuss his Blackness on Instagram, but as he navigates his undergraduate career, his posts begin to articulate the complexities of his race and sexuality. Autochoreography, like the fluidity of identity itself, takes shape over time. It cannot be confined to one post, cannot be defined through one home dance video, and cannot be represented by one self-expression.

Part 3. Circulating the Moving Selfie

The discussion of autochoreography through moving selfie demonstrates how home dance videos online might come to be read as personal, familiar, and intimate—both a reflection and an expression of the performer. These efforts produce an intimaesthetic image of the dancer's personhood, primed for viewership—a viewership that is then activated by the decision to post the media. Such a decision launches the performer's image into mass circulation online. Thus, while part 2 unpacks techniques involved in producing an image of oneself, part 3 delves into its nuances of circulation. Indeed, many aspects of performance change when it is initially mediatized and then again when it is posted online.[20] Yet, it is the shift in its scale of exposure that most acutely harnesses the ways in which one's autochoreography adjusts to the media's online circulation. A living room dance by oneself, for instance, becomes a locally stored video with an audience of one, which then, once uploaded to a platform, becomes a public artifact with an audience of hundreds, thousands, or even millions. This manner of *leaping scales* prompts a shift in the selfie's ontological register.[21] As it moves from the inside to the outside, from the home to the world, and from the individual body to the body of the public, the moving selfie opens itself up to new possibilities of autochoreography—a new "social life."[22] Once online, the media circulates the feeds of followers, thereby inviting an audience; it accrues social and cultural capital in the form of quantifiable views, likes, and comments; it contributes to a larger public persona of the performer by continuing—or, alternatively, disrupting—the trajectory of their previous self-expressions; and it bumps up against other worlds of media content through its incorporations of hashtags and mentions.

Considering these activities, it is useful to approach the moving selfie's social life through three distinct layers: its life in the feed, its place on the personal profile, and its integration with enterprise. Unlike the circulation of candid dancing, the ethos of the moving selfie's online life is less obviously political, as it does not originate with the overt theft of the performer's authority and agency. Nonetheless, the platform enacts its own forms of theft, its own forms of authority over the homebody. Continuing the focus on Mar and Donté, the three layers of digital activity together reflect the online manifestation of one's autochoreography. While these layers do not exhaust the many facets of the moving selfie's social life, they suggest a range of its social, cultural, political, and economic operations.

The Feed

Once uploaded to a platform, a moving selfie may encounter a winding, unpredictable pathway of circulation. It might, for instance, get aggregated into various search results; viewed once, twice, or a thousand times; reposted by a follower; shared to another platform; or locally downloaded and saved to a device. However meandering its circulation, the social life of an image on social media begins at a particular digital locale: the feed, a general term used across platforms to refer to a stream of content, typically including material that was recently published. As the gateway to wider circulation, the feed activates the accumulation and exchange of capital. That is to say, because the feed is where users typically encounter the media of those they follow, it is also where they first engage with that media and where that media begins to gain algorithmic traction. For a video on Instagram, the user's possible interactions include watching (and rewatching), liking, commenting, sharing, and saving the media. Those interactions then "teach" the algorithm—because such algorithms "learn" the behavior of users and then adjust accordingly—how to serve up content to a user, thereby commanding the flow and degree of exposure of a particular post.[23] Ultimately, this process determines the *currency* of an image.

The use of the term "currency" to describe the feed on new media platforms is especially appropriate. The term refers to (1) the constant flush of new content and (2) the ways in which content accrues social, cultural, and economic capital for its producer, thereby catapulting the user into what Jansson and Fast call a "click economy."[24] Interestingly, at different points in time, Instagram's feed has harnessed both of these notions of currency (i.e., both as nowness and as a medium of exchange). When it was first launched in 2010, Instagram organized its feed in a reverse chronology so that the most recent post was at the top, and as the user scrolled down, they encountered less recent content. However, in July 2016, four years after Facebook (now Meta) bought the fledgling company, Instagram announced that it was changing the organizing logic of its feed. The content would no longer be ordered by recency but instead through "relevancy sorting": a complex system determined by machine-learning algorithms. When the company announced this change, they explained how the notion of relevance was "based on the likelihood you'll be interested in the content, your relationship with the person posting and the timeliness of the post." This new system would, according to Instagram, allow users to see content that they "care about most."[25] Such a shift in how users encounter the media of those they follow cemented Instagram's move toward personal data collection and targeted advertising, as the algorithms that determine the circulation of media relied upon behavioral data about users. Yet the behavior metrics the company uses to determine what content users "care about most" are not made available but are instead part of Instagram's *black box*: a system wherein the inputs (images) and outputs (content moderation) are distinct, but the processes that occur in between are obscured.[26]

Indeed, Instagram users (and the public at large) are excluded from information about how the company's algorithms work. In 2018, however, after backlash from users regarding the changes in the feed, Instagram released information on the data points that determine relevance. They cited three core factors: interest, or how much Instagram predicts a user will care about a post, which is determined by "past behavior on similar content and potentially machine vision analyzing the actual content of the post"; recency, or how recently a post was published to the platform; and relationship, or how close a user is to a person, determined by how much they engage with previously posted content. In addition to these data points, Instagram also revealed three signals that influence the ranking of a post in the feed: frequency, or how often a user accesses Instagram's platform; following, or how many accounts a user chooses to see content from; and usage, or the amount of time a user spends on the platform.[27] In short, this information reveals that Instagram's relevancy algorithms learn users' likes and dislikes, their clicking and scrolling habits, their level of engagement with those they follow, their duration and frequency of accessing the platform; and their taste in media (whether they like videos or still images, for instance), among many other data sets. Systems may also gather personal and behavioral data across different platforms and different devices.[28] However, like the algorithms on its platform, Instagram offers little to no information about how its system—and the ecosystem to which it belongs—functions.

The 2018 reveal by Instagram, aimed at demystification, largely avoids specificity and reiterates Instagram's algorithmic power.[29] Remaining nebulous, for instance, are the components of "behavior," the weight of each factor in relation to the others, and the degree to which a shift in habit might change the organization of content on the feed, among many other questions. Despite the uncertainty around Instagram's algorithms, users nonetheless tend to take what little information they have in order to make sense of their online practice, contributing to what Taina Bucher calls "the algorithmic imaginary."[30] They may, for example, find that particular days of the week, as well as times of day, are likely to gain more algorithmic traction than others.[31] They may read a blog about how a post on a Wednesday afternoon—when followers are eager to check their feeds—may garner more views, likes, and comments than a post on a Friday evening—when followers are typically busy with social events. Another technique users may adopt is the "like-for-like" approach, wherein they strategically engage with the content of others in order to activate the law of reciprocity toward engagement in return. These techniques, and many others like them, compose a system of tacit knowledge, all geared toward demystifying algorithmic behavior toward greater agency—even if that agency exists solely in the user's perception of their online practice.[32]

These techniques reach new media dancers and impact their orchestrations of media and online identity. Performers learn to choreograph their image within the confines established by Instagram's code. The cases of Mar and Donté illustrate this point. After all, both dancers accrued hundreds of thousands of followers and rose to a status of "micro-celebrity" with some sort of understanding of or confidence in how Instagram functions.[33] In Donté's posts, the view count and comments on videos might indicate which videos went viral and which ones enjoyed a smaller audience. The video analyzed in the previous section accrued, for instance, over 1,250,000 million views (at the time of writing), whereas other videos on his profile did not break 20,000 views. This exceptionally high number of views reflects the wide audience that Donté's moving selfie reached, perhaps due to its nonspecific address to all viewers, its universally appealing content, and the intimacy the homebody garnered. Following the post, Donté continued to share similar content, perhaps in response to the algorithmic treatment of that particular home dance video, as it resulted in a remarkable number of views compared to his content not related to dance. This point is evidenced in how Donté reposts videos that have performed well for the algorithms, an approach that allows him to take advantage of existing content to gain new followers, keep the existing ones interested, and continue his media output. One home dance video in particular was posted three different times, undoubtedly reaching new viewers each time. Indeed, Donté seems to understand the value system that Instagram cultivates and enforces through its relevancy sorting.

Like Donté, Mar also appears cognizant of Instagram's inner workings. Though they do not repost the same home dance video multiple times, as Donté does, Mar provides meta-critiques of Instagram's platform, as in one post wherein they highlight the power of its algorithms. In an Instagram *story* shared on December 10, 2020, on their separate personal account (an account that is discussed in greater detail below), Mar compares the algorithmic traction of two posts: one with their girlfriend and another one talking about deactivating their Instagram account.[34] In this story, Mar writes, "good morning let's get an algorithm check," and below that text, they include screenshots of the two separate posts from their account. Written on top of the post with their girlfriend is the text "being gay and selling stickers with a hot pic," with the like count of 4,212 circled. On the post of an image about deactivating a social media account is the text "telling you how to leave this app with a graphic," with the like count of 187 circled. As Mar points out, the post about their intimate relationship and commercial ventures outperforms the one that subverts the dominance of the platform. The post that draws attention to this discrepancy not only reveals Mar's awareness of Instagram's algorithmic preferences but also represents its own subversion. It, in essence, uses the platform to shed light on the silent powers of that platform. At the same time, Mar also benefits from Instagram's way of ranking posts.

The observations that Mar shares, alongside the tactics of Donté, reflect how dancers navigate Instagram's revised algorithms, an additional layer of work they perform. With every update to the platform, dancers update their approaches to satisfy, complicate, or otherwise transgress the value system that Instagram has enforced through its algorithms. One such case is the addition of Instagram TV (IGTV, for short): a sister application, released in June 2018 and later rolled into the main Instagram app as a feature, that allows users to record and upload video content that is longer than sixty seconds. Like typical Instagram media, IGTV videos appear on the feeds of followers and also reside on the user's personal profile. This feature of Instagram offers new autochoreographic possibilities for users, as it enables the posting of lengthier content. Updates such as these reflect Instagram's encouragement of users to perpetually adapt to its system of values and currency.[35]

While Instagram continues to implement changes to its platform, prompting users to constantly tune their practices to those changes, the 2016 update to its ordering of content on users' feeds prompted a seismic shift in how dancers share their content and how viewers encounter it. Though it may seem minor in the arc of Instagram's development since its launch in 2010, this change prompted an upheaval of user behavior, encouraging new habits to form in how users might share their media and how they might engage with others' media. It must be noted, too, that by establishing a new system of values, this revised mechanism also shapes the content that users produce in the first place. In other words, the relevance feed impacts the levels of not only circulation and consumption but also production. If pictures of food tend to get more likes and comments, then users are going to post more pictures of food. If videos of cats tend to get more views, then viewers will likely post more videos of cats. Similarly, if intimaesthetic expressions of the home dancing body attract more interest, then users may produce more content of that nature, leading to what Martin Gibbs and colleagues call a "platform vernacular," or the "affordances of particular social media platforms and the ways they are appropriated and performed in practice."[36]

The implications of a platform vernacular for the moving selfie, and for dance on new media at large, are manifold. Dancers tailor their expressions to the system of values that Instagram has created, and continues to adapt that vernacular anytime the platform affordances change. Chief among such tailorings is how the notion of branding has shaped dance on social media—particularly the entanglements of the self as a brand and a brand as the self. This phenomenon manifests, unsurprisingly, through the circulation of moving selfies on Instagram: a circulation that makes up the dancer's autochoreography and is represented not only through the feed but also through the personal profile.

The Personal Profile

If the feed represents the currency of a singular post, the personal profile represents the longevity of one's performance of self over time. The user often crafts this performance longitudinally, perhaps deleting media that no longer satisfies their evolving self or simply letting the profile accumulate media over time to represent the expansiveness of their identity. Through this work, the performer extends their autochoreography, creating somewhat of a record of the self across time yet not without limitations and complications of the platform.

Separate from what Instagram designates as a professional profile, the personal profile includes the following information at the top of its page: a singular profile picture, a 150-character-limit biography, an outside website (if the user chooses), and a count of the individual's followers and followings. Below this introductory information is a gridded repository of images that the individual has posted since the creation of their account, with the most recent image at the top. Depending on what additional features the user utilizes, there may also be tabs for IGTV posts, content that the user has been tagged in by others, media placed in a *series* (a feature added in 2019), and *effects* that other users are able to download and use in their own images. Instagram users treat these features of their profile with varying levels of depth and frequency. Donté, for instance, utilizes the gambit of features, not just photos and videos but also IGTV media, series, and effects. By contrast, on their home dance account, Mar mostly refrains from those additional features of the profile and only has photos and regular videos on their profile (i.e., not IGTV videos, but videos under sixty seconds).

It must be noted here that, while Mar takes a more minimalist approach to their account, they complicate their relationship to the profile, and thus to their Instagram portrait at large, by having more than one account (which is made obvious by tagging and mentioning across accounts). In addition to their dance-centric account, where they solely post home dance videos, Mar is also the owner of a self-named personal Instagram account, which they describe as a "planetarium" with the signature "artist, writer, dancer." On this account, Mar not only has a vast collection of photos and videos but also has many IGTV posts, links to their personal website, and ads for their quilting class and radio show. What is especially noteworthy here is how, by creating and managing multiple accounts, Mar is managing multiple public personae: each one highlighting different aspects of themselves and each one targeting a different audience. This phenomenon is, of course, common practice on Instagram and is arguably something the platform encourages. Such a notion is evinced by Instagram's February 2016 announcement that users would have the ability to add up to five accounts (with separate email addresses for each one) and switch among them without having to log out. This change not only promoted the creation of new accounts but also facilitated how users like Mar might approach the management of their multiple accounts. In other words, if Instagram makes it easier to switch between different accounts for the same individual, then it also makes it easier to maintain multiple personae.

The phenomenon of creating and managing multiple profiles on Instagram is couched within a wider movement of personal branding. Indeed, the notion of the personal brand is integral to the ethos of Instagram: the platform encourages both selfie-ism and commerciality, effectively integrating those two categories to an extent that they are inextricable. Of course, personal branding is not a new phenomenon, nor is it intrinsic to new media. While the notion of self-branding is often attributed to the 1997 article "The Brand Called You," written by Tom Peters and published in *Inc.* magazine, examples of branding the self may be found throughout modern history.[37] Nonetheless, the phenomenon enjoyed even greater growth with the expansion of new media, particularly the advent of reality TV.[38] Under the influence of neoliberalism, the individual is subject to the same rules that govern any other sector of the capitalist marketplace. Expounded by Boltanski and Chiapello, the neoliberalist logic encourages the "instrumentalization and commodification of what is most specifically human about human beings."[39] Along these lines, one's character, body, and thoughts may be subject to commodification, just as any other product on the shelf at the market, so that branding culture sees a rise in the "self brand."[40] The notion that one individual may create "products" of themselves is very much within the bounds of neoliberalism.

If branding the self on Instagram is well suited to flourish under the terms of neoliberalism, then the advent of new media only further fosters its growth toward cultural ubiquity. With its rapid transmission of information, infiltration of everyday life, and image centricity, new media makes for a prime instrument in the production, circulation, and consumption of *personae*. Individuals "give themself"—to borrow the language of Boltanski and Chiapello—to their production, whereby the "construction of [their] identity [is] a product to be consumed by others."[41] Then, concepts like *domesticity*, *intimacy*, *interiority*, and the *dancing body* become fitting material for this work, as each of those concepts provides "raw" composites of personhood. The home dance selfie, then, simultaneously produces a concrete image of the self and contributes to a perceived authenticity of that self.

Granted, not all selfies on new media represent one's self brand. Rather, as both marketing experts and cultural studies scholars maintain, creating a personal brand requires a consistency of messaging about one's self.[42] Along these terms, the branded selfie must contribute to a stable image of an individual so that their personhood is more easily "consumable" to viewers.[43] The Instagram personal profile is primed for such a task, as it frames an individual through a gallery of images, each of which provides a variation of one's branded character: different activities, different places and spaces, and different props, all mapped onto the same body with the same, consistent character.[44]

Through their respective Instagram profiles, Mar and Donté demonstrate how branding the self in new media requires a consistency of messaging about one's personhood. True to the strategies of branding at large, both of these dancers capture their moving selfies and, over time, create a stable representation of themselves, each reflecting their own "authentically unique personality."[45] While Mar manages multiple personal profiles, and thus multiple public personae, their account devoted to home dance videos is an integral aspect of the persona they construct through that account. Dance, in other words, is fundamental to the personal brand Mar choreographs on their home dance account. Donté, on the other hand, takes a different approach to his personal profile. Instead of honing his brand to his home dance practices, he provides a broader image of this life, as he shares content that reflects a wide array of activities. Indeed, Donté's moving selfies mingle with other aspects of his everyday world: eating, shopping, socializing, and spending time with family, among other activities.

Alongside their approaches to the scope of their personal profiles is how the respective identity positions of each dancer become integral to the brands they construct. Through the posts on his personal profile, for instance, Donté presents himself as a hip, fun-loving, good-humored yet somewhat mysterious young Black man who performs an ambiguous sexuality but later references his queerness. Like the example discussed above, Donté's other moving selfies convey a sentiment of buoyancy. In one video, which initially appeared on January 8, 2019, and was reposted on June 30, 2019, January 12, 2020, and June 10, 2020, Donté congratulates his audience on "[waking] up today" and encourages them to "KEEP GOING!!!" Digital confetti explodes across the screen and heart emojis fly through space as Donté grooves to the upbeat melody of an electronic song—

perhaps one composed by him. Donté's poppy style of movement, light-heartedness of character, and use of motivational text and emojis reflect a similar sentiment and persona as that which he performs in the video discussed in part 2. This maintenance of Donté's character—along with his performance of identity—demonstrates the notion of consistency that is so integral to branding the self.

It must be noted how the events of 2020 allowed Donté to further complicate his personal brand, as his nondancing posts began to contain more overtly political messaging, thereby revealing more detail regarding his identity positioning, cultural affiliations, and personal history. Following the murder of George Floyd, Donté expressed his support for the Black Lives Matter movement, his disapproval of the state of politics in the United States, and his frustrations with the social and cultural effects of the COVID-19 pandemic.[46] Amid this shift in tone and content, Donté's moving selfies still largely refrained from any political messaging—anchoring his personal brand by maintaining a level of consistency across time. So, as Donté's collection evolved over time, thereby demonstrating the evolution of his identity, his personal brand gained greater texture. His consistently motivational, inspirational, and lighthearted homebody came to mingle with content that was both more personal and more overtly political.

Like Donté, Mar also uses their home moving selfies to provide a consistent message about themselves and thus cultivate a personal brand. Their content on their home dance profile situates them as a white, middle-class, queer individual who uses pop music, the ethos of the home, and their witty charisma to construct an image of raw yet fantastical domesticity. Across their profile, they move through the home with a casual virtuosity; express their relationship to whatever song is playing; comment on their current state of mind and life; and perform their identity as a queer person about to embark on a transition—a process that viewers begin to see on Instagram in 2021. This evolution of their persona (and person) becomes evident across their many moving selfies, while remaining consistent in the ethos of their home expressions.

On November 1, 2015, Mar posted a video of them engaging in a floor exercise, stretching across the hardwood floor of their home. The caption reads: "slow sunday practice with james brown and new shampoo and doing my best." Here, Mar performs wit and charm through the caption; trained dancerly experience through the floor movements (in the style of Bartenieff Fundamentals, a technique commonly taught in university dance programs across the United States); and affinity toward an array of music genres. With many moving selfies in between, Mar posted a video on April 11, 2016, of them dancing in front of a large window and cluttered desk, with an ironing board resting beside them and a swinging chandelier overhead. The caption reads: "a reminder that when you're a grown woman—having sleepovers with ur best friends and listening to alanis are still just as important as they were 20 years ago. Thanks @eliza.hernand for not letting me 4get."[47] Here again, Mar provides some intimate detail of their life while revealing their musical interests. Features available in these two examples may be seen across their oeuvre of home dance videos on Instagram. The media illustrate how, through their everyday movement practice, Mar has determined what domestic interiority looks like, how to capture it, and how to build a brand around it. Through this project, Mar cultivated a postfeminist audience that can indulge vicariously through their everyday wonderings and witness their back-to-the-basics expressions of self.[48]

While Mar and Donté each cultivate their own unique brand, they together reflect the power of the personal profile as a way of organizing one's long-term autochoreography in a fashion of Instagram's neoliberal personal brand. The ways in which these dancers post and organize their moving selfies demonstrate how easily self-expression slips into self-promotion on platforms like Instagram. Moving selfies, that is, illustrate not only the ubiquity of personal branding on new media but also the commercial co-optation of notions like dance, domesticity, intimacy, and authenticity. The following section addresses this trend through a discussion of *hashtags* and *mentions*. Through these tactics, dancers incorporate their media into/with other bodies—other individual users, as well as larger bodies of enterprise. Once again, Mar and Donté serve as examples in how home dancers circulate their images on Instagram. They, as people, may be the *products* of their labor; but also they engage with and align themselves to other products in the Instagram marketplace.

The Hashtag and the Mention

The mechanics of the hashtag and mention are not inherently market driven. Instead, these instruments reflect a way of organizing data and communicating with other users. A hashtag, indicated with a *pound* symbol before it, aggregates posts together around a particular idea, event, movement, or theme; and a mention, indicated with an *at* symbol before it, references another account and links to the associated profile. There are many reasons why a user might incorporate a hashtag in their post or mention another user's account: to participate in some dialogue, either interpersonal or more broadly public; to add an explanatory or comical addendum to one's post; or to gain the attention of a wider audience. Across their many uses, these two instruments contribute to how one's content circulates on a platform: to whom the user directs their thoughts; where all their posts might be aggregated; and what new audiences might be exposed to their content.

Because the inclusion of hashtags and mentions influences patterns of circulation, they contribute to the performer's autochoreography. When attached to a moving selfie, for instance, the hashtag and mention function to incorporate that dance and that dancer into a wider network, extending the audience and further entangling the self-expression into the nodes of Instagram. Dancers like Mar and Donté utilize these instruments to varying degrees and with varying frequency—and those utilizations have different social, political, and economic implications. Mar, for one, seldom incorporates hashtags or mentions, but when they do, the tags often link to a fellow artist. Interestingly, after Mar amassed a wide following on their home dance account, they began to mention their personal account. After all, it is on their personal account where they post about various artistic endeavors: advertise episodes of their podcast or the stickers, pins, and shirts they design; promote their books or articles written about them; and call attention to online courses they teach. In a post on February 24, 2017, for instance, Mar is pictured writing in what looks to be a journal (see fig. 12). The caption states:

> dear LA, I'm comin 4 you next month to teach at my favorite place on earth: @otherwild
>
> 3/16 : how to not always be working—building a spiritual & practical toolkit
>
> 3/18 : improvisational quilting : or how there is no messing up ☐ ▫ ☐
>
> Details on both classes & to sign up via link in bio click workshops xoxox
>
> Stay tuned also for a practice and process movement class AND one on one creative mapping sessions—STOKED ✨ photo by @maestier

Illustrated through this use of their account and the incorporation of hashtags and mentions, Mar's relationship to neoliberal capitalism is complex. Affiliated with a culture of both DIY and small business enterprise, Mar uses Instagram not only to link themselves to other artists, writers, and small business owners but also to make a living selling the things they

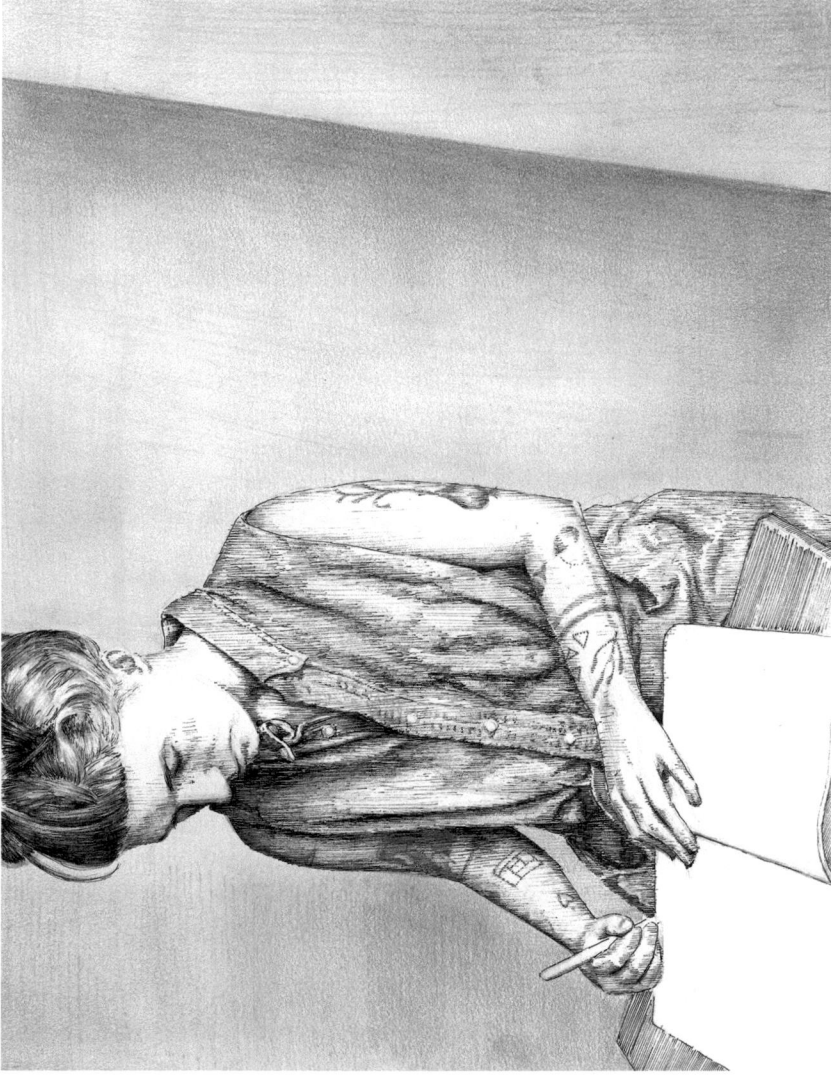

Fig. 12. An Instagram post from Mar's personal account that advertises an upcoming event and collaboration (Meagan Willoughby)

make, the words they write, and the classes they teach. Through their online endeavors, they have tapped into a not so small online community. If this community is the fabric of Mar's online life, the composition of that fabric is equally social and financial.[49] Mar relies on their network of followers and artist friends to help promote their latest project or creative endeavor—tapping into their friends' networks and vice versa. This element of reciprocity, combined with Mar's explicit promotion of products, demonstrates how the moving selfie might flow in and out of gift and commodity systems of exchange.[50]

Like Mar, Donté, too, utilizes hashtags and mentions to draw his homebody into other networks and initiate various transactions through his media. Donté's approach, however, is more explicitly commercial, as he makes clear that his videos are advertisements for particular products. By partnering with companies as well-known as LG, Axe, Ugg, Prada, GoDaddy, and Reebok, Donté aligns his dancerly content with the many different products available in the capitalist marketplace. As his hashtags and mentions of these companies indicate, Donté unabashedly "incorporates" himself, monetizes his dancing, and conveys his profit-seeking motivations.[51] While this orientation may seem uncritical, Donté's relationship to capitalism is more complex than what is immediately available in the media he posts.

Donté's complex comportment may be found in a home dance video that he posted on July 10, 2019, in which he dances with a virtual Starbucks drink. Similar to other content on his account, Donté incorporates text and emojis as he spins and grooves in his home: the strikes and circles of his arms correspond to the appearance and movement of messages like "IT'S TIME TO CELEBRATE TODAY," "LIVE YOUR LIFE IN COLOUR," and "SUMMER VIBES." A large virtual Starbucks cup appears to be a colorful "tie-dyed" Frappuccino drink that the international coffee chain offered in the summer of 2019. The cup dances along with Donté, but it often eclipses his movements. The caption below the video reads: "#StarbucksAmbassador The @Starbucks @TieDyeFrappuccino is out now! What a beautiful day. Let's celebrate!! Sending love your way. Live your life in COLOUR" (see fig. 13).

This video reflects one of Donté's first major corporate partnerships and initiates his trajectory toward many others. His inclusion of the hashtag #StarbucksAmbassador and the mention of @starbucks indicate his transactions as a "brand ambassador," a marketing strategy wherein companies invest in everyday individuals to represent their company by asking them to wear, use, review, or otherwise consume particular prod-

Fig. 13. Donté's Instagram advertisement for the Starbucks Tie-Dye Frappuccino. (Meagan Willoughby. Example of nonchalant gestures)

ucts. These companies tend to select individuals with many social media followers—often referred to as *influencers*—so that their brand and products cast a wider net of exposure that is also focused on a target audience, determined by the follower base of the influencer. Perhaps Starbucks chose Donté to be a brand ambassador because of his universal appeal and his lighthearted personal brand. In return, Donté receives payment from Starbucks, likely augments his own following, and begins to build an influencer portfolio that will attract other paid sponsorships.[52]

One result of this transaction is that Donté's homebody and intimaesthetics get subsumed into a corporate advertising scheme. This effect may be gleaned in the relationship between his body and the virtual Starbucks cup. For much of the dance, a greater emphasis is placed on the dancing drink, as it moves throughout the screen, at times obscuring Donté's own dancing figure. Positioned in the foreground of the image, with Donté dancing behind it, the virtual cup is quite literally upstaging Donté's performance. Moreover, the emojis and text he incorporates seem to describe the *beverage* rather than Donté or his movement, as the words and emojis frame and then drop into the cup. These stagings, though they may have been enacted and produced by Donté himself, represent how his body and autochoreography have been co-opted by the commercial forces of new media.

For Starbucks, the post likely represents a successful sponsorship. The semiotic and technical anchor of the representation is, after all, the mentioning of @starbucks and the hashtagging of #StarbucksAmbassador in the caption of the post. Viewers, in seeing Donté dance with the cup and recognizing the Starbucks brand, associate the new beverage, and possibly also the Starbucks company at large, with Donté's fun-loving humor and positive energy. They may also feel inclined to click on the hashtag to explore other videos in that aggregation, further impressing the product in their memory. True to the notion of a transaction, the hashtag and mention benefit not only Starbucks but also Donté. Both of these technological instruments improve the locatability of the video by creating additional avenues for users to stumble upon the content, perhaps through Instagram's Explore page. Additionally, because Donté worked in an official capacity with Starbucks, the company featured his post on their account as well. Thus, any one of the eighteen million followers of the @starbucks account (at the time of writing) who did not already know of Donté was then exposed to his content. It is possible that Donté received many more followers as a result of the transaction.

While Donté appears to orient himself toward capitalist enterprise through his partnership with Starbucks, his commercialized moving selfie reveals more about the platform itself than Donté's intentions or predilections. Donté's case in particular demonstrates how Instagram has created the conditions by which a major corporation can easily co-opt personal, intimaesthetic content and use it to sell more products and increase its bottom line. This sort of product placement media, pervasive across Instagram, disguises its own scheme through the fun-loving face, personality, and dancing of Donté. At the same time, advertisements such as these are effective for both the dancer and the company/organization, as described above. Rather than contemplating the social, economic, and political implications of a home dance advertisement, viewers might instead see this video, muse at Donté's dancing, and then think, "I sure could go for a Tie-Dye Frappuccino right about now."

As Donté's and Mar's cases illustrate, the circulation layer of one's autochoreography, particularly in and through Instagram, is steeped in the logic of capitalism, which works to commodify the dancing body and subject: their character, their domestic world, and the intimacy they construct. While Mar to some extent resists explicitly capitalist pursuits, their account nonetheless participates in the practice of personal branding. Donté, on the other hand, makes obvious his corporate partnerships and economic dealings. While he offers up his homebody and media for money, exposure, and social capital, he maintains a personal distance from his global audience. Both dancers, though they each occupy different orientations toward the neoliberal capitalist marketplace that powers Instagram, together reflect the ways in which dancers choreograph themselves on new media. By posting their moving selfies, they fold their autochoreographies into the feed, the personal profile, and hashtags and mentions. They may develop tactics around these features of Instagram, or they may merely give themselves and their media to the forces that conduct those features. Regardless of their intentions, Instagram dancers use the platform to continue shaping their public personae.

Conclusion

Moving selfies, created through the performer's recognition of the camera and the resulting semiotics of self-capture, come to represent the individuals who post them online. The techniques of this production allow the performer to frame themselves in a specific way, under a specific light, and for a specific audience. For moving selfies set in the home, in particular, the manner of framing the self initiates the dancer's autochoreography—and the techniques for autochoreography vary by dancer and situation. Mar's techniques of exposure point to their ways of pulling back the curtains on their life, self, and body as a way to construct an authenticity of image and cultivate a sense of closeness with the viewer. Donté approaches the production of his moving selfie through techniques of buffering, which allow him to create an expression of himself while maintaining a cool distance from the viewer. And then, once uploaded to a social media platform like Instagram, Mar's and Donté's respective autochoreographies acquire a new dimension. The platform establishes boundaries and feature sets that direct users where to go; it uses algorithms to determine who sees what content; and it enables (if not promotes) the commercialization of the dancers' productions. In this way, the dancer employs autochoreography in production, but that autochoreography extends to the platform in ways that complicate and compromise the performer's sense of agency over their image and online persona.

However complex the online life of the moving selfie may be, the home remains at the crux of the dancer's autochoreography. Not only does the home provide the ideal backdrop for the dancer's cultivations of an authentic persona, but also it enables them to contour to their personal brand(s). The domestic objects and orientations in space, the level of cleanliness or disarray, and the signs of other inhabitants all convey intimate data that shape the performance and give it meaning. The viewers read this data and may feel closer to the performer by means of the intimacy they produce. The home's intimaesthetic potential means that this space will continue to be leveraged as an instrument of closeness toward the marketization of self, and all other things, on new media.

While the domestically situated moving selfie and its politics of autochoreography capture a wide range of media that is self-captured, it does not include *all* content that is produced for oneself and by oneself. That is, self-produced media on platforms like Instagram include that which was created not only through an *acknowledgment* of the camera but also through an apparent *disregard* of the camera. Fitting with the logic of intimaesthetics, this difference in the dancer's orientation toward the camera cultivates a separate semiotic character and opens out to a distinct online life. The next chapter approaches this manner of self-capture, wherein the dancer ignores the camera but nonetheless makes obvious their role as both subject and creator of the image. This type of intimaesthetic, which

I refer to as *nonchalant gestures*, articulates how performing nonchalance models privacy while allowing the dancer to engage in public dialogues and cultural memory. On the heels of a thorough analysis of moving selfies, the *nonchalant gestures* type of intimaesthetic points toward other modes of self-capturings, particularly ones that illuminate the dancer's role in dialoguing with, intervening in, and complicating cultural memory.

THREE

Nonchalant Gestures

Danko claps his hands and drops his head, nodding to the beat of Beyoncé's "Deja Vu." His hips rock to the rhythm of the music as he belts out "Heeeeeeeeeey!" and claps once more. Dancing in his bedroom, he remains absorbed in the moment, not paying mind to the camera in front of him and not acknowledging the scene as any sort of spectacle.

Does he know we're watching him? Surely he does. But why does he act as though he doesn't?

Separately, in another home and in another video, we see the lower half of Liv's body moving in her living room. She repeatedly swings her legs and pivots her standing foot, which alternates as she continues. With a fireplace and mantle in the background, the camera captures the scene from the floor, limiting the frame and highlighting Liv's leg work.

Did she drop the camera on the ground, forgetting that it was recording? Of course she didn't. But why does she utilize this vantage point?

Introduction

The ways in which dancers like Danko and Liv capture themselves dancing in the home—performing an obliviousness of and for the camera—reflect a provocative type of intimaesthetics that I refer to as *nonchalant gestures*. The dancers disregard the camera as if they forgot about its presence; yet their way of performing suggests the preparedness of the image, thereby complicating the obliviousness of their body, space, and media. Similar to how the aesthetics of candid dancing and moving selfies open out to a politics of twenty-first-century softening of surveillance and choreography of the self, respectively, nonchalant gestures media speak to wider implications as well: those wherein privacy *is the subject* of one's performance. Dancers leverage this image of privacy not only to engage with the public sphere but also to dialogue with larger cultural phenomena, figures, and events. The nonchalant gestures intimaesthetic thus demonstrates how dancers utilize new media to navigate, eschew, and promulgate cultural binaries like margin and center, private and public memory, and forgotten and remembered narratives.

The home dance videos of this type link the domestic space to threads of public discourse, thereby drawing the homebody into the fabric of cultural memory. This maneuver engenders a provocative paradox: on the one hand, it relies on the character of the home and the sole dancing body to construct a sense of the forgotten, marginal, and rogue—qualities that develop outside of and in tension with dominant culture. On the other hand, this performance reveals itself for public visibility and global circulation, flirting with those elements of dominant culture against which it had previously oriented itself. This paradox of the home dance video reveals the ontological complexities of aestheticizing privacy.

In this chapter, I pry apart this paradox, first—in part I—by discussing the aesthetic and semiotic features of nonchalant gestures. Here, I address how media of this type may be read as a performance of both intimacy and oblivion. An investigation into the historical and cultural factors, such as antecedent media like closed-circuit television (CCTV) footage and subject-camera relationships in Hollywood cinema, demonstrates how the subject's disregard of the camera draws from divergent cultural instances with varied social and political intricacies. The section then attends to the notion of the *choreography of oblivion*, a collection of techniques that dancers employ to engage with, against, and toward cultural memory. It is here that notions of the forgotten, marginal, and rogue are unpacked, as they each bring some aspect of memory into focus.

In part 2, the aesthetics and semiotics discussed in part 1 become animated through an analysis of two home dance examples on Instagram. This discussion illuminates how Danko and Liv, introduced above, engage nonchalance to rework elements of dominant culture, particularly through their play with aspects of cultural memory. Danko performs an homage to Beyoncé and in doing so "scribbles in the margins" of the text of celebrity.[1] Liv creates a tribute to postmodern dance choreography icon Trisha Brown that ultimately works on/against the canon of American modern dance. An analysis of these two home dance videos on Instagram thus reveals how dancers dialogue with, complicate, and intervene in aspects of some cultural center—which, for Danko and Liv, become celebrity and canonicity, respectively. Celebrity, for instance, suggests mass appeal, knowability, and an accumulation of cultural, political, and financial capital. Its bastion, *the* celebrity, manifests these features and comes to embody particular values. Similarly, canonicity functions to concretize and maintain through historicization a collection of texts and authors that at once reflect and propagate a system of values. Both of these concepts are bound to a visible and established center of cultural production and thus represent the hegemonic structures toward which dancers might position themselves and their performances.

Threaded throughout part 2 and taking focus in part 3 are the roles that the forgotten, marginal, and rogue play in shaping nonchalant gestures to reveal the mechanisms of one's choreography of oblivion. First, forgottenness articulates a picturing of privacy that is embedded in the dancer's seeming unknowingness of the camera. The resulting media presents a duality of privacy: on the one hand, it provides evidence of some sense of privacy through its documentation; on the other hand, it negates that privacy by making its contents known and visible. Distinct from forgottenness, marginality emphasizes a displacement of focus from some recognized center of activity or phenomena and subsequently redirects it toward the embodied practices of individuals *beyond* that central locale—toward the fringes, or margins, of cultural production. Finally, rogueness refers to a resistance to and isolation from a collective. The dancer who "strays from the pack" assumes the role of rogue actor and, in publicizing their activity, challenges some established understanding of *who* and *what* may define cultural repertoire.

These qualities of the forgotten, marginal, and rogue are not only available in the videos themselves but also imbricated in the politics of digital culture. Thus, as with the previous chapters, part 3 exhibits a reading out from the examples analyzed in part 2. It brings digital culture into focus to unpack the ways in which cultural memory is established, promulgated, and complicated in new media. Notions of the forgotten, marginal, and rogue thus remain integral to the logic of part 3. This analysis provides a counterpart to both the moving selfie (with its techniques of self-capturing) and candid dancing (through the dancer's lack of contact with the camera) to unpack how the home dancer engages with cultural memory through intimaesthetics.

Part 1. Defining Nonchalant Gestures

The nonchalant gestures intimaesthetic reveals a particular relationship between dancer and camera, wherein the dancer is aware of the camera but does not demonstrate their awareness. Their movements and disposition thus present as nonchalant. As with everyday situations, nonchalance indicates the *appearance* of calmness or coolness, suggesting that such a way of being does not necessarily match some underlying sentiment or psychological state. That is, one might *seem* nonchalant but not *feel* nonchalant. In other words, nonchalance is externally derived and does not speak to the perceptions of the individual. It is, thus, inherently performative, activated through choreographies of body, space, and media. Through their orientation toward the camera and their cultivation of narratives of the forgotten, marginal, and rogue, the dancer activates nonchalance to contribute to, intervene in, and subvert systems of cultural memory. This work ultimately captures a play with, and indeed choreography of, the notion of oblivion. The following discussion attends to this proposition, focusing on the antecedent practices that feed into the aesthetics and semiotics of this type of intimaesthetics.

Genealogy of Nonchalant Gestures

The nonchalant gestures type draws on a subject-camera relationship that, due to its prevalence across the history of film and television, seems obvious and unremarkable. Yet, aside from comedy and musical performance, the technique of ignoring the camera has dominated narrative cinema since the origin of the filmic medium.[2] Cinematic performers, that is to say, use their gaze to help construct a narrative *within* the scene: an approach that has led to the trope of ignoring the camera by default. The dominance of this approach is reflected in discourses on film style. David Bordwell, in his review of the history of subject-camera relationships across the twentieth century, for instance, traces stylistic qualities in staging but does not discuss techniques of departure like, for instance, the direct address.[3] Instead, Bordwell's review of staging in film attends to the various ways in which performers use their gaze within the scene to construct a narrative.[4] Bordwell's omission of the direct address suggests its scant use and the ways in which it was, at least in twentieth-century cinema, exceptional to the wider rule of ignoring the camera.

Of course, the rise of documentary and amateur filmmaking—each with its own distinct historical arc—brings major departures from the dominant tropes of narrative cinema. News broadcasting, reality television, and, now, self-produced videos on new media usher the direct address more deeply into public consciousness and more prominently into the maker's toolset.[5] Thus, with the rise of Instagram as a popular tool for creating self-produced media, users create videos in a more expansive landscape of production. As exemplified through the discussion of selfie culture in chapter 2, twenty-first-century media production not only heavily incorporates the direct address but also widens the field to allow for a more diverse range of gaze tactics in general. This expansiveness in techniques complicates the dominance that ignoring the camera held in twentieth-century narrative cinema. It also opens up opportunities to infuse the styles of one genre into another—that is, that of narrative cinema into that of new media productions.[6]

The mapping of stylistic trends here suggests how the aesthetics of nonchalant gestures largely reverts back to the norms of antecedent cinema in which actors would by default ignore the camera. The emergence of selfie-style productions has created a new standard for self-produced media—one engendered through the subject's recognition of the recording device and thus their audience. In a way, then, the performer's manner of disregarding the camera on a platform like Instagram articulates a departure from the direct address, similar to how the gaze of comedy and musical performances was a departure from the styles of narrative cinema. Regardless of how conscious this decision may be, home movers draw on this actorly technique to create a particular mood and tension with their audience. Someone in front of the camera, for example, immediately recognizes that if they turn their back, the viewer will not be able to see their face and thus might feel disconnected from the performance. As this chapter elucidates, the use of such a tactic defines the choreography of oblivion.

Of course, home dance videos that imitate the subject-camera dynamic common in cinema occupy a different place in culture than images on the big screen. The low-cost and prolific nature of new media production means that creators can play with techniques without much economic or social risk. Moreover, a dancer creating a video for social media might not have the filmmaking vocabulary or experience to contemplate the subtleties of their "blocking," a term used in the professional performance culture to describe the orientations of the body. They also might not have the knowledge of the history of film and the history of filmmaking to knowingly reference, uphold, subvert, or completely disregard certain styles and techniques. In other words, the dancer in a nonchalant gestures production is oblivious not only to/of the camera but perhaps also to the historical work of their bodily orientation.[7]

Alongside the historical prominence of particular styles of staging or blocking in cinema is a separate stream of antecedent practices: the aesthetics of surveillance footage. Video surveillance practices have a relatively short history that congeals around the rise of CCTV.[8] The term "closed-circuit television" represents a broad category of technology wherein a video feed is not openly transmitted, as is the case with broadcast television, but is instead displayed on a limited number of machines. Certainly not a monolith, CCTV represents a range of practices toward a range of purposes—and as such, its contexts of use vary remarkably across institutional, geographical, and cultural milieus. From recordings of royal ceremonies of the British monarchy in the 1950s to oversight of activity in the streets of New York City in the 1980s (and beyond) to surveillance of shoppers in retail stores across the globe since the mid- to late twentieth century, CCTV indeed serves a variety of functions.[9] Across these functions, CCTV is used to capture spaces that are both public and private, activity that is both ordinary and extraordinary, and people that are both particular and anonymous.

Considering its varied use, CCTV has contributed to an aesthetic sensibility around the idea of video surveillance. As illustrated through the instance of candid dancing discussed in chapter 1, popular culture and public conceptions surrounding the television program Candid Camera have helped cultivate a "surveillance aesthetic" that establishes a collection of visual qualities and technical sensibilities that influence how individuals understand surveilled spaces and subjects. In particular, chapter 1 addresses how surveillance has moved beyond the bounds of government control and seeped into popular media and commercial enterprise through advertising and marketing tactics.[10] Building on that discussion, the genre of CCTV—if we might indeed consider it to be a genre—effectively bridges this transition. Deployed within governmental, corporate, and residential spheres, CCTV has facilitated the spread of surveillance practices into all levels of social practice—imbricating itself into both public and private life and establishing a collection of aesthetic and semiotic tropes. Abstracted out of its context, for instance, CCTV conjures images of moving bodies doing seemingly everyday, pedestrian-like things: traveling between destinations (by foot, bike, bus, train, or car), entering and exiting buildings, purchasing goods, and waiting for someone or something, among other activities. While variations in this aesthetic certainly exist, such images nonetheless contribute to a wider picture of how video surveillance is *aestheticized* in culture.

CCTV has indeed contributed to an aesthetic surrounding surveillance, but perceptions of this technology also impact its life in the public imaginary. Video surveillance, that is, elicits reactions of support toward public safety as well as a resistance to being captured.[11] In terms of the former, crime dramas tend to paint a portrait of surveillance as an instrument for public good.[12] In terms of the latter, the practice of *sous-veillance*, wherein the subject subverts the apparatus by turning the gaze back on itself, reflects a powerful mode of antisurveillance.[13] Of course, a resistance of or support for this technology does not capture the entire field of orientations toward surveillance. Resting in the middle of this range is a sense of *apathy* in the subject.[14] This sort of subject, which Shaul Duke describes as a "nontarget," reflects a passive comportment and indifferent positionality toward surveillance.[15] In theorizing this archetype, Duke acknowledges how the nontarget is imbricated in the *privacy paradox*, or the "false tradeoff between privacy and security."[16]

While Duke does not call out the nontarget's gaze as a facet of their surveillance apathy, one might imagine how a subject who does not look toward the surveillance device may be apathetic toward it. This same lack of eye contact with the camera might even play out for a "targeted" subject (to take the inverse of Duke's concept). If someone is concerned about getting caught doing something, that is, they might refrain from acknowledging the surveillance device so as to not seem guilty of any hypothetical crime. Thus, if the nontargeted do not care, then it would seem that the targeted do not want you to know that they *do* care.

Crime, security, and protection may not figure into how dancers who create nonchalant gestures comport themselves in relation to the camera. However, those performers allude to—or perhaps even craft—a surveillance aesthetic by embodying the comportment of the nontarget when creating their productions. Their sense of ease in front of the device suggests their consent to being watched while also offering an image of protection. Their way of not returning the camera's gaze articulates how the camera is not a threat to them. However, this way of not looking at the camera, but then uploading the video to a new media platform, ultimately ruptures whatever sense of privacy might otherwise imbue the scene. In this way, the nonchalant gestures intimaesthetic epitomizes the privacy paradox in a surveillance society.[17] Such media aestheticize privacy and, in doing so, compromise the very existence of that privacy.

The historical and theoretical aspects of CCTV and narrative cinema demonstrate how their respective aesthetics flow into nonchalant gestures in distinct ways. Though home dancers may not intend to draw on these histories, they nonetheless create images that allude to the sensibilities of these antecedent media. More specifically, the dancer's relationship to the camera borrows from blocking and the avoidance of a direct address in narrative cinema as a way to not compromise the narrative within the scene, and borrows from the laid-back, complicit comportment of CCTV's nontarget. Reviewing this genealogy helps lay the groundwork of nonchalant gestures so that we might investigate the subject-camera dynamic that defines those antecedents in the first place. Toward such an effort, the following section addresses the aesthetic and semiotic nuances of nonchalant gestures.

The Aesthetics and Semiotics of Nonchalant Gestures

Expressed at the outset of part 1, the notion of nonchalant gestures is constructed through a nonchalance of the performing subject. As a performative quality or state, nonchalance is located in the body of the performer. It may be understood, for instance, through one's relaxed posture, steady voice, and focused yet unassuming gaze. These characteristics and their semiotics may also be understood through the environment and situation in which one acts. Nonchalance is, namely, produced through a discrepancy between, on the one hand, an individual's disposition and, on the other hand, the behavioral expectations of that person's surroundings. The definition of nonchalant as "unconcerned" suggests that, in a given situation, there would be something *to be concerned about*—something in/about one's environment that would typically invite such a comportment. Yet, someone who does not exhibit concern in that situation stands out in their cool and collected disposition. Here, we find how nonchalance may create a tension between expected behavior and perceived behavior.

When considering home dance performances in which the dancer does not acknowledge the camera, that dancer may be understood to be nonchalant precisely because they ignore the recording device. The suggestion here is that the landscape of self-production on new media creates the expected behavior of how one is to orient themselves toward the camera: to make eye contact with it and, thereby, suggest that the production is of their own. The tropes of selfie-ism discussed in chapter 2 represent the field from which that expectation is derived. The nonchalant dancer, however, stages their scene, prepares their camera, but acts as though they were merely dancing in their home with no one watching or capturing their performance.

Following this logic, the reading of a nonchalant gestures video as a self-recording entertains a degree of ambiguity. The nonchalant dancing body and its borrowing of a surveillance aesthetic articulate the possibility that the image is *not* self-produced. Perhaps someone else was behind the camera filming the dancer but that person had secured the device so that the frame would remain static. Another possibility is that the dancer is actually not aware of the recording, aligning it with the candid dancing type of intimaesthetic. Despite these possibilities, the performance of nonchalance is more complex than merely a *deliberate self-capture* posing as *nondeliberate* might suggest. Even though the audience does not see the dancer move away from the camera as if they had just pressed the record button, and they do not see them return to the camera to end the recording, the subject's role as both subject and operator, though obscured in the technical sense, is read as obvious in the semiotic sense.

Nonchalance manifests through three features of the dancing body: a gaze that does not meet the camera's eye; a casual, introspective comportment; and a use of space that only partially adheres to the delineations of the frame. Regarding the first element, the dancer may glance aimlessly around the room, as if to not look at anything in particular but to allow their head to be part of the dancing; they might close their eyes, as if lost in thought; or they might sustain their attention toward a particular point in space, suggesting a sense of focus in the moment. Such choreographies of the gaze might overlap with the second feature mentioned above: the assumption of a casual, introspective comportment. Introspection manifests, for instance, through the dancer's eschewing a sense of "forwardness," meaning that they might not direct their movement toward the camera, disregarding any notion that the lens may stand in for an audience-to-be. Instead, they orient themselves in no particular way and rotate in various directions, sometimes to the point that their movement is mostly obscured. It is worth noting how these features of gaze and spatial orientation resemble those seen in candid dancing. However, unlike the candid dancer, the nonchalant dancer appears to be aware of the camera's framing—the third feature of the body. That is, the dancer more or less adheres to the confines of the frame. If they did not know they were being filmed, they might move in and out of the frame or remain completely outside of it. However, in nonchalant gestures media, the mover generally abides by the delineations in space that define the frame. However, because they are not watching their captured image on a monitor or screen, as is the case with many dancing selfies, they might slightly breach the borders of the image, but only momentarily. The dancer who *does* leave the frame for a second or two, but then returns, further constructs a sense of spontaneity and nonchalance. This play with the frame subtly suggests to the viewer that the camera is an incidental feature in the home dance occurrence and has little bearing on the dancer's movement, as if the dancer says, "*This would be happening regardless of whether you were watching me.*"

Alongside the corporeal elements of nonchalance are the contributions of the setting to the construction of this type of intimaesthetic. The image and semiotics of the home function as an especially prime space for the framing of one's nonchalance. For one, the concept of home is seemingly so mundane, ubiquitous, and universal that it tends to fall out of sight and out of consideration as a space of cultural production or even as a social space at all.[18] As discussed in the introduction, Heidegger's notion of "dwelling" as a space of consistency, neutrality, and staticness for the development of human perception speaks to this sense of the home.[19] It allows its inhabitants to attach their own meaning to it and to the objects in one's surroundings. In tandem with Heidegger's dwelling is Bachelard's notion of home as a space for the imagination to flourish, which comforts and nurtures its inhabitants. While these conceptions of home should be viewed with a critical lens, they nonetheless hold sway in the public imaginary, perpetuating a sense that the home does not itself require attention but instead gives way to introspective musings, imaginative preoccupations, and proprioceptive immersions.

Heidegger's and Bachelard's views of the home contribute to the dancer's nonchalance—not necessarily by a neutrality or imaginative wandering for the dancer, in some true or authentic fashion, but instead by establishing a semiotic vocabulary and aesthetic character from which they might create such an image, ultimately also allowing the viewer to read the scene as such. In a Heideggerian fashion, the dancer seems oblivious to the setting they have choreographed, as if the space is neutral. At the same time, in a Bachelardian sense, they articulate an imaginative dimension to their performance through their apparent improvisations; their wandering, introspective gaze; and their non-forward-facing positioning.

Of course, an understanding of the dancer's self-capture hinges on how media are understood in contemporary digital culture. While the dancer may consider aspects of this culture when creating the video, the actual upload of the video online gives it a new social life. This seemingly minor action of sharing a video opens that media up to a robust web of cultural production wherein infinite threads of discourse cross every which way: from this person to that event, this event to that object, this object to that person, this event to that meme, this meme to that dancer, and so forth. Considering this *leap in scales*—from the seemingly nurturing, imaginative home to the infinitely frenetic web—prompts us to focus on the meaning of the dancer's nonchalance in the online space.[20] Through such a lens, nonchalance starts to gesture toward the connections that the dancer makes between their at-home worlds and the innumerable nodes of people, ideas, cultural objects, discourses, and temporalities online. The following section approaches this layer of the media to describe how the production embeds a sense of forgottenness, marginality, and rogueness.

The Choreography of Oblivion

The dancer's nonchalant comportment gives way to the choreography of oblivion, or their way of engaging with larger dialogues, themes, events, and people through the modeling of a world *forgotten by, marginal to,* or *rogue from* dominant culture. This concept harnesses the notion of oblivion and its associations of obliviousness to reveal how, in seemingly forgetting the camera but uploading the video online, the home dancer choreographs an image that stretches across worlds of cultural memory. This choreography ultimately allows them to intervene in, dialogue with, or complicate facets of dominant culture. Though certainly not *all* home dance productions in which dancers ignore the camera engage with cultural memory in this way, the choreography of oblivion represents a wide range of videos that do this work. The concept thus articulates an important type of intimaesthetic. When creating nonchalant gestures, dancers aestheticize intimacy as a way to both publicize and complicate their worlds of the forgotten, marginal, and rogue. Their choreographies of body, space, and media show how the domestic setting might be small in size and minor in how it is valued in a contemporary mediascape but is nonetheless a stage that allows bodies to shout into and groove with the archives of new media. And perhaps in doing so, they may also feel that their voices have been heard. While the choreography of oblivion involves layers of the forgotten, marginal, and rogue, the concept of the forgotten takes focus first.

The choreography of oblivion relies on an understanding of both oblivion and obliviousness. In considering these two terms, it is important to recognize how they are both undergirded by the concept of memory. The common root, *oblivio*, emphasizes this link to memory, as it refers to "forgetfulness, a being forgotten." Embedded in this rooting is the dual sense that, on the one hand, forgetting can be a force that a person experiences ("they forget"); on the other hand, forgetting can be a force that acts upon a person, place, thing, or event ("they are forgotten"). Thus, the shared root indicates how forgetting is both active and passive. Those who move within some oblivion may be actively forgetting and/or are passively being forgotten; they are oblivious to something, or that something is oblivious to them; they are lost to memory, or memory has been lost to them.

More than just markers of memory's active and passive qualities, these twin terms also connote the inextricability of absence and presence, forgottenness and remembrance. A state of obliviousness or a space of oblivion is, after all, marked in relation to a particular thing or idea that one may be *expected to remember*. A subject is oblivious *to* something, just as the idea of oblivion becomes activated *against* a recognized space of remembrance. As Marc Auge argues, the concept of oblivion shapes memory more than it evades it: "Oblivion is the life force of memory, and remembrance is its product." This paradox may be likened to how a gap or a hole is a thing itself, even though it refers to a loss. In a similar fashion, obliviousness and oblivion both harbor the presence of some absence. A state or space of forgottenness, in other words, is intimately coupled with the remembrance of that which is forgotten.[21]

The ways in which forgottenness requires remembrance prompt notions of how performance is already defined by a tension between presence and absence, remembering and forgetting. Joseph Roach, through his notion of "surrogation," prominently theorizes how the performing body harbors the unwritten past—that which is largely *forgotten* by Western structures of memory.[22] Then, for Rebecca Schneider, the notion of "remaining" aptly extends Roach's concept to describe how performance harbors a paradoxical relationship between remembering and forgetting. Schneider asserts:

> If "to remain" means to endure or even to stay behind, "to remain before" is to endure as both *ahead of* and *prior to*—a phrase that clearly tangles or crosses temporal registers. In this sense, before and behind cannot be plotted in a straight line, and so memory *remains* a future act: not yet recalled, if also never yet forgotten.[23]

Schneider's discussion of that which *remains* nicely embeds a sense of oblivion. Even more, Schneider's linking of this function of performance to the body further expresses the corporeal dimensions of oblivion/obliviousness and of forgottenness. Such a notion is apparent in Schneider's mentioning of flesh. "The place of [performance's] residue," Schneider writes, "is arguably *flesh* in a network of body-to-body transmission of affect and enactment."[24] The flesh of the body, following Schneider, harbors and transmits both knowledge and memory, contributing to the performance's nonlinear spatio-temporalities. It links the unknowable, absent qualities of oblivion to the knowable presentness of the moving, gesturing body.

As suggested through Roach's and Schneider's conceptualizations of performance, when activated through the performing body, oblivion/obliviousness speaks to the ontology of performance as well as to knowledge production at large. Since performance relies on a visual economy, when something that was forgotten *appears*, it may presumably no longer be forgotten. Articulating a state or sense of being forgotten, then, makes that state a tangible reality, available to be recognized, known, and remembered by others. This process draws from the principles of speech act theory, as set out by J. L. Austin and expounded upon by Judith Butler.[25] According to this theory, a spoken proclamation has the power to affect the change that it proclaims. However, unlike the performative speech act to which Austin refers, a performance of forgottenness prompts a transformation, and therefore a negation, of that forgottenness. In performatively expressing a state of forgottenness, the subject reconfigures that defining trait into its opposite: a sense of the remembered. This degree of inverted performativity, if we might name such a concept, demonstrates the ontological complexities of the performing body and its relation to presence/absence, as well as remembrance/forgottenness.

Extending the theoretical richness of oblivion, the *choreography of oblivion* articulates how the dancer plays with the paradoxes of memory through their home dance productions. The dancer's nonchalance *looks like* forgetting, yet the fact that they uploaded the video online suggests their self-documentation, and the act of uploading enters their performance into a space of public memory/remembrance. The dancer's subsequent engagement with online dialogues, people, events, and cultural objects through the platform articulates how their narratives and their bodies stretch across worlds of activity: from some domestic oblivion to a locus of cultural production and a network of cultural memory. As discussed in part 3, the dancer incorporates hashtags and mentions other users to engage in wider dialogues, they make references in their captions, and they reply to comments on the video. Their way of harnessing the tensions of memory reflects their choreography of oblivion.

While the notion of oblivion highlights the theoretical dimension of forgetting, the choreography of oblivion harbors other facets of cultural memory that are *not* etymologically linked. Namely, the concepts of marginality and rogueness also play into how dancers choreograph oblivion through their home dance videos. Marginality, first of all, embeds divergent meanings, applications, and uses. For instance, it might refer to the value system of artistic practice and cultural production (as in the marginality of the avant-garde); to the spatial sense of the margin as an edge or borderland (as in the margins of a page or defined territory); or to the sense of being left out of a conversation or phenomenon (as in the marginality of socio-politics). Undergirding these variations in marginality are, on the one hand, an impression of the concept as a state of disenfranchisement and, on the other hand, a generative, subversive quality that engages a productive, agonistic tension with "the center." Discourses on art history and literature engage both senses of the term, as marginality is frequently used to refer to practices and aesthetics that fall outside of mainstream venues, styles, and ways of working.[26] People, activities, and objects along the margins are at once *left out of* and *resistant to* dominant practices, making this notion powerful in its ambiguity. Antunes, Craveiro, and Gonçalves describe this power in terms of its liminality:

> The condition of marginality implies that of liminality, with limits and thresholds engaged in various forms of interaction between the official and the marginal, the norm and its transgressions, erudite culture and folklore, the privilege and the excluded, the normalized and the bizarre. . . . In each case, liminality enhances contact as much as ambiguity and hybridism, two other categories particularly treasured by contemporary art, art history, and visual studies alike.[27]

According to this perspective, marginality not only reveals a binary logic of *this* versus *that* but also gestures toward the spaces in between those categories and the ways in which those spaces create productive tensions. So, while the notion of marginality represents a range of meanings, its imbued sense of liminality most profoundly speaks to how performers might dialogue with and complicate notions of the center—from the margins.

Understood through this framing of marginality, the choreography of oblivion speaks to new media productions in the home, wherein dancers move through spaces of liminality. They create records of oblivion and use those records to engage with the public sphere and aspects of cultural memory. Integral to this understanding is how home dance videos mobilize a sense of marginality through the video itself rather than through the personal histories of the dancers in the video, the lives they lead, and their world and selves beyond their digital identities. While the dancers might certainly identify with some status of marginality, it is their media that perform a sense of marginality. Thus, while the notion of nonchalant gestures resonates with theories like José Muñoz's concept of the "minoritarian counterpublic sphere," in that performers construct a space where individuals may work "on and against" dominant culture, the off-screen realities of new media users are obscured by/through their intimaesthetics.[28] To what extent is a given performer a "marginalized" subject? And who determines that status? The viewer? The dancer themselves? The platform? Whatever sense of marginality that a person might experience remains unknown to the viewer. Thus the category of nonchalant gestures, in focusing on the production itself, might capture or collide with the everyday realities of the subject in the video—but the certainty of that possibility is lost to the image.

Alongside and in concert with the forgottenness and marginality embedded in the choreography of oblivion is a sense of *rogueness*, or the display of a "straying from the pack" ethos. After all, the figure of the rogue agent is one who severs themselves from an establishment and is thereby deemed a threat to that establishment.[29] Their singularity and separation challenge the hierarchy of the collective from which they depart. Abigail de Kosnik provides a helpful lens through which to consider these operations, specifically, by situating the rogue within a field of fandom in digital culture. For de Kosnik, rogueness online represents the redistribution of public, cultural, and collective memory. "Memory has gone rogue," de Kosnik writes. "[It] is now the basis of a great deal of cultural production."[30] Such memory reclaims dominant narratives and resituates them within archives of a new sort—digital archives. Conceptualizing these *rogue archives*, de Kosnik argues:

> One of the greatest political potentials of rogue digital archives is that groups that have occupied the margins of "mainstream" society, and have consequently been largely marginalized by traditional memory institutions, can build their own robust cultural memory sites, as something like counterinstitutions, akin to the counternarratives told by postcolonial, ethnic, and feminist writers who archontically rewrite the stories of dominant culture.[31]

As de Kosnik expresses, denizens of network societies have the capability to offer counternarratives that work against dominant narratives of public consciousness. In this manner, everyday performers may become, as de Kosnik would say, rogue archivists who singularly resist hegemonic processes of recording.

Extending this logic, media of the nonchalant gestures type may contribute to rogue archives as a way to comment upon, complicate, or reclaim some official record, image in the public imagination, discourse, or movement. Rogueness, in this way, becomes available to the performer-agent as they engage in a choreography of oblivion. Their ways of framing, deploying citations and references, positioning themselves toward (and away from) the camera, and capturing their domestic situation, among other techniques, reflect both their resistance to a collective whole and an embodiment of individual positionalities. In other words, the performer who strays from the pack assumes the role of cultural producer and, in publicizing their production, challenges some established understanding of *who* and *what* may define cultural repertoire. Their solitude and soloness, two distinct yet related prongs of their rogue singularity, are integral to this understanding: the former reflects a sense of being alone, which manifests through the singular moving body and its domestic situation, and the latter articulates a theatricalization of being alone, one in which the sole figure is spotlighted to be watched and consumed. The performer's choreography of oblivion mingles these two notions of the singular moving body, thereby amplifying the rogue character of their production.

The home dancer in a nonchalant gestures video manifests some sense of forgottenness, marginality, and/or rogueness as they choreograph oblivion. Through this work, features of their production correspond with/against elements of dominant culture. Here, dancers not only aestheticize intimacy (and oblivion, for that matter) through their choreographies of body, space, and media but also invite components of public memory into their homes and personal practices, remix its features, and then release that work back into the public sphere. In doing so, performers stretch across worlds of memory—not just drawing the arc between the private and public, personal and communal, unseen and seen, but also moving through the liminalities between the forgotten and remembered, marginal and center, rogue and sanctioned. The choreography of oblivion traces that arc.

A conceptualization of the choreography of oblivion is most powerful through application. Part 2 offers this consideration through an examination of the home dance productions of two dancers: Danko and Liv, referenced at the outset of this chapter. It is primarily through an in-depth study of Danko's and then Liv's media that nonchalant gestures and its corollary choreography of oblivion take shape. Of course, the videos considered here do not exhaust the field of nonchalant gestures. Instead, they provide two distinct models of how everyday performers might choreograph oblivion through distinct approaches. Danko's performance corresponds with celebrity, while Liv's calls forth canonicity. The dancers may engage in different operations, but together their videos represent the techniques involved in the choreography of oblivion.

Part 2. Screening Nonchalant Gestures

Home dance productions on new media remind the public of certain bodies, lives, and experiences that reside beyond the focus of dominant culture; and through nonchalance, home dancers image these worlds and aestheticize some sense of oblivion. Part 2 exemplifies these theories through an in-depth analysis of their media. In the first example, Danko, dancing in what appears to be his bedroom, composes an homage to music icon Beyoncé and in doing so maintains a cool distance from the camera. His production expresses his fandom, demonstrates how celebrity becomes domesticated, and indicates how home performances contribute to and intervene in digital cultural memory. In the second example, Liv performs a tribute to choreographic icon Trisha Brown—but only shows the bottom half of her body. The posting of this video occurs just after Brown's death, which prompts questions around how the legacy of public figures become absorbed into a personal, private, everyday domesticity—but one that is staged for publicity. Together, these two home dance videos not only exemplify the nonchalant gestures type of intimaesthetic but also reveal how the media complicate dualities of memory and thereby articulate the choreography of oblivion.

Whose Celebrity? Danko's Celebrity

Danko is already in mid-dance when the video begins. He moves in a Beyoncé-like fashion: alternating heel lifts, as if he were dancing in stilettos, while casually swinging his arms forward and backward. I think I saw that same movement in a Destiny's Child music video. Head down, eyes closed, and tongue out, Danko bounces to the beat of Beyoncé's "Deja Vu," which plays in the background. He jumps and claps his hands, then lands in a grounded position rocking his head—all while grinning and singing along. Danko is shirtless and wears red athletic shorts and a yellow bandana around his head, revealing his muscular physique. His figure is bathed in natural light, perhaps emitting from a nearby window. He appears to be in a bedroom, as there is a mattress barely in view at the edge of the frame. The chest of drawers in the background holds various objects, most of which are unidentifiable, save the one vase holding three yellow roses. To the left of the dresser, and behind Danko, sits a large weightlifting dumbbell atop a pillow on the floor.

Danko continues moving in an improvisatory fashion for about one minute—leaning back and forth, swinging his arms, rotating away from and toward the camera, moving slightly in and out of frame. Occasionally, he lifts his left fist to his chin, as if to imitate a microphone, and lip-syncs to the song's lyrics. Other times, he sings along while caressing his face and emphatically pulsing his hands in front of him, fingers spread. He then performs a modified grapevine, turns his back to the camera, and sharply looks over his shoulder toward some unknown focus (not the camera). With an intense elation, he revels in the music, matching his movement to the energy of the lyrics and rhythm. The video ends with Danko still in movement. The caption below the video reads: "Beyoncé at Coachella was EPIC. OMG OMG OMG OMG Beyoncé I love and I know is right, if something I'm doing right in my life is LoVe Beyoncé What A Performance what a dancers what a musician, what a costumes. Beyoncé 🫶" (see fig. 14).

What is most immediately striking about this home dance video is its unremarkable character: Danko's cool, casual comportment; the smooth effortlessness of his improvisation; his all-consuming engagement with the music; and his quotidian "home attire." Such an impression is linked to Danko's performance of nonchalance and his drawing of a connection between autobiography and cultural memory. Danko creates an image of himself in his home, performing as if no camera were present, and then subsequently publishes that image online for public viewership and engagement. In doing so, he pictures his world at once from the outside looking in and the inside looking out. On another level, Danko, in performing a personal home tribute to Beyoncé, contributes to a robust cultural discourse around Beyoncé's performance in 2018 at Coachella, a popular music festival that occurs annually in Palm Springs, California. This engagement, however, begins with Danko's nonchalance through movement, media, and space.

A prime feature of Danko's nonchalance is his gaze and orientation in

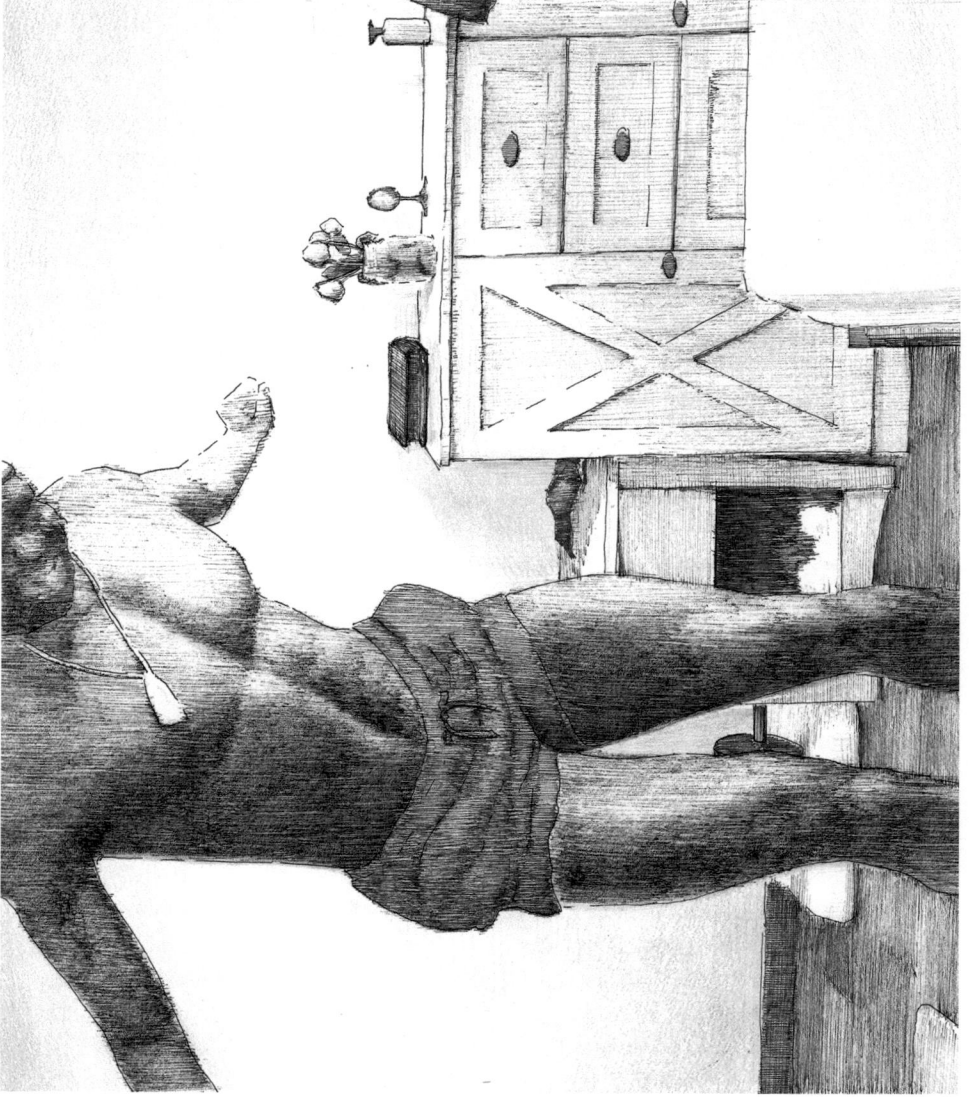

Fig. 14. Danko grooving to Beyoncé. (Meagan Willoughby)

space. Though his body occasionally turns toward the camera, much of his dancing is directed at other parts of the room, constantly shifting directions and even at times facing the backside of the room, thereby obscuring his movement. His gaze never meets the camera's lens but instead drifts with his movement, engaging in a separate choreography: closing his eyes, reopening them, gazing down toward the ground, then toward the ceiling, looking beyond the camera, and so forth. This constant shift in gaze not only demonstrates how Danko's focus is untethered from any particular thing but also suggests that his untethered gaze is choreographed. As if he is actively trying *not* to look at the camera, Danko's ways of looking and facing seem both incidental and purposeful.

Along with Danko's cool relation to the camera, the domestic scene itself also contributes to his choreography. The setting of the performance looks to be Danko's bedroom, as a bed and other personal belongings occupy the space. Perhaps he has a roommate and does not feel comfortable dancing in the common spaces of the home. Or maybe the bedroom has the most adequately stable structures on which to place his recording device. Regardless of whatever practicalities contributed to Danko's decision to record in the bedroom, the video carries signifiers of intimacy that contribute to his choreography of oblivion. The bedroom itself, after all, serves as a symbol of solitude and personal privacy. It is a space where people get dressed and undressed, where they rest their bodies, where they reflect on the day's events and anticipate those of tomorrow. It is also a space that invites uninhibited, unseen dancing. The logic of this space, then, is both intimate and forgotten. In other words, the bedroom is so germane to some common understanding of humanness, so imbued with a sense of neutrality, that it is often disregarded as a space completely—a metonym for the home itself.

While these elements of Danko's home dance contribute to an impression of both intimacy and nonchalance, they also reveal how the performance is choreographed: how the camera is not incidental and how the framing is part of the logic of the production. For instance, in watching the video, it initially appears as though Danko disregards the spatial boundaries of the frame. However, upon closer inspection, it becomes evident that while parts of his dancing go in and out of view, he never fully leaves the camera's boundary of capture. The disappearance of half of his body into the surrounding, unseen domestic space is followed by a complete reappearance milliseconds later. A limb might momentarily leave the frame, but Danko's body remains, to some extent, within the boundaries of the image for the entirety of the video. This frame play occurs continuously and reveals how Danko largely concedes to the gaze by perpetuating its rule over space and the body. So, while he performs some freedom from the disciplining forces of the camera, he nonetheless reinforces its power to command the performance—even in the "comforts of his own home." Ultimately, this concession enables him to activate the affective potential of his dancing to frame some sort of subjective reality and publicly express his admiration for Beyoncé.

Considering the intimate logic of the bedroom along with the dancer's relation to the frame, Danko's decision to dance in such a space wearing shorts and no shirt is fitting. One might imagine how such attire is typical for "around the house" kinds of activity. Whether doing laundry, cleaning dishes, tidying up, or merely lounging around, a pair of athletic shorts and a bandana might be appropriate, as the shorts provide an ease of movement and the bandana would catch any sweat caused by that activity. Of course, this attire is also fitting for a home dance experience, a moment of getting lost in the music of Beyoncé without inhibition. Choreographies like these—not just the attire but also the gaze, the relation to the camera, and the space of the bedroom—casually suggest to the viewer that the camera's presence is merely incidental, that Danko would be doing this dance regardless of whether it was being captured. At the same time, the semiotics of the movement, space, and attire articulate an intentionality. These simultaneous readings reveal the ways in which Danko is, on an aesthetic level, playing with dualities of memory—namely, absence and presence, forgottenness and remembrance.

The *form* of Danko's choreography of oblivion, primarily its corporeal, cinematographic, and spatial compositions, is contoured by the *content* of the video: the tribute to Beyoncé and his relation to the discourse around "Beychella." Indeed, as the caption and exuberant improvisation illustrate, Danko's home dance video is a celebration of Beyoncé's performance at Coachella. A brief review of this event will enable a greater understanding of the discourse with which Danko's media engages.

Beyoncé's 2018 Coachella performance almost immediately became a global sensation, as it incited the circulation of countless in situ videos capturing the performance, of media coverage around the event, and of memes created by fans. Her role in the festival was momentous from the start, as it was the first time in Coachella's twenty-five-year history that a Black woman would be the headliner. According to reports, the performance exceeded expectations, with its incorporation of countless costume changes and the appearance of many high-profile guest performers, including Kelly Rowland and Michelle Williams, two other members of

Destiny's Child. News outlets as diverse as Forbes and CNN offered the momentousness of the occasion, marking it as one of the most culturally important events of 2018 (along with, among others, the royal wedding of Prince Harry and Megan Markle).[32] This sort of buzz resulted in the entire event being referred to as "Beychella"—a proclamation that often accompanied tribute videos by fans across the globe through its hashtagging.

Danko's home dance video was one of many such tributes that asserted the momentousness of Beychella and expressed admiration for Beyoncé. Unlike the more widely circulated news media buzz around the event, Danko's performance has a more personal and situational quality to it. His orchestration of a particularly intimate scene centers his own everyday, domestic experiences of Beyoncé's performance, enabling him to express his admiration for Beyoncé. Through this expression, viewers understand that Danko is indeed a fan of Beyoncé; but even more so, they get to experience his own creative expression in response to Beychella. After all, as a nonchalant gesture, this home dance video is its own cultural product: its own dance with its own meaning and intentionality, one that is distinct from but in relation to some other more widely recognized concept, person, object, event, or idea. This is Danko's dance, not Beyoncé's.

This way of engaging in public dialogue with a public figure while shifting the focus to the subjectivity of the fan resembles what Gunther Kress calls "writing back": "The affordances of the new technologies of representation and communication," Kress writes, "enable those who have access to them to be 'authors,' even if authors of a new kind—that is, to produce texts, to alter texts, to write, and to 'write back.'"[33] This notion of "writing back" is quite appropriate to our concerns here, as it articulates how individuals along the margins of activity simultaneously cite a public figure and create a distinct work of their own making: one that enters its own cultural economy.[34] Perhaps this phenomenon of centering one's experience of and writing back to a celebrity—as Danko has done with Beyoncé—is performance's answer to literature's trend of fan fiction.[35] Like the latter, the former "[blurs] the boundary between reader and writer," according to Henry Jenkins, so that a fan respondent of a text also becomes an author in their own right.[36] As Jenkins explains, the fan is "scribbling in the margins of the text" and in doing so is creating their own text.[37] In other words, a correspondence is its own unique product with its distinct meaning and intentionality. Notably, de Kosnik engages this approach to fan fiction but applies it toward an understanding of digital cultural archives. As de Kosnik suggests, the creation of fan fiction in digital culture exists because something or someone is absent in the archives of mainstream culture.[38] Thus, a contribution to a fan fiction archive reflects how one might not just *write back* but *rewrite* the codes of dominant culture, which in de Kosnik's terms is a rogue act.

The logics of both writing back and rogue archives illustrate how the marginal, rogue, and forgotten performances that take place on new media platforms activate fan fiction's thrust of re/writing codes, of prompting a remembrance of something forgotten, and of refashioning public discourse. These qualities are integral to the choreography of oblivion in Danko's home dance video. Though his dance is imbued with a playful, lighthearted, and seemingly apolitical quality, his engagements with celebrity emphasize the rogue nature of his production—specifically, through his reorientation toward the home, toward the embodied practices of the fan, and toward the everyday remixing of celebrity. Danko is reverent toward Beyoncé and her performance, but also, in performing that reverence, he accrues his own aspirational capital and activates his public persona.[39] In a neoliberal fashion, consistent with the mechanisms of intimaesthetics, this maneuver indicates how Danko is not just performing a tribute to Beyoncé but also borrowing from and repurposing her celebrity toward his own narrative—however minor, potential, or imaginary it might be. In this way, he ensures that his moving body, his geographically removed experience of Beychella, and his domestic situation are *not* forgotten.

It is worth noting that, in considering Danko's rogue rewritings of celebrity repertoire, he creates somewhat of a *living* dialogue with and around a *living* artist. Though Beyoncé may not directly respond to his performed correspondence, there is nonetheless a potential for Danko and other fans to influence, in a grassroots-like manner, Beyoncé's reputation, career, and public image. The viral nature of Beychella is, in part, a testament to the perceived excellence of Beyoncé's performance, as each post that expresses such excellence only reinforces that evaluation, culminating in a digital consensus. While Danko's video is a mere pixel in this larger portrait, the weight of the collective fan base impacts the artist's status in culture and her future professional trajectory. Of course, not all nonchalant gestures influence the public image of a living artist; and not all direct their attention toward celebrity. The following example captures such a scenario wherein nonchalant gestures are performed toward a nonliving artist. In this performance, Liv creates an homage to choreographer Trisha Brown following Brown's passing. Though, like Danko, Liv also performs in the home, her choreography of oblivion differs in many ways from Danko's. As opposed to harnessing and transforming the powers of celebrity, Liv plays with canonicity and calls forth themes of life and death, while also gesturing toward the paradoxes of cultural memory in digital culture.

Living with Liv

Liv's video opens with her in mid-step. She places her right foot on the ground and immediately shifts her weight back onto her left foot, pivots, and then steps in the other direction. Wearing loose black pants that barely show her ankles, Liv primarily remains on the balls of her feet, only occasionally touching her heels down to the ground. She takes a large step backward with her left leg to subtly change directions again, lifts her right leg forward, then swings it back while pivoting her standing leg. Liv rebounds from one side of the frame to another, keeping her movement mostly along one plane—left to right, right to left, left and right. She chugs to the left before scooting back on both feet, then once again swings one leg while the standing leg pivots and then steps forward. She continues in this fashion for the length of the thirty-eight-second video: constantly shifting her weight, constantly changing direction.

Throughout this uniplanar dance, we only see Liv's lower body, no higher than the hip. The camera appears to be sitting on the floor, capturing a scene with Liv in the foreground and a living room scene in the background: a couch and two chairs all situated around a fireplace with a mantel that holds some candles, a record player, and several vinyl albums. Photos and framed images are affixed to the wall above the fireplace. There is no music and the room is silent, except for the sound of the wood floors creaking with every step or the slightest shift in weight. Below the video is a caption that reads: "A small and imperfect tribute to #trishabrown 🕺 🎐 🏃 " (see fig. 15).

Liv's home dance video was posted on March 20, 2017—two days after the death of American postmodern dancer and choreographer Trisha Brown. Given this information, along with Liv's naming of the dance as a "tribute" to Brown and the explicit reference to the choreographer through the hashtag, Liv's home dance video embodies a particular ethos of nonchalant gestures. Unlike Danko's example, Liv's performance foregrounds themes of life and death—which, as a result, shifts the ways we might understand the levels of forgottenness, marginality, and rogueness that appear in and become activated through her media. By contributing to Brown's legacy within the repositories of digital cultural memory, while also centering her own experiences, Liv uses her own life force to play with

Fig. 15. Liv's floor-view dance in the living room. (Meagan Willoughby Example of home concerts)

the canon of postmodern dance. As demonstrated here, this work becomes evident through both the aesthetics of the video and its critical implications in digital culture.

Several elements of the video reveal Liv's choreography of oblivion. First is the verbiage in the caption of the video—namely, the choice to describe the dance as "small" and "imperfect." Despite the subtleness of its mention, there are multiple levels to this articulation. For one, these descriptors allude to the "minor" qualities of Trisha Brown's work—work that is often described as being "minimal" and "pedestrian."[40] Liv matches Brown's aesthetic by limiting her movement to directional changes, pivots, subtle steps of the feet, and small leg lifts. While Liv may have extensive dance training, she does not present virtuosic movement here. The movement also does not appear to be rehearsed and tightly structured. These seemingly spontaneous elements of the video suggest that the dance was a minor occurrence in an otherwise active day—that it was perhaps, we might imagine, followed by activities like doing laundry, preparing a meal, or reading a book nearby a favorite window. Considering these characteristics, harnessed by the performing body, the video reads as an in-the-moment improvisation stylized to reference and pay homage to a lost figure.

Another dimension of the "minor" and "imperfect" that Liv constructs is the conceptual and value-based qualities of the video: the fact that the tribute is not an event orchestrated by the gatekeepers of high art but rather an action imbued with the character of the everyday; the short duration of the video with a low number of views, especially compared to the extensive oeuvre and iconicity of Brown and her work; and the use of a popular media app, Instagram, to share the work. The minor, marginal character of the video is only reiterated through its setting. The space of the living room, in particular, articulates a marginality grounded in its ubiquitousness, commonness (quite literally, in that a living room tends to function as a common space for residents), and understood place in the public imagination. Even the image of the room tends to strike a chord of familiarity, as it includes furniture and fixtures typically found in a communal living space. The mantle is adorned with domestic objects and personal momentos; the fireplace presents a protective grate over it with Polaroid photos strung above the grate; the couch, chairs, and side table together function as a quintessential living space backdrop. This setting is primed for what I refer to in chapter 2 as autochoreography. One might imagine, for instance, Liv curled up on the couch sipping a cup of Darjeeling tea while chatting with a friend who just stopped by to return a borrowed vinyl.

Perhaps Liv plays another vinyl by the same artist while the two engage in a conversation that seems to organically swirl through topics—from the latest farce in politics to the best hiking shoes to the week's funniest memes. Regardless of whatever imaginative character the scene might evoke, the living room space in which Liv dances is imbued with a sense of intimacy: one that is familiar in how the viewer might access information about the scene but unfamiliar enough to dwell on its imaginative possibilities. While this distant but close sensibility is certainly linked to the intimaesthetics of the video, it also characterizes Liv's choreography of oblivion—both in its marginal and forgotten dimensions. Her scene, that is, reflects a familiarity that is easily disregarded in cultural memory and public discourse. It also articulates a tension between a remembrance of domestic life (both Liv's domestic life and domestic life at large) and a forgetting of its specificities. Of course, this reading of the scene is harnessed through Liv's own language and its relation to her aesthetic choices.

The language that Liv uses to describe her tribute to Brown is especially appropriate when considering her relationship to the camera and orchestrations of space. Compositionally, Liv's dancing body is foregrounded in the image and thus speaks to the semiotics of the home to construct meaning. Most obvious about Liv's dancing figure, however, is the fact that only the lower half of her body is visible. The camera, which appears to be resting on the floor, captures only the movement of her legs and feet. Without picturing her torso, arms, and face, the viewer is left with a partial image of the dancer's body. The exclusion of her face, in particular, forecloses the opportunity of the viewer to decipher Liv's gaze or read her performance through how she acknowledges the camera. This lack of visual information suggests her nonchalance, as if she haphazardly recorded the dance without any need or care for an instrument to prop up the camera. Then, her movement utilizes an x- and y-axis, but not a z-axis, as she repeatedly rebounds from left to right, and back again, as if the frame of the image were the boundaries of a wrestling ring against which she repeatedly throws herself. When captured in the form of a video, Liv's play with the frame produces a two-dimensional rendering, as she does not approach the camera or recede away from it. Such a uniplanar, torso-obscuring approach conveys simultaneously her cool attitude yet careful preparation of the video.

These techniques, though they convey the dancer's nonchalance, also articulate another element of the production: the suggestion of *more beyond*. As discussed in the Introduction, the intimaesthetic product offers the viewer a sense of closeness while also indicating that the image is merely a snapshot within a larger life. In this video, Liv utilizes her movement and space to harness the qualities of her everyday world without actually revealing that world. In both a literal and figurative sense, then, she suggests that there is more beyond this one particular portrait. With this technique, Liv leaves room for the viewer to speculate about the movement, form, and situation that all remain to be seen. Such imaginative possibilities capture the viewer's attention while creating a tension between that which is familiar and unfamiliar, inside and outside the frame, and ultimately part of the record and beyond documentation.

Like Danko's post, the formal dimensions of Liv's choreography of oblivion are complemented by the content of the post—that is, Liv's engagement with the persona and legacy of Trisha Brown through the caption. In creating a tribute to the choreographic icon, Liv renders herself within a wider digital portrait and legacy of Brown. In particular, Liv's use of #trishabrown places her performance in a dialogue surrounding this figure. While the hashtag itself is the subject of greater discussion in the following section, it is a key aspect of Liv's on-platform choreography. By invoking Brown through a hashtag, Liv positions her own body, persona, domestic space, and narrative within a digital archive of Trisha Brown. Liv's dance then comes to reside next to other tributes, homages, and expressions of grief from a slew of other users. This collection of media comes to enjoy both currency in the moment of Brown's passing and posterity through ongoing additions as time passes. In this way, the hashtag allows Liv to combat some sense of her own domestic forgottenness, from the private margins of her living room toward some locus of digital cultural repository.

It must be noted, too, how the particularities of Liv as a person (a *living* woman) invoking the spirit of Brown (a figure who is *no longer living*) add an additional layer of complexity. Specifically, this observation imbues Liv's choreography of oblivion with a necropolitical character so that she is producing not only a tension between the margin and center, the private and public domains, but also a sense of life and death.[41] In other words, Liv's intervention in and work on memory is harnessed through the activation of her own vitality in response to the loss of another's.[42]

While the hashtag draws the tribute out further into public catalogs and dialogues, the personal account from which it was published simultaneously envelops it into Liv's everyday life and domestic situation. As in the case with dancing selfies, discussed in chapter 2, the autobiographical home dance video sits on the dancer's personal account page, mingling with other slices of life. Through this positioning, it links the individual's expressions of admiration for a public figure to other everyday activities, events, thoughts, or experiences embedded in the user's profile. In this way, the performer personifies their engagements with/on cultural memory through images of their own life—or how they *depict* their life on new media. Through this maneuver, the dancer may be able to link themselves to the artist's "reputational capital" and mobilize it toward their own ends, perhaps transferring it into their own capital.[43]

Indeed, Liv's use of #trishabrown articulates many layers of her engagement with/on cultural memory. Among the formal qualities of the performance, this engagement points to how Liv's production becomes part of a network that is perpetually shaping the cultural afterlife of Trisha Brown and the status of Brown's work, gesturing toward the implications for canonicity in digital culture. After all, the public figures toward whom individuals perform their grief might be recognized for their contributions to disciplines with an established canon. This possibility is certainly the case with Trisha Brown: Brown's persona and choreography are and have been central to the historicity of postmodern dance as they have been narrativized in both academic and nonacademic environs. Ironically, Trisha Brown was part of a group of performers in 1960s and '70s New York who were working *against* the canons of ballet and modern dance. However, their iconoclastic approaches became iconic in their own right, thereby catalyzing their induction into the canon of Western concert dance history, alongside the dancers, choreographers, and productions of ballet and modern dance.[44]

Integral to Liv's work on canonicity is how canons have typically been maintained by individuals, groups, and organizations in power: cultural arbiters like art patrons, museums and galleries, and governing bodies that determine funding schemes.[45] In contrast, dance practices located in or associated with mass culture, often those problematically considered *social* or *popular*, tend not to satisfy the palates of cultural tastemakers and as a result come to reside outside the canon.[46] The tendency of new media, however, to open channels of production, as well as to cultivate a potential for more bottom-up organization and discourse, demonstrates a threat to the historical operations of canonicity. So while new media itself might be "popular" in its mass utilization, assigning value to its content is not so easily accomplished, as its structures tightly mingle "low" and "high," so much so that the two categories become indistinguishable.[47] De Kosnik appropriately emphasizes how digital archives manifest new archival styles and repertoires and, thus, have a different relationship to the canon: "The rise of digital culture has thrown the very concepts of canon, canonization, and canonicity into question."[48] Indeed, emerging systems like those undergirding new media platforms refigure the landscape of canonicity, as well as the figures and works that reside in the canon. This transformation, de Kosnik suggests, is a rogue activity. Like Danko's engagement with celebrity repertoire, Liv's tribute to Brown operates in a rogue archival system that eschews the formally exclusive procedures and mechanisms of canonicity.

Indeed, Liv's tribute—however "small and imperfect" she might claim it to be—engages in a choreography of oblivion that complicates existing structures of cultural memory. Her nonchalance toward the camera, her home setting, and her dancing body make up her techniques, all while establishing her contribution to digital repositories on Instagram. The social (after)life of Trisha Brown will continue to evolve in these repositories, as more and more individuals reflect on her persona and life's work. Such a "living archive," if we might refer to platforms like Instagram in such a way, maintains a particular pulse of Brown that will not only continue to define her legacy but also demonstrate the revised mechanisms of canonicity and the ways in which everyday performers orient themselves toward, and perhaps also intervene in, the canon.

Both Danko and Liv compose their *nonchalant gestures* through different means and toward different ends, yet these examples both underscore how the dancers in everyday settings dialogue with, challenge, and remix forces of the hegemonic center. They demonstrate the popular, quotidian, and embodied pulse of both celebrity and canonicity, and in doing so, they begin to refigure the structures of power that shape those manifestations of some dominant locus of cultural activity.

Part 3. Circulating Nonchalant Gestures

Though Danko and Liv help to animate nonchalant gestures, their media provide only a surface trace of some key complexities and contradictions of their respective online lives. This section thus delves deeper into how new media denizens dialogue with public culture and embody cultural memory and how that work might be couched in an ambiguity and ambivalence pervading digital culture at large. The structure of the forgotten, marginal, and rogue continues to be a helpful critical lens and organizational device. Part 3 addresses how forgottenness might be in need of protection rather than deconstruction; how marginality in digital culture embeds a double-edged sense of equity; and, finally, how rogueness reveals a growing complacency toward new media, thereby reaffirming hegemonic structures. These considerations thus complicate the subversive rhetoric of *nonchalant gestures* by focusing on the mechanisms of power that pervade new media platforms like Instagram.

Forgetting to Remember

While the notion of forgottenness embedded in home dance videos is shaped by the phenomenon of social, cultural, and political disregard, and as a result becomes something to challenge and transform, the concept of nonchalant gestures articulates another register of this concept: a need or desire to safeguard forgottenness. Particularly in an era of governmental and commercial surveillance, mass collection of data, and the routine and ongoing archiving of digital content, the *forgotten* might acquire a desirable quality. It becomes, that is, something to locate after someone or something has been *remembered* by digital systems. Lewis Hyde's treatise on the virtues of forgottenness and forgetfulness contours this sense of forgottenness. In *A Primer for Forgetting: Getting Past the Past*, Hyde offers a catalog of examples from a range of cultures to propose that "forgetfulness can be more useful than memory."[49] Though Hyde does not explicitly relate this proposition to the memory machines of our contemporary digital landscape, this view nonetheless resounds with recent policies and conversations regarding online privacy, ownership of data, and dataveillance. For instance, legislation and dialogue surrounding what is referred to as "the right to be forgotten" point to a surge of interest by individuals wanting to exercise their authority over what information about them is available on the internet.[50] Such interest came in response to several legal cases in which individuals charged that search engines like Google had preserved information about them and, in continuing to make it available, had harmed those individuals. These legal disputes and their ripples of discourse across the globe demonstrate how digital repositories—including search engines but also extending to social media platforms—might *not* forget, perhaps to the detriment of its users who supply data. George Brock aptly captures this dilemma when writing, "The public is the creator of most new data and both the beneficiary and, sometimes, the victim of its retention, processing, and deployment." Brock summarizes, "In twenty-first-century life 'to exist is to be indexed by a search engine.'"[51] The right to be forgotten, then, becomes a direct challenge to how search engines determine and document the "existence" of its users.[52]

While, for the most part, these debates lie beneath the surface of new media practices, and those of Instagram in particular, they occasionally come into view. In October 2019, for example, Instagram found itself paying a "bug bounty" to security researcher Saugat Pokharel when he discovered that his deleted content was still being stored on Instagram servers.[53] Pokharel located the bug when he used the "Data Download" feature to download all of his content but then found that the media package included content he had deleted at least a year earlier.[54] Of course, it is not unusual for platforms to temporarily store deleted data on its servers—Instagram itself claims that it keeps deleted data for up to ninety days before that data is completely purged.[55] Yet, Pokharel's case of discovering data many months after deleting it reveals the inconsistencies between what Instagram claims it does and its actual practices.

The policies and conversations around remembering and forgetting data fold into performers' choreographies of oblivion and their resulting nonchalant gestures. New media users who create their own images of forgottenness use their setting, camera, and movement to manifest the complications with how their images *may* or *may not* be forgotten: *Who—or what—is doing the remembering here?* In asking such a question, performers might try to contribute to their forgottenness by deleting certain videos or perhaps by deleting entire accounts. *I am asking you to forget this dance.* Or, realizing the unknowingness of the user, in terms of the online life of their image, they might perform nonchalance to subtly engage in a dialogue around what it means to be forgotten—and, by extension, what it means to be remembered—in the age of new media. *What is the dancing body remembering and forgetting, and how is it being remembered and forgotten?*

Regardless of whether Danko and Liv leverage this angle with their home dance videos, they nonetheless complicate the meaning of their image merely through its capture and circulation. By uploading their content to Instagram, for instance, they might not be participating in any legal action or contributing to political discourse regarding the right to be forgotten; yet their nonchalant gestures illustrate how, through the choreography of oblivion, their media capture the conundrums of contemporary digital identity. Sometimes producing a likeness of their state of forgetting and sometimes staging an image of them being forgotten, Danko and Liv demonstrate how machines remember to forget and forget to remember. Through this work, the dancers end up creating a representation that performs in its own way, circulating through digital spaces as a testament of digital memory's complexities.[56]

The Marginalities of Marginality

Just as forgottenness bears contradictions, so too does marginality. The ways in which Danko and Liv illustrate marginality primarily rest with their situation in the domestic environment, a space that is so quotidian and seemingly ubiquitous that it is often painted as an asocial space; (1) with the fact that they are *not* the celebrity or canonical figure they address, but instead construct their identities as far from such stature; (2) with the production of their videos beyond the heralded methods and devices of cultural production; and (3), among other aspects, with the mere presence of their casual dancing bodies, which are clothed in everyday garb and move in ways that appear indiscriminate. However, also at play in digital cultural memory's marginalities is how media productions suggest a level of accessibility, capital, and literacy that not everyone possesses. For instance, undergirding Danko's and Liv's productions is how both dancers have access to the device they used to record their respective scenes, understand how to operate Instagram, and speak the "language" of digital culture to create a post that makes sense to their audiences. These features require literacy of and immersion in mobile communication devices (i.e., smartphones, tablets, laptops) and the media platforms to which they connect. Such a consideration indicates how *nonchalant gestures* are thus *already* part of a system that reinforces marginality rather than dismantles it.

The ways in which Danko and Liv are imbricated in a marginaliz*ing* machine, rather than a marginaliz*ed* one, may be framed within the ongoing debate regarding the degree to which the internet enables democracy, grassroots activity, and empowerment among the masses. Henry Jenkins captures this debate through a discussion of "grassroots convergence," which reflects "the increasingly central roles that digitally empowered consumers play in shaping the production, circulation, and reception of media content."[57] For Jenkins, grassroots convergence opposes corporate convergence—a dichotomy that forms a "bottom-up" versus "top-down" dynamic. While this relationship between two forms of convergence reiterates a sense of digital-cultural marginality in relation to some dominant center, it also subtly points to worlds beyond that dialogue. That is to say, Jenkins's reference to consumers who are "digitally empowered" gestures toward a separate yet related question: What contributes to "empowerment" in the digital sphere? Jenkins's language here not only gestures toward the privilege that is embedded in access to digital tools but also suggests that there may be individuals, groups, and cultures who might be *digitally disempowered.* The concept of the digital divide harnesses this point by indicating notions of marginality embedded in access to digital tools and knowledge.[58] Of course, as Jan van Dijk notes, access to digital tools is defined not just by physical or material access but also by "motivational access," "skills access," and "usage access."[59] Digital and media literacies—alongside political restrictions, economic conditions, and cultural orientations—thus impact how a person might access and navigate information technologies. Robinson and colleagues capture this notion when arguing that digital inequalities embed "traditional axes of inequality such as race, class, and gender."[60] This narrative emphasizes the ways in which digital culture—alongside its promotion of practices that might *challenge* the dominant center—might also simultaneously *reinforce* marginalities.

Platforms like Instagram effectively promulgate this paradox of marginality through its approach to issues of access. For instance, in acknowledging the digital divide (in terms of material/physical access), founder and CEO of Instagram's parent company Meta, Mark Zuckerberg, announced a plan in 2013 to bring free internet to countries across the globe. By 2016, the program was active in forty-two countries, half of which are in Africa. While Zuckerberg has expressed a belief that access to the internet is a "basic human right," his efforts have been determined as opportunistic: a "marketing ploy."[61] Though individuals are able to use the program to gain access to the internet for educational, social, and occupational needs, their data and online activity become part of Meta's repository, if not their property—and the extent to which that data may be utilized by the company is not made known to those users. The effects of this bait-and-switch approach become especially palpable in the case of Meta's withdrawal from India. Only one year after launching Free Basics, users in India found charges on their accounts for viewing videos that were deemed to be paid content. The Telecom Regulatory Authority of India then prohibited service providers from charging discriminatory fees for users accessing data solely based on content. While this instance is not the only case that reflects the opportunism of Meta's Free Basics program, it aptly epitomizes the ways in which the company obscures how it benefits from such seemingly altruistic endeavors aimed at resolving the digital divide. Part of Meta's wider strategy of leveraging "free" access and content for user data, that is, only exacerbates existing tensions between margin and center.

Nonchalant gestures must be understood through this nuanced sense of marginality. While home dancers' choreographies of oblivion might resist and intervene in the hegemony of cultural memory, their multifaceted access to tools and knowledge, which have enabled them to produce those narratives in the first place, articulates the privilege of their performance and of their being able to aestheticize their forgottenness. Of course, gone unseen are innumerable experiences and productions yet to be that remain in the margins of oblivion, beyond the capturings of the camera and the recordings of digital cultural memory and foreclosed by the digital divide.

The Other Side of Rogue

Alongside the complexities of forgottenness and marginality are those that rogueness presents. As expressed in the previous points in this chapter, rogueness is intrinsically resistive. While the margin cultivates this potential, it may not necessarily activate, mobilize, or manifest resistance. The rogue individual, however, practices agonism from the outset. The ways in which Danko and Liv present their rogueness rest with their individual dancing bodies working against forces of hegemony as they enact their own productions and intervene in digital repositories of knowledge and cultural memory. This argument, however, must also be understood within a contemporary digital landscape that is often characterized by ambivalence.[62] Similar to how the nontarget of CCTV might feel apathetic about being the subject of surveillance, as discussed in part 1, the new media user might feel ambivalent about the structures of power that undergird digital culture. Read within such a field, the home dance video might not land as a subversive intervention by the solo dancer, in solitude, but ultimately as a reinforcement of the larger collective that the dancer is ostensibly resisting.

The rogue performer, alongside its possible ambivalence, also harbors an ambiguity in its characterization: that is, by "straying from the pack"—a defining feature of the rogue—the performer also references (and perhaps even *relies upon*) the whole from which they depart. In other words, by marking themselves as a singular figure that *was* part of a larger collective, the rogue individual maintains their association to that collective. They may be seen through their relation to the group—as someone who has left the group, perhaps in a critical manner; yet in doing so, they inadvertently indicate the power of that group. The question that follows, then, is whether that individual is subverting the hierarchy, symbolized through the established group from which they depart, or reinforcing it.

In their editorial, Harmony Bench and Simon Ellis reveal this conundrum of the rogue when they interrogate the meaning of the solo dancing body. They ask, "Does solo performance reflect an impulse to withdraw from the world and amplify the self? Or conversely, does solo performance offer a space from which to critique such withdrawal?"[63] The ambiguity between spotlighting the self and critiquing their own departure, which Bench and Ellis identify, indicates the inherent complications of the solo performer's relation to the larger collective. How might drawing away to perform one's solitude both highlight the self and also reinforce one's association to the group?

Considering the rogue character's ambivalence and ambiguity within the landscape of Instagram allows for the nuancing of the "group" or "collective" from which the rogue departs, references, and perhaps ultimately reinforces. Such a consideration gestures toward the relations of power that exist between the individual dancer performing solo-ness (and solitude) and the larger collective. The sole dancing body on new media, despite its performed solitude, initiates an engagement with others through the posting of their dance online. The viewer, the discourse, and the platform with which the dancer engages may be understood as a collective body, if not an establishment—perhaps one that is imbricated in the systems from which they have withdrawn. In such an instance, then, the dancer's withdrawal is only symbolic, as it ultimately becomes negated by the sharing of the performance. In this regard, perhaps the rogueness that they express through the media functions as another layer of their aestheticized intimacy—a theatricalization of an interiority that at once complicates and reaffirms problematic binaries of body, space, and subjectivity.

This complication of the rogue is evident in the home dance productions discussed in this chapter. In Danko's case, though he remixes celebrity repertoire in a way that reclaims public memory, his interventions might not shift the discourse around Beychella or reach an audience that might be compelled to do so. Instead, his performance may underscore the power of celebrity to infiltrate individuals' homes and bodies. Under this logic, Danko's departure from the group, his straying from the pack, is just a way to reincorporate himself back into it. Liv's case, on the other hand, is a bit different in terms of her on-platform choreography of oblivion. In using the hashtag #trishabrown, Liv engages in a separate performance of rogueness. Though the hashtag is just Trisha Brown's name, when the viewer clicks on it, they will see a sizable collection of *other* images (both photos and videos) that *other* users have decided to link to Brown, her persona, and her legacy. The hashtag in this case is quite interesting theoretically, as it links a singular image to a number of different repositories of knowledge (depending on how many hashtags are used in the post), while indicating a bridge between the individual dancer and digital cultural memory. However, Liv's incorporation of this hashtag takes the viewer away from her expression and toward a repository of expressions from other users. That is to say, by incorporating the hashtag, Liv has at once embedded her performance into a collection of other expressions (thereby pulling herself into focus) and directed attention away from her profile (thereby pulling the hashtag collection into focus). So, while the hashtag serves as a performative mechanism that reflects the dancer's straddling between worlds, it also functions to envelop the potentially rogue dancer back into the collective.

These intricacies of the rogue, as well as those of the forgotten and marginal, may point to the layers of ambiguity embedded in nonchalant gestures. However, considering the already paradoxical character of non-chalant gestures—with its stretching across worlds of the forgotten and remembered, marginal and centered, rogue and established—the com-plexities discussed above are fitting. Though they may complicate the arguments presented in parts 1 and 2 of the chapter, they also extend the semiotic and ontological intricacies of one's choreography of oblivion to a more nuanced sense of digital culture. In this way, the safeguard-ing of forgottenness, the marginality of marginality, and the other side of rogue continue to underscore the ways in which dancers negotiate digital identity and its relationship to digital cultural memory. The contours of digital culture and of intimaesthetics are already laced with ambiguity and ambivalence—this section only reinforces that notion.

Conclusion

Nonchalant gestures, though sourced with a particular relationship be-tween the subject and the camera, open out to a number of social, cultural, and economic intricacies. This type of intimaesthetic harnesses the power of the gaze, the domestic setting, and the dancing body to both model surveillance and complicate notions of privacy in a network society. Once online, these images participate in systems of cultural memory through the dancer's imaging of forgottenness, marginality, and rogueness. Danko's homage to Beyoncé and Liv's tribute to Trisha Brown are merely two in-stances wherein the home dancer initiates these choreographies. The danc-ers remix culture to then toss their works back out into public circulation to collide against, dialogue with, and exist beside other expressions, many of which are from other domestic stages around the globe. Thus, their choreography of oblivion might *represent* the unseen, private, and forgot-ten corners of cultural production, but the vibrant online life of those performances underscores the fact of their public-facing aestheticization.

Chapter 3 harnesses the dynamic in which the dancer creates an image of themselves but acts as though they *did not*. Chapter 4 focuses on a slightly different dynamic: the dancer who does not create their own image but acts as though they *did*. The intimaesthetic that emerges from this dynamic, referred to as home concerts, represents a family-oriented approach to home dance performance and its mediatizations. In particular, the next chapter focuses on parent-managed accounts of children to reveal a set of techniques called minor choreography. Distinct from choreography of oblivion, minor choreography requires the collaboration and consent of another person: an informal agreement of sorts between the dancer and the camera operator. So, as the former's complications of cultural memory recede from focus, the latter's complexities of authorship and child autonomy come into view.

FOUR

Home Concerts

*"Wait! I know this music!" Declan yells from the living room. He slides
into the kitchen and begins dancing to the Nutcracker music playing from
the television. Danielle quickly grabs her phone and opens the camera app.
She knows by now when she might capture some good content for her son's
Instagram account—and with Declan dancing a fierce ballet improvisation in his pajamas, Danielle has a feeling it will be prime content.*

Is this how the scene unfolded? We do not know, but the image
suggests so much.

*Declan spins and, almost frantic with excitement, flitters through his
balletic footwork. He drops his jaw and tilts his head back in a dramatic
appeal. This is golden. Declan's followers will love it, Danielle thinks
as Declan continues to imagine he is the principal dancer of a renowned
company.*

Does Declan know Danielle plans to put this video online?

*Elsewhere, and at least two years later, Gemma, a seven-year-old as-
piring ballerina, didn't expect to ever attend her dance classes from home,
but, alas, the COVID-19 pandemic has disrupted her studio's rehearsal
schedule and performance plans, among many other facets of life. Focused
on the teacher's cues emanating from the laptop speakers in front of her,
she rehearses a routine that she had been learning for an upcoming dance*

*competition. As she strikes her arms to the left and then right, launches her
leg up by her ear, and spins tightly around, Gemma feels the difference in
rehearsing at home.*

Gemma knows she's being recorded, but did her parents tell her
about the account in her name? Would she perform any differently
if she knew this video would be posted to that account?

*Gemma sharply turns her head toward the screen, circles her arm, and
launches into an attitude leap toward the corner. This is the ninth time she
has rehearsed this dance, but she stays focused on perfection. Upon finish-
ing, she looks toward the camera with stoic exhaustion as if to say,* Was
that good enough?

Introduction

Amid the sea of self-produced media on Instagram—colliding with candid
dancing videos, circulating in tandem with moving selfies, and bumping up
against nonchalant gestures—are media of a different type: media wherein
the dancer is a knowing subject of another's recording. That is to say, the
dancer is not the one filming the action, and yet they are aware of the
camera, the cameraperson, and the fact that a recording is taking place.
As is the case with the media of Declan and Gemma captured above, the
viewer gets the sense that the dancer would be performing in such a way
regardless of whether they were being filmed by their parents.[1] Unlike the
media discussed in chapter 1, the subject of a home concert production
is cognizant of both the audience and the camera. This cognizance aligns
the form with the moving selfie explored in chapter 2—though notably,
the image here is *not* self-captured. Instead, as the examples of Declan and
Gemma illustrate, the home concert type of intimaesthetics results from
a familial engagement.

This sort of production-through-collaboration represents a wide swath
of content on platforms like Instagram. Performers may acknowledge the
camera, but the semiotics of the image suggest that someone else was
involved in the production. Then, when set in the domestic environment,
such a production constructs an intimaesthetic imbued with familiarity
and familiality. These *home concerts* are staged for an audience, embedded in the home, and produced in concert with others in the space. There
may be only one person in the frame, but the presence and sentimentality
of the cameraperson is suggested through the fact of the recording, the
framing of the scene, and the camera movement. These semiotics combine
with those of the performer and the home to suggest the relationality of

those involved in the production. Its subsequent online circulation then contributes to reproductions of systems of value, including those of the nuclear family.

This chapter considers media produced through this relationship between performer, camera, and cameraperson and the values those media inadvertently reproduce. I unpack the home concerts type of intimaesthetics by focusing on a particular phenomenon on social media wherein children become the subjects of images crafted by their parents/guardians or some other supervising adult(s). In these media, parents often create the image, upload it to the internet, and manage the account on which it lives—an account that often features the name of their child. The intimaesthetic articulated through this phenomenon points to a blurring of roles involved in new media production, particularly as it pertains to families. In these images, the children are being modeled—that is, they are the subjects of media that work to capture some moment, sentiment, or dimension of their childhood. And yet, the posts tend to disguise the role of the parent(s) behind the supposed authorship of the child. While this phenomenon does not capture the wide range of home concert media, it poignantly represents not only the techniques of production involved in this particular arrangement of performer-camera-cameraperson but also the cultural attitudes and ethical complexities around posting images of individuals with close relationalities, particularly media in which minors are involved. Attention to this subset of media reveals the strategies by which gender and other social categories are reiterated through family dynamics—a collection of strategies I refer to as *minor choreography*. This theory captures the techniques and approaches parents use to fashion their child's public personae online, while also shaping that child's personal identity. The content of this choreography, once it ends up online, becomes susceptible to the platform's own mechanisms of establishing and influencing contemporary youth culture. Home dance videos uploaded to Instagram are a prime space to uncover and unpack these layers of minor choreography. Two videos come to epitomize the home concerts intimaesthetic and its display of minor choreography: one featuring a seven-year-old boy whom I refer to as Declan and the other one capturing a young girl around the same age as Declan, whom we will refer to as Gemma. These media, introduced above, at once reflect exemplars of the home concerts type of intimaesthetic and present distinct models of choreography. Gender, in particular, becomes part of the aspect of these children's identities that is being both *modeled* and *reproduced* on their Instagram accounts.

Like the previous chapters of this book, this chapter begins with a definition of the intimaesthetic in question: home concerts on Instagram and its associated phenomenon of minor choreographies. Part 1 approaches this effort through a discussion of the theoretical, historical, and aesthetic anchors of these concepts. Part 2 exemplifies these practices through the choreographic analysis of dances featuring Declan and Gemma, as well as their respective accounts. Part 3 rounds out this analysis with the study of the contexts surrounding the online circulation of minor choreography. This final section displaces the focus from the parents to the platform, emphasizing the ways in which apps like Instagram work to establish a culture that encourages the oversharing of media that features or targets children. Ultimately, I argue that Instagram institutes its own version of minor choreography.

Part 1. Defining Home Concerts

A defining feature of the home concerts intimaesthetic is the ambiguity of authorship embedded in the media. These videos capture the domestic world of a particular subject, yet they are clearly recorded by someone else. Still, the profiles on which the videos appear are often staged to suggest that the subject is also the account owner. This tension is especially pronounced on parent-managed accounts, where a child's face serves as the profile picture, their name is used as the handle, and the bio describes their hobbies, their interests, and perhaps even their age. Every post on such an account features the child and their apparent preoccupations. To an unfamiliar viewer, the profile may appear self-managed; yet, a closer look reveals the invisible hand of an adult. The language of the caption often reflects a tone and sophistication beyond the child's likely capacity, while the editing and camerawork demonstrate a level of technical proficiency unlikely to belong to the subject themselves. Ultimately, such accounts exhibit new media strategies and literacies that exceed what the child-subject could reasonably achieve. This blurring between the subject of the content and its true author lies at the crux of home concerts.

A post featuring a child may indeed suggest the involvement of another actor, particularly a parental figure, thereby complicating the culture of self-production that pervades social media; yet the centrality of the child here is tinged with its own set of politics. Specifically, the phenomenon of parent-managed kids accounts has stakes in a larger conversation about how new media industries configure content *of* and *for* children. With their influence of commercialization, their development of *echo chamber*–like communities (what scholars call *homophilies*), their ambiguities of age appropriateness, and their ease of impersonation, new media platforms elicit an abundance of questions and concerns regarding how minors produce, circulate, and consume media online.[2] While these complexities are discussed in further detail in subsequent sections of the chapter, they are important to point out here because they emphasize the active role of a parent creating, authorizing, and managing an account on behalf of, or otherwise representing, their child. It also points to a compelling genealogy wherein parents have been involved in the performative productions of their children across various media. The following section thus traces historical and cultural antecedents of home concerts through a few cultural threads that collectively shape its place in digital culture today.

Genealogy of Home Concerts

The home concerts intimaesthetic represents a convergence of myriad social, cultural, and technological influences. This discussion focuses on specific media or technologies that have helped give rise to this phenomenon: the advent of the home movie and the reality television show *Dance Moms*. Each of these examples not only represents a different point in the history of technology but also reflects variations in scope and scale. The first example, for instance, is a broad cultural movement and arguably also a genre of filmmaking, with a lengthy history of development featuring many technological changes and sociocultural shifts. The second example is one particular series on television that lasted eight seasons. Despite the variations in framing, a review of each antecedent adds depth to an understanding of home concerts.

The phenomenon of home movies captures an impetus to record the everyday realities of a group of individuals, to mark milestones big and small, and to exercise creative autonomy as a way to produce an object of one's making. While the term "home movie" evokes the domestic setting, the practice has always extended beyond the home—part of the wider heterogeneous practice of amateur filmmaking.[3] Still, when we foreground the domestic associations of the home movie, we can better understand how this legacy informs the aesthetic and affective registers of contemporary home dance videos. For instance, viewers often assume that the individuals appearing in such videos know each other intimately, often on a familial level. This impression does not suggest, however, that the video is unmediated, raw, or authentic. As with any filmic medium, home movies—past or present—are carefully constructed representations of one's experience. Visual anthropologist Richard Chalfen articulates this point when writing that "what is supposed to be a documentation of daily family life, isn't at all."[4] Instead, the content of home movies is often selective and tends to capture extraordinary events like "vacation activity," "holiday activity," "special events," and "local activity," as Chalfen maintains.[5] For Patricia Zimmerman, however, the constructed sense of familiarity and relationality embedded in home movies is more nuanced, historically contingent, and linked to normative family dynamics in capitalistic societies. Rooted in the development of leisure time and disposable income amid a postwar economic boom, home movies came to represent the idealization of the nuclear family through "togetherness." Home movies, in Zimmerman's words, were a "mirror image of the disciplined, skilled, coordinated world of work, enveloped and ameliorated by the leisure activities of the nuclear family."[6] Togetherness, in this way, was couched in middle- to upper-class normativity.[7]

Similar to home movies, home concerts offer the *impression* of unmediated realities, but they are indeed structured representations. Through their expressions of togetherness and familiality, that is, both forms create a sentiment and aesthetic of some domestic reality—a reality that may be selective, as Chalfen points out, and culturally rooted, as Zimmerman argues. Of course, these two media differ in their audience and mode of dissemination, thus giving home concerts a different tinge of "realness." While parents in a network society might not always intend to post a video of their child when they record it, the possibility of that outcome is nonetheless present. In other words, the culture of quotidian content across new media shapes the way users record *any* material, regardless of whether they intend at the moment to upload it. This culture thus impacts how new media users capture "home movie" footage. They might, for instance, encourage activity that they know their followers will like or, alternatively, record only the situations, things, or activities that they have been conditioned to conceive of as culturally or socially valuable. This thrust differs from pre–new media home movie production. Instead of anticipating the possibility of mass circulation and public exposure, home movies of the twentieth century opened out to small audiences that were often limited to the family and close friends of the subject. Such a limited audience then determines the subject's and the cameraperson's approach to the scene, the media, and the production of the media.[8]

While the intentionality behind the productions of, on the one hand, twentieth-century home movies and, on the other hand, new media's online iterations certainly differs, there is a clear thread of aesthetic practice that can be traced from the former to the latter. Creating home movies, that is, promoted a certain technological literacy that would be required to produce a video that others might want to watch. For instance, it allowed a person to navigate situations like how to hold a camera while recording; when to move with the camera versus when to position it ahead of time; what the optimal distance from the subject might be, for both audio and video quality; how to frame a close-up as opposed to a full-body shot; what types of accessory devices might enhance the image; and what that "white balance" button even does. While the recording devices have evolved since the early days of home movie production, the skills developed through those practices remain transferable to the craft of self-produced home videos in the twenty-first-century new media landscape.

Alongside the importance of the twentieth-century home movie phenomenon is a more specific antecedent for home concerts on new media: a particular television program that names and reflects the social archetype of the "dance mom." Titled after this archetype, *Dance Moms* reflects parental involvement in crafting not just the mediatized representation of a child but also that child's social identity.[9] The show premiered in 2011 on the television network Lifetime and enjoyed eight seasons of viewership. It follows the pursuits of a competition dance studio in Pittsburgh, Pennsylvania, focusing on the drama that ensues among the studio owner, Abby Lee Miller, the dancers' moms, and members of rival studios. As these dramas ebb and flow from episode to episode, the show articulates the social and cultural intricacies of gender, the body, family, and childhood. Scholars have, for instance, pointed to the show's treatment of both girlhood and motherhood, calling attention to the damaging effects of the program's competitive focus and how the values it instills have shaped the larger landscape of dance education in the United States.[10]

Being a reality television show created by producers with TV ratings in mind, *Dance Moms* exaggerates cultural particularities that exceed the typical and venture into the sensational. It, for instance, is likely made up of many scenarios, conversations, and events that were fabricated and scripted. At the same time, the culture that the show sought to broadcast was, at the time, an underexamined yet pervasive movement in the United States and other wealthy nations. Through its airing, then, *Dance Moms* provided a glimpse into the culture of competition dance studios and in the process also captured how the genre of competition dance has become a powerful tool to shape the bodies, minds, and social circles of young girls.

Alongside *Dance Moms*'s representation of a cultural movement, it also sheds light on the figure of the competition dance stage mom: an archetype that many characters on the show embodied. As the namesake of the show, these women performed the managerial duties required to develop a star-dancer-in-the-making, often resembling a talent agent for their child. Though the show does not focus on it, the viewer presumes that these women also played a significant role in the typical caretaker duties involved in being a parent. The personality of the dance stage mom was portrayed as calculating, competitive, and fiercely attentive to her child's needs. This figure might be concerned, for instance, if she felt her daughter was not getting enough attention from the teacher or the other dancers were getting in the way of her daughter's success. Characters exemplified variations in personality, yet the overarching type that the show established undergirded their individual idiosyncrasies.

While shows like *Dance Moms* articulated a character that was certainly an exaggeration of the individuals they were based on, they also reflected qualities found in upper-middle-class culture (particularly in the United States) and found a way to reiterate and reproduce those qualities. Thus, when pulled out of her televisual context, the stage mom was able to maneuver through other platforms. Social media, in particular, provided a fresh playground/workspace for the mom-manager archetype to explore. Platforms like Instagram allow her to exercise more autonomy in the shaping of her child's public image—away from the script-writing, drama-cultivating hands of the reality television producer. She may utilize platforms like Instagram to create and manage a profile that expresses the child's personality and positions their identity in a particular way. She also might engage with other content, post media, remove media—all on behalf of her child. She can *become* the child's online persona.

Another key difference is that, unlike *Dance Moms*, social media *invisiblizes and abstracts* the figure of the mom-manager. In the case of home concerts, the manager of the dancer's media is, first of all, not always explicitly a mom. Instead, the account may be run by a different parent figure, both parents, or perhaps some other family figure or guardian. While the cultural reference of the dance mom prompts a reading that the mother is involved in such productions, the content on the child's account often excludes adults and appears to capture the perspective of the dancer, thereby obscuring the role of the parent-producer.

The convergence of twentieth-century home movies and the archetype of the dance mom reflects troubling implications for both parent and child. These implications come into focus in the following section, which reveals the mechanisms through which a parent might shape their child's online image. While these mechanisms might not be tethered solely to the home concerts intimaesthetic, they nonetheless reflect a system of broad strategies that parent-producers might employ to shape—through both the production and circulation of media—their child's public persona, online image, and social identity. The theory of minor choreography captures such a system. What follows, then, is a description of this theory and the techniques that compose it. Ultimately, minor choreography points to how home dance productions become the medium through which a child's image and identity are *choreographed*.

Minor Choreography

The choreography of or involving minors is a delicate subject. It points to the subtle yet nonetheless powerful processes that shape a young person's identity, image, and persona/e. The delicacy of the matter is sourced with the fragility of the population: they are not deemed economically or developmentally self-sufficient enough to enter into contracts of their own accord. A theorization of their choreography is thus anchored to both the legal designations determining their public status and the sociocultural sensitivities surrounding their development. Thus, to better understand how mediatizations of children are produced and shared through new media productions, it is necessary to first review the legal dimensions of this group.

The designation of *minor* is indeed a category referring to the age of an individual and their corresponding rights, freedoms, protections, and responsibilities. The age cap of a minor varies by country and context. A minor in the United States, for instance, is anyone below the age of eighteen for most purposes and contexts, like voting in an election, owning property, suing or being sued, or consenting to medical treatment. However, for the contexts of gambling and consuming alcohol, a person must be at least twenty-one. This rule generally applies to all states, except for Alabama and Nebraska, where the age of majority is nineteen, and Mississippi and Puerto Rico, where the age of majority is twenty-one. Other countries have other specificities for the categories of minor and major, which then open out to legal parameters for those groups. For example, New Zealand, Thailand, and Taiwan all have the nationwide age of majority at twenty. In Cambodia, Palestine, Vietnam, and Cuba, among others, the age is set at sixteen. Countries with the age of majority of twenty-one include Gabon, Chad, Honduras, and Kuwait. Iran has theirs set to nine for girls and fifteen for boys. Japan had theirs set to eighteen until March 2022, when they increased it to twenty. Aside from these outliers, most countries across the globe have established the age of majority at eighteen.[11]

The variations in the legal status of minors are important to recognize, as they may be in tension with the seemingly border-transcending and legally amorphous nature of the internet. Even though the civil law of a given context prescribes certain activities to certain age groups, network society tends to play by different rules that govern the actions of its users, thereby impacting both legislation and subsequent due process. As Jan van Dijk notes, the terms of legal protections in network society shift across geographical, and thus legislative, boundaries. As van Dijk explains:

> The effectiveness of all privacy legislation is uncertain as personal data in networks are transferred across borders with different jurisdictions and because the legislation has a low status: it is most often civil and common law rather than criminal law, so prosecution and punishment for privacy offenses are rare.[12]

While van Dijk refers specifically to privacy concerns, the legal ambiguities are concerning for all users, much less users with the status of "minor." For example, a person posting a video may be of the age of majority in the place where they produce the content but a minor in the place where someone else in the world receives the content. And the laws that protect those categories of users might also shift in transmission. Age of minority/majority is thus not only mutable by its geographical context but also made especially ambiguous when considering the implications of online transmission and the status of legal protections in a network society.

The legal definitions of a minor not only provide a grounding for the term—however mutable it may be—but also emphasize the very distinction between a minor and an adult. That is, these two parties are not only defined *against* one another (a minor being someone below eighteen and a major being everyone else) but also inextricably *linked* in their social, cultural, and economic activity. Specifically, a minor must be legally under the care and decision-making authority of a major—often the parent but sometimes someone else who serves as a legal guardian. Among other expectations, a minor's parent/guardian provides sustenance, housing, and safety for the child under their care. Those individuals often also manage the child's social calendars, oversee their recreational endeavors, and facilitate their education. They instill grooming habits; teach the child the specificities of a language or multiple languages; and impress upon them the etiquette of public culture, the mechanisms of dressing oneself, and the rules of a family, neighborhood, community, or nation-state. They may also demonstrate the differences between categories of gender, race, and class, among others. A parent/guardian, in other words, often does much more than provide the basic necessities that are required by civil law. These actions may generally be understood as minor choreography.

The concept of minor choreography indeed captures the extra-legal nature of shaping a young person. This theory, with its explicit reference to the concept of choreography, particularly addresses how the techniques and patternings instilled in a child take place in and through the body: they are enacted through the body of the parent/guardian, they are received through the body of the minor, and then that minor rehearses them through bodily movement. This sensibility extends the notion of the homebody, as discussed in the introduction to the book. The homebody proposes that the body's development of identity and subjectivity is linked to the spaces it inhabits, and in particular embeds those formations and deviations of the habitus in one's habitat—in their home. Minor choreography further applies this focus on the body, its movement, and its habituations to young people: a population who is especially in a state of perpetual development.

While all bodies are constantly in a state of re/construction, the conditions of being a child entail remarkably more physical and cognitive changes than adults experience.[13] Their homebodies, that is, are especially malleable. On a neuroscientific level, children are rapidly forming synapses and new neurological connections. On a musculoskeletal level, their bones, muscles, and connective tissues are taking new shape and becoming stronger. They might not be able to throw a ball one day, and the next day will launch one across the room. While these layers of human development capture the more measurable and externally recognized modes of growth and change, they nonetheless serve as an apt indication of other corporeal processes of becoming.[14] Like the tip of the iceberg, these markers represent an amalgamation of less obvious forms of bodily constructions: those pertaining to the social and cultural layers of one's development.

Contrasting the measurable evidence of growth, the concept of minor choreography reflects the ongoing processes by which young people learn the codes and conventions of their surroundings, which gradually shape their personae: the etiquette of their class, specificities of their race, characteristics of their gender, meaning of their citizenship, relationship to authority, and rhetorical approaches to language, among others. Regardless of the degree to which a child may subscribe to or deviate from the accepted conditions of their surroundings, these codes and conventions shape their identities, self-understandings, and worldviews.[15] The complex psychological and sociological threads involved in this process are beyond the purview of this consideration; however, it is important to recognize that the processes involved in identity formation, though they are housed in the individual subject, are heavily influenced by the collective bodies in that individual's sociocultural orbit.[16] That is to say, the processes of construction that take place with a young person's self and identity rest with the people and cultural attitudes in the realm of exposure for that individual. Whether it be through more abstract entities, like the media that a child consumes, or through their interaction with particular people, like family and friends, the child receives cues and deciphers codes from their surroundings. A minor is immersed, that is, in systems of "social choreography," to borrow Andrew Hewitt's term, through bodily techniques, patterns, and sequences that are part of a social fabric.[17]

The ways in which a minor is embedded in their surroundings and susceptible to the influence of others, the ways in which they absorb and perform social codes and conventions, and the manifestation of those processes through cultural products reflect the tenets of minor choreography. This theory, however, approaches the social and cultural development of minors specifically through the lens of media: media production and media semiotics. Such a lens offers an understanding of how minor choreographies are activated, circulated, and consumed into public consciousness—from one body to many bodies. Attention to these operations emphasizes, then, how minor choreographies enable the reproduction of value systems. Images, in particular, may manifest ideals of beauty, enable the performance of personae, construct personal narratives, express one's identity, mark a particular stage in the formation of that identity, and document relationalities. Considering the meaning-making possibilities of images, it is no surprise that new media platforms—with their image centricity and ease of public circulation—have become a prime mode for parents/guardians to craft narratives of their children, to influence how others perceive those children, and to play a role in shaping the children's identities.

Creating a personal account online *for* and *on behalf of* a child has become an easy and popular technique for minor choreographies to flourish.[18] Through these profiles, parents/guardians can post videos and pictures that reflect the child's interests, activities, social world, and other minutia of their existence. They can frame the child in particular ways and narrate their world in a manner that suits the values to which the family subscribes.[19] They can curate a profile to capture the fluidities of their child's identity formation, adding to or deleting particular media that no longer captures some ethos of that portrait. The possibilities for minor choreographies to appear through new media are indeed abundant.

In many ways, the home concerts intimaesthetic demonstrates these capacities of new media. By honing in on dance media that appears on parent-managed accounts *about* and *featuring* a child, this movement reveals the mechanisms of minor choreography. As noted above, the ambiguity around who is doing what in these productions is central to media of this type. That ambiguity obscures the reproduction of values that occurs in and through the young dancer's body and image. Once aestheticized, the home dance performance comes to represent—and ultimately propagate through its circulation—the social construction of gender, race, class, sex, and ability, among other social categories. The reception of these media then relies on codes and conventions, producing what Roland Barthes calls "a mirage of structures" through which the dancer's image passes.[20] These instances, from production to consumption, reveal how dance functions as social practice, as it is, in Hewitt's words, "the aesthetic medium that most consistently [seeks] to understand art as something immanently political; that is, as something that derives its political significance from its own status as praxis."[21] The dancing child, in the case of home concerts media, embodies systems of value through bodily movement, representing both the production and reiteration of values.

While parent-produced media of children dancing in the home reveal minor choreographies, their online circulation acquires a new character. That is to say, once uploaded to a new media platform, the performances of identity expressed through the media fall into largely undetermined circuits and pathways. The media is orchestrated by a complex system of settings, algorithms, and features of a given platform. In this sense, minor choreography gives way to what I call *minor orchestration*: a collection of systematic properties on a platform that determine the social life of media *of*, *about*, or *for* children. This notion suggests that the minor orchestrations of one platform are distinct from those of another platform.[22] Of course, these orchestrations, like most data in a network society, are black boxed, wherein distinctions may be viewed only through their outputs, as the systematic intricacies that determine them are not publicly available or accessible but belong to the platform itself. Whether it be Meta, Google, Microsoft, or ByteDance, the user provides the data but cannot see the criteria, scripts, or rules that command its circulation. Aligned with the principle of platform specificity, minor orchestration is a result of technological specifications of a proprietary application, website, or tool, such as its options, settings, algorithms, restrictions, or relation to commercial enterprise. These particular elements then open out to cultures of production, circulation, and consumption that are also particular to each platform.[23] As discussed in part 3, for instance, the feature set and system properties of Instagram reflect a neoliberal attention to children and the generational expansion of its user base. These, along with other minor orchestrations, articulate the handoff of *parental control* to *platform control.*

The techniques of minor choreographies and strategies of minor orchestration may be subtle, if not undetectable, to most viewers, but they undoubtedly play a role in how viewers perceive the subject. It is worth noting, too, that even if the viewer perceives the role of the parent/guardian in a given production, they may not conceive of it as remarkable. Instead, minor choreographies that are made obvious to viewers may be understood as part of contemporary parenting. In an effort to gesture toward this culture of parenting, the following section reveals the many complexities of home concerts and the minor choreographies that appear through them.

Aesthetics and Semiotics of Home Concerts

Like other approaches to intimaesthetics in this book, home concerts may be understood primarily through the relationship between the dancer and the person recording the action. Several features of the production indicate that these two individuals are indeed separate actors. Similar to the case of candid dancing, a telling characteristic of a home concerts image is the camera movement. The fact of a moving, often jostling frame indicates that someone other than the dancer is holding the recording device. This suggestion then conveys a relational dynamic at play in the scene, as the role of the cameraperson becomes a collaborator in the scene and also likely a familiar face to the performer. Perhaps the subject and camera operator are, for instance, siblings or maybe child and parent. The two parties came together and, for whatever reason, decided to create a production. The dancer would perform the action—perhaps to rehearse for an upcoming performance, to imagine themselves in a fantastical narrative, or merely to experiment with movement—while their accomplice would record the scene. Regardless of the specificity of their relationship, the viewer of the image, once identifying the camera movement, immediately would presume that (1) there is someone behind the camera and (2) that the camera operator has a relationship of familiarity with the subject.

The notion of *familiarity* of the video recorded by someone other than the subject develops into a suggestion of *familiality* when the production is set in the domestic environment. Several aspects of the scene indicate that the setting is the home: the appearance of lived-in furniture or fixtures—a couch with throw pillows, a half-made bed, a desk adorned with objects, a dresser; the personal objects situated in the frame; and even the architectural features of the room, among many other features. Though these indicators vary widely across different videos and also gesture toward different social, cultural, and economic specificities, they nonetheless work together to create a sensibility of domesticity. This sensibility impacts the meaning of the image as well as the impressions viewers get of the residents. Namely, the domestic setting enables the blurring of familiarity and familiality, particularly in terms of how one might figure the relationship between the dancer and the cameraperson (and whoever else may be involved in the production). Representations of the home, in particular, cultivate what Bex Harper and Hollie Price call "domestic imaginaries" that contribute to readings of the domestic setting as a place for family activity, dialogue, and memories.[24] In this sense, the home's inhabitants not only are familiar with one another but articulate a kin-like relationship.

The camera movement adds to the setting to construct a guardian-like dynamic between the cameraperson and the subject of the image. Typically, when camera movement is present, the viewer understands that another person is recording the action. However, this sensibility becomes more contoured in cases where the subject is a young person and the setting is in the home. Unless otherwise stated, the viewer will read the relationship between the dancer and cameraperson as a parent-child one. The visual focus and way of framing the child's performance further underscore this reading. For instance, a guardian-like attention may be perceived in the way the camera follows the dancer as they move through the space. Such a technique of/with the camera ultimately ensures that the dancer remains somewhat centered in the frame, centered in the production, and centered in the viewer's attention. It allows, in other words, the cameraperson to create a video that effectively showcases the minor under their care.

Despite the influence of the cameraperson-guardian over both the production and the domestic life surrounding it, their authorial role is quite ambiguous. Their invisible contributions are known only through the performance of the child, the true focus of our attention. This individual is looking in on the scene, supervising its unfolding and managing its mediatization from afar (or at least from beyond the delineations of the frame). At the same time, they are part of the scene at the moment of production. While this role may be akin to that of a film director, who manages many aspects of the scene but whose work primarily lies outside of the frame, the figure of the cameraperson-guardian is embedded in the reality of the space. For instance, aside from the familiality with the dancer, they are involved in the domestic affairs that determine the child's social, cultural, and economic life. They likely provide some sort of financial assistance or security for the child, may sleep under the same roof, provide sustenance for them, ensure their education, and manage their social and recreational affairs. In other words, the cameraperson-guardian, despite their seemingly directorial role, is likely a key figure in the domestic world that gives the production meaning, further highlighting the ambiguity of their role.

Alongside the cameraperson-guardian's role in the production, they often also have a hand in the online life of the image. That is, whoever runs one of these accounts often demonstrates a keen understanding of the operations of new media: what content tends to gain algorithmic traction, how to leverage personal narratives, how hashtags and mentions might attract more followers, how to implement a "like for like" strategy, and how to establish a personal brand, among others. While this feature of home concerts is the subject of a more detailed discussion in part 3 of the chapter, it is important to recognize here, as it is a direct extension of the authorial ambiguities of the image. Specifically, the child sits at the center of the content and serves as the face of the profile, the cameraperson-guardian plays a major role in the the content's social life, further blurring the lines between subject as author and parent-manager as author.

With both individuals indicated as the author of the image, there is the suggestion of mutual consent in the production—a sense that is linked to the understanding that the dancer appears to know they are being recorded. Unlike the ambiguities of authorship discussed in chapter 2 with the case of candid dancing, the blurring of authorship for home concerts has a different ethical dimension. Instead of the dancer being unaware of the camera and onlooker, home concerts media depicts a seemingly cooperating child, suggesting that the child is both aware of the camera and has agreed to be filmed. Of course, the viewer's presumption of a consensual recording is not without issue. Specifically, the child may be aware of the recording, but they may not be aware of its subsequent publicization.[25] While it is difficult to discern their level of understanding in terms of the cameraperson-guardian's intentionality or how the dancer may negotiate their own intentionality with their parent's, the suggestion of their consent is nonetheless embedded in the image.

A consideration of the child's knowingness of the recording opens out to a number of other aspects of their performance, further defining the character of this intimaesthetic. Alongside the role of the cameraperson-guardian, the dancer helps construct the meaning of the production. They are, after all, the individual who is most visible and made to be the subject of the video. Through their bodily comportment, gaze, and relationship to the camera/cameraperson, the dancer provides the viewer with additional information about the affective and relational dimension of the scene. A review of these aspects of the production will add greater depth to this type of intimaesthetic.

Several bodily techniques structure how a home concerts dancer might relate to the camera and viewer and ultimately aestheticize intimacy. One of those techniques is to engage a focused, performative gaze, wherein they seem to disregard the camera altogether and focus their attention inwardly or along the trajectory of their movement. As discussed in chapter 3, this nonchalant gaze may either model a style of postmodern and contemporary performance or perhaps demonstrate concentration. However, unlike the steady nonchalant gaze, the focus of the home concerts dancer is often not continuous throughout the entire video. Instead, in many cases, the inward gaze is briefly interrupted by a glance toward the camera. Such a rupture is evinced through some sort of eye contact with or toward the camera. For instance, a dancer absorbed in their performance may suddenly shift their gaze, either through a sustained look or a fleeting side-eye. The break is typically momentary, as the dancer often refocuses their attention and, once again, disregards the camera and their in situ audience.

This shift in the dancer's attention not only marks a break in their inward gaze but also reflects a relational dynamic at play in the scene. Much like how the camera movement of the cameraperson-guardian gives the impression of an attention to and care toward the dancer, the dancer's way of breaking the inward gaze points to their cognizance of the audience in the space—the cameraperson or parent/guardian. In looking toward that person, the dancer might reveal an eagerness to please, a search for feedback, or a signal to continue or stop the recording. Thus, depending on the context, their way of looking at or beyond the camera might convey a range of messages to the viewer. One common instance is when the dancer glances toward the camera at the end of the dance, indicating that they are checking the expression of the cameraperson, perhaps to sense that person's reaction to the performance or maybe to let them know they can stop the recording. The intricacies of the relationship between the dancer and the cameraperson are abundant, and yet one might understand how the dancer's changes in gaze are part of a larger conversation between the collaborating individuals.

Collectively, through the dancer's ways of looking and the cameraperson's work with the recording device, the resulting home dance video becomes a work of minor choreography. It demonstrates the techniques employed to create a piece of media that might subtly contribute to the child's public portrait. Once on the platform, that media comes to both represent the child and shape their identity. Of course, this process is best understood through example, a task of the next section. Through the choreographic analysis of Declan's and Gemma's home dance videos, part 2 not only pictures the phenomenon of parent-managed accounts of kids but also animates the techniques of minor choreography and its intimaesthetics.

Part 2. Choreographing Childhood, Logging Gender

While part 1 reveals both the home concerts type of intimaesthetic and the mechanisms of minor choreography that run through it, part 2 illustrates media that exemplify those concepts. The publicly available media on the accounts of Declan and Gemma help in that endeavor. While the productions of these two dancers stand out in their representation of distinct approaches to minor choreography, they do not capture the entirety of the phenomenon of parent-managed social media accounts, nor do they plumb the depth of minor choreography. Nonetheless, these examples represent the landscape of such concepts through a few critical distinctions. For one, the media on the two accounts demonstrate variations in how the parent/guardian constructs their child's online portrait. Declan's mother, Danielle, makes her presence obvious, whereas Gemma's parent, an unnamed and unknown entity, disguises their role. Also, each account expresses a different set of values surrounding gender and how the dancer's performance of gender is enveloped in a logic of class. Namely, Declan's account articulates a gender inclusivity through the affordances of an upper-class ethic, while Gemma's account articulates a gender normativity shaped by the logic of a competition dance paradigm. In other words, the former logs gender through difference, while the latter logs gender through sameness, particularly in terms of how each dancer models systems of value. Together these approaches not only reflect the envelopment of gender in a matrix of social values but also reveal the mechanisms by which they are reproduced.[26]

Declan's Transgressions

Declan, with his legs in sous-sous and arms in fourth position, peers to his left with his chin up and eyes down, harnessing the confidence and poise of the principal dancer of a renowned ballet company. He briefly glances toward the camera before swinging his left leg out and back while lifting his left arm, wrist broken at the top, with overexcitement. He completes a rond de jambe to the front and then reverses it to the back toward another broken wrist pose. Declan lifts both arms before bowing to the right, then to the left. He sautés to the back, left leg flying backward, to then spin back to the front. Passé, passé, step, step, jump, step, jump, tendu, passé. Another big bow to the right with his right arm floating up and down, Declan then soutenus to land in a deep plié.

Despite the terminology used here, Declan's movements only approximate ballet. Dancing in his dinosaur pajamas in what looks to be the dining area/living room of his home, this four-year-old child improvs to Nutcracker music playing somewhere in the room. Clothes are scattered across the wooden dining table just behind him. On the television in the background is some indiscernible cartoon, and just below it is a mantel holding a collection of Christmas stockings—six, maybe seven, of them.

Declan's steps are jumbled at times, but his comportment and the character of his movement is indeed "balletic," even though it is not precise in its form. Frenetically moving his feet as if performing a complex allegro sequence, but without any discernible ballet steps, Declan wears an expression that is intense with focus—his gaze wandering and lips pursed as if processing his next move. Occasionally, he glances toward the camera and the person behind it. The camera, too, moves to keep the dancer within the frame. We hear a voice: "Honey, you're so graceful. Beautiful dancing."

As if recharged by the praise of his audience, Declan lifts his front leg in attitude and sways to the right with his arm floating up and then down. As the music rises in energy, his expression becomes more intense, with his eyebrows furrowing and mouth frowning with dramatic appeal. He continually sways back and forth as he enhances the drama in his face, almost appearing as if he is going to cry. "Gorgeous!" says the voice behind the camera.

With the high-pitched, emphatic "ding" of some bell-like instrument, Declan once again changes his tone to a softer comportment. He draws his legs into sous-sous, bringing his arms to high fifth position before floating them back down to his sides, and then gazes upward. All of a sudden, the video cuts and loops back to the beginning.

The caption of this video reads: "This is what Declan feels when he wakes up. It's 7am and the music sings to his soul! #boysdancetoo #boydancer #dancelife @traviswall @allisonholker #childhoodunplugged #dancelife #dancersofinstagram @evolutiondance." Notably, the bio of the personal account states (in November 2021), among other biographical information, "Account run by mama 🧸" (see fig. 16).

Fig. 16. Declan singing and dancing in his pajamas (Meagan Willoughby)

Since December 12, 2019, when this video was posted to Instagram, Declan has tremendously grown his following and become an Instagram sensation. While Declan is at the center of the posts, his account is managed by another individual: his blogger mother, Danielle. Through Declan's dancing, the domestic setting, and the media, Danielle crafts Declan's public image, highlighting his gender identity and cultivating his personal brand for public consumption. The particular video described above reflects Declan's persona near his online debut, before his brand had been established and before his following rose to over half a million. While the video seems to be about Declan, it also demonstrates his mother's role in the production and reveals the minor choreography involved in shaping the media and account.

Several key features of the video indicate the role of the cameraperson, and primary among those features is Declan's relationship to the camera. Throughout his performance, Declan maintains his attention in the direction of the recording device. The constant return of his gaze toward the device—using it as a marker to spot while spinning, for instance—makes clear that the camera defines his point of forward/front. While this sort of attention to the camera is common among self-produced videos on social media, subtleties of Declan's gaze help define the intimaesthetics of his media. When looking toward the camera, Declan slightly shifts his eyes between the camera and a point of focus just behind the camera. This shifting gaze suggests that Declan's audience rests not only with the camera (and the prospective viewers it represents) but also with the cameraperson.

In tandem with Declan's gaze is the audible commentary in response to the performance. At two moments in the video, someone offers Declan feedback and support: "Honey, you're so graceful. Beautiful dancing." and "Gorgeous!" These comments are heard at a volume that seems to be in close proximity to the camera's microphone, suggesting that, indeed, the subject of Declan's occasional focus is both the speaker and the cameraperson. It is important to note the nature of the comments as well. For one, they suggest a familiar, supportive relationship, as they function to offer Declan enthusiasm and encouragement. The fact that the speaker calls Declan "honey" and cheers him on as he dances helps to construct this relationality. Often used as a term of endearment, "honey" functions in this video to suggest that the speaker is older than Declan and in a position of support and care toward him. The praise, too, supports the familiar qualities of the commentary. Comments like "you're so graceful," and "beautiful dancing" gesture toward the speaker's interest in Declan's confidence and how he might perceive himself. Perhaps, for instance, the speaker wants Declan to feel good about his dancing so that he continues his expression. These pieces of information, all available in the vocal commentary of the on-scene audience/speaker/cameraperson, suggest that the invisible individual behind the camera is Declan's caretaker.

The setting of the video only underscores the evidence of a parental force involved in the making of the video. The fact that Declan is seen dancing in the home articulates the relational dynamics embedded in the scene. First, Declan's home attire—his dinosaur pajamas—grounds the familial dimension of the video. As if he just got out of bed—an occasion that would often not invite outside guests—Declan dances for an in-home audience who seems to support him, care for his self-esteem, and nurture his interests. Second, the objects and actions in the space construct an everyday quality of the scene. The cartoons playing in the background and the laundry on the table help to convey the domestic character. They also suggest that bodies live in and move through this space regularly: that those bodies are familiar with one another, that they are in rapport, and possibly that the nature of that rapport is familial. These elements of the space combine with the affective dimension of the speaker's commentary to contour the familiality of the scene.

The relation between dancer and cameraperson expressed through the home and the on-scene commentary is made more obvious by the fact that this same voice can be heard in *other* videos on Declan's account, some of which feature Declan's mother, Danielle, as the speaker *in the frame*. In many of these more conversational videos, Declan will carry on a dialogue with his mother, whom he calls "Mama Gorgeous." Danielle will often ask questions from behind the camera, and Declan will respond in typical Declan fashion, usually expressing his love of dance and all things "fabulous."[27] Such dialogue, also evident in Declan's Nutcracker dance video, compounds with the outright recognition of Danielle's account management in the bio to connect Danielle to the roles of cameraperson, mother, and manager.[28]

The above evidence of the camera operator's presence and identity indicates not only Declan's cognizance of the camera but also a vague understanding of family relations surrounding the recording. The ways in which the Nutcracker improvisation is embedded in a larger, longer scene and domestic world evince the contextual nature that Declan's videos construct, ultimately contributing to the media's intimaesthetics. For instance, because the video begins with action and ends with action, the audience gets the impression that the recording is part of a larger movement experience. It is very likely, for instance, that Declan had been dancing long before Danielle started recording the scene. The video, then, does not articulate a beginning and end but presents itself as an excerpt from a domestic world that is full of *many* stories, relations, and family goings-on. The details of the surrounding family narrative might not be known, but the video manifests the existence of a context. Along similar lines, the video gives viewers the impression that there is more to the relational dynamic between Declan and his mom. Though Declan does not respond to Danielle's comments in the video, the audience understands that Danielle's attention to his performance is merely a minuscule sliver of their mother-son relationship, the wider family dynamic, and the culture of their family. These aspects contribute to a sense of *more beyond*—a cozy tension between the text and the context of the post.

Through the production of Declan's video, Danielle creates an image that harbors the tensions of the frame, while also enabling Declan's self-expression. While it may be difficult to discern this effort through one particular post—as such shaping occurs gradually through the curation of hundreds, if not thousands, of media posts—Danielle's minor choreography, particularly concerning Declan's gender, is nonetheless apparent through this one post. Her commentary, as discussed above, suggests her support for Declan's interest in ballet. It is important to note here, too, that Danielle is praising her son's ballet improvisation while noting the historical feminization of the dancer.[29] That is, in addition to her comments, Danielle calls attention to Declan's boyhood through the use of hashtags, particularly the incorporation of #boysdancetoo and #boydancer. These hashtags operate on multiple levels. First, as expressed in chapter 2, they help circulate a post more widely for greater locatability, so that others might be more likely to stumble upon the content, which would then lead to more views, comments, and follows for that user. Second, a hashtag can help align a piece of content with a larger movement, event, or collection, as discussed in chapter 3. Finally, hashtags add more information, detail, or commentary to the post in a way that punctuates the prose of the caption. They often enhance the meaning of the post in a succinct manner. While these functionalities may certainly overlap, it is the final one in particular that demonstrates how Danielle frames Declan's gender expression. The use of #boysdancetoo articulates the predominance of girl dancers—as in "sure, girls dance, but *boys dance too!*" This phrase also subtly conveys an argument for greater inclusivity and cultural acceptance of dancers who are boys. It is as if the person writing it is aware of the gender imbalance in dance and is casually issuing a public service announcement or subtly embarking on some cultural awareness campaign. The subsequent hashtag, #boydancer, reiterates this intentionality by underscoring

Declan's gender in a more matter-of-fact way. Through the incorporation of these two hashtags, Danielle leaves no ambiguity: Declan is a boy; Declan does ballet; ballet is "for girls," but boys can (and should) do it too.

A momentary hypothetical situation allows us to more closely examine the strategy that Danielle is employing in her use of the two hashtags described above. One might speculate, for instance, how these hashtags might not be necessary if it were Declan's sister dancing in the video, as there would be no need to point out her gender or argue for the acceptance of her dancing. By the phenomenon of *exnomination,* or Barthes's concept that enables power to hide in the removal of certain signifiers, the hypothetical case of Declan's sister dancing reveals the hegemonic structures that both align dance with a particular gender and dictate the cultural expectation of the dancing body as a female one.[30] Considering this case reveals how Danielle is employing *reverse exnomination* in Declan's Nutcracker video described above. In the way that someone might say "the woman mechanic" to describe someone who repairs cars and who also happens to a woman, but not identify the gender of a mechanic who is a man (suggesting that the speaker's audience will, by exnomination, automatically presume the mechanic to be a man), Danielle calls out her son's gender. The use of this strategy provides the reader with information about the culture in which Declan lives, the normative gender roles that Declan faces, and perhaps also Danielle's familiarity with (and possible resistance to) that normativity. By another comparison, Danielle might not feel the need to include these hashtags in a culture where dance was acceptable for people of all genders. However, their use here places this video in a context where the dualities of gender pervade the dancing body, manifesting themselves through the young dancer who becomes incorporated in processes of minor choreography.

While Danielle authorizes (and authors) Declan's subversions of gender, thereby enabling his performativity, she also reinforces the binary logic of boy-girl that Declan himself deconstructs through his dance. As noted above, Danielle's inclusion of the hashtags #boysdancetoo and #boydance matter-of-factly defines Declan as a boy, while also reasserting that dance—especially ballet—is a femininized domain. These hashtags, framed as calls for inclusion nonetheless rely on and reproduce the very gender norms they claim to challenge. Though her support for Declan's balletic moves (and his associated passion for ballet) aligns to some degree with critical gender work, the post also effectively reinforces the distinctions between boy and girl by invoking them as fixed identity categories. Similarly, Danielle's challenge to the feminization of dance, though it is aimed at greater inclusivity, ultimately maintains the gendered logic of the dancing body.[31] In these ways, her minor choreography is both resistive and reiterative.

The minor choreographies embedded in Declan's Nutcracker video are further complicated by the suggestions of affluence expressed through Declan's posts and what that affluence means for the gender work of the post. Evident through many of their posts, Declan and his family live in San Diego, California, an area where the average income and the cost of living are well above the national average. Declan's mother is a blogger and his father is a cosmetic dentist, occupations that articulate an upper-class status. Moreover, the domestic setting of many of Declan's posts demonstrates the family's socioeconomic standing, with its marble-surfaced kitchen and high-end appliances, its spacious bedrooms with large walk-in closets, outdoor entertaining space, and posh furniture and decor. The large family—Declan is one of four children—frequently goes on vacations, the tales of which are described on Danielle's blog and sometimes also appear on Declan's Instagram page. In posts on Declan's account, there are references to housekeepers, nannies, and other domestic workers. The lifestyle of Declan's family exudes wealth, and with that suggested wealth comes privilege.

The socioeconomic positioning of Declan's family indicates their relative ease of acquiring social and cultural capital on platforms like Instagram. In other words, their social standing in offline settings means that they are in a position to speak out and to be heard in online settings as well.[32] While they may not have sought to create a platform around a greater acceptance and inclusivity of all genders in dance, that position has become the message of Declan's account. The video described above offers a glimpse of that message, but as his profile and public persona evolve through subsequent posts, the message of inclusivity and acceptance becomes more overt. For example, one post on August 21, 2021, shows Declan wearing a wide-brimmed black hat, leopard-print shirt, cut-off jeans, and sneakers covered in red sequins. The caption reads:

Everyone is different and unique! 😄 *Whatever you bring to the table makes you special.* 👯👯👯 *From dolls and dresses, to footballs and video games, it is important that [Declan] and all of our kids know that whichever they may choose is okay.* 👗 🩰 🎮 *If [Declan] wants to dance around in a dress because that is what makes his [sic] happy and unique then so be it! If any of my kids want to step outside their gender norm it is okay.* 💅 *In this family we celebrate uniqueness and difference because it allows you to shine and be a light for oth-*

ers #limitless #shine #light #uniqueness #dance #boysdancetoo #tinydancer
#littlelegend #different #beyourself #loveyourself #love #shine #shinebright
#genderneutral #gender #dancelife.

The acceptance of Declan's gender and the support for his interest in dance are made obvious in posts such as this one. To a certain extent, the socioeconomic position of Declan's family enables them to create such a platform, to openly foster Declan's subversions of normative gender roles, and to ensure that he is surrounded by individuals and engaged in institutions that will also allow him to "shine."

Indeed, Declan's account provides broader messages around acceptance of all genders, while also cultivating a public portrait and persona for Declan. The minor choreography shapes this image through Danielle's on-camera dialogue with Declan, the suggestions of more beyond that are expressed through Declan's gaze and relationship to the camera, and Danielle's hashtag work. Collectively, these techniques create an intim-aesthetic that allows the audience to gain a sense of closeness with Declan and his family. The viewers may feel as though they know him and may engage with his posts through likes, shares, and comments to express their appreciation for his zeal for life and dancing, as well as his messages of greater acceptance. Of course, Declan's rise to Instagram stardom is in part because, as Danielle writes in the posts, he is "unique" and "different." His difference that is articulated through the media not only enables his profile to stand out among a sea of content on Instagram, and therefore gain algorithmic traction, but also gestures toward what Declan is *not.* He does not embody normative gender codes and conventions that are typically instilled in children in the United States. The suggestion here is that plenty of content on Instagram *does* represent such codes and conventions and thus provides a snapshot of the ways in which Instagram circulates dominant culture. The next analysis stands to represent this more reiterative collection of media. The profile of Gemma demonstrates a version of minor choreography through a more ambiguous role of authorship, while also expressing a more rigid binary logic of gender. An analysis of Gemma's at-home rehearsal articulates these points and gestures toward the breadth of techniques that play into minor choreography on Instagram.

Gemma's Reiterations

Gemma steps out to the right as both arms lift, gaining tension as they
move upward. With the sound of clapping, which seems to be playing from

a video Gemma watches on the screen in front of her, she strikes her arms down and jumps, lifting her right leg, then left. Her arms move in a sharp sequence: elbow out, arm down, wrists clap together. She steps onto her left leg as her right leg drags to meet the other, left arm flying up, around, and back down. From a kitty-corner squat, Gemma shoots her right leg toward the camera and then to the side, now facing forward. She piqués onto her right leg as she lifts the left knee above her hip, her left shoulder rolling toward the back in syncopation with the knee. Popping her chest out and back in, she steps together before clasping her hands together and rocking her forearms like a seesaw. The movements themselves are balletic, but their delivery is quick, sharp, and showy—consistent with the style of contemporary ballet found on the American competition dance stage. Bam, bam, boom.

As Gemma dances, her body's sharp movements are contrasted with the stillness of her red hair bow, which is about half the size of her head. She moves within a small room, staying within the bounds of what looks to be a black vinyl mat on a hardwood floor. Behind her is a closet door, and next to that is a collection of accessories hanging on the wall. There is a small, child-sized table sitting in the corner with two child-sized chairs tucked under it. At one point, we see a laptop on a table in front of Gemma, which seems to be the source of the sound to which she dances. In addition to the faint music emanating from the speakers, the video also captures the sound of someone—an adult—giving direction and clapping their hands emphatically. Gemma remains focused on this device as she moves through the phrase.

Gemma hops forward before piqué-ing on her right leg to circle her left knee up and back. She pops her chest out and in as she jerks her elbow back. She pauses for a moment to wait for the next beat, remaining focused on the screen situated in front of her. Drawing her fingers together to create a straight line with her forearms, she toggles her elbows up and down in a rapid seesaw-esque motion before circling them around her head. Stepping backward in preparation, Gemma executes a tight double pirouette into three piqué arabesques, posing in the final one. She quickly draws her right leg forward, out and in, and then jerks her forearms again right and left.

Gemma continues the sequence, striking certain movements with great force and then hastily moving through others with little attention. Strike, pose, step, step, step. She undulates her torso and steps off the black mat, out of frame. The camera shifts to recapture her figure as she does a high kick with her left leg and steps out of the frame once more. Gemma is now almost hitting the table against the wall. With that last kick, Gemma casu-

ally, blankly approaches the camera as she looks toward the person behind it, punctuating her dance.

The caption below the video reads: "Thank you Miss @chelsebes for an amazing class. I had so much fun learning this combo #contemporarydance @evolvedancecomplex #alwaysevolving #dancefromhome #socialdis-DANCING" (see fig. 17).

This home dance video was uploaded to Gemma's Instagram account on December 14, 2020. The profile identifies the name of the individual, and just under the name, it also states "Dancer—Parent Run Act." The parental involvement in Gemma's production described above, however, is not obvious. There is no on-camera conversation to consider, no indications in the caption, and no cameos in the video. One subtle yet profound indication of another person's involvement, however, is the camera movement. For much of the video, the frame is quite still. At the end of the video, though, the camera operator moves the device to get Gemma back in the frame and then moves it once more. Such camera movement might indicate that the operator either has a remarkably steady hand or is using a tripod with a panning capability. While both scenarios are possible, the control of the pan at the end of the video appears too steady to be a hand-operated gesture, making the use of a tripod likely. After all, tripods for smartphones are now relatively inexpensive (less than ten dollars) and can be purchased from a variety of stores, both online and in person. Such equipment may also now be considered part of common practice for new media users who frequently create videos, as it allows for a more efficient use of space—for instance, with the camera sitting close to a wall. This technique is helpful in small spaces like bedrooms—perhaps those that have been made into multipurpose rooms, as seems to be the case for Gemma. Most importantly, however, the use of a tripod would indicate the intent to create videos with what the producer might perceive to be a higher production value. A tripod is an *investment* in something, or someone, it would seem.

Aside from indicating the possibility of equipment in use, the camera movement in the video highlights attention to the dancer, a most telling aspect of the producer's minor choreography. On the most superficial level, the viewer might see how the panning of the camera demonstrates a desire to maintain more or less continuous footage of the dancer's movement. On a more metaphorical level, the camera operator is working to keep the dancer in the center of the image, at the center of the viewer's attention.

Fig. 17. Gemma rehearsing a dance combination during the COVID-19 pandemic. (Meagan Willoughby)

The care reflected in this camerawork suggests that the cameraperson is invested in the dancer's movement, her image, and her digital identity.

The fact that the video is set in the home amplifies the relational connections between the dancer and the cameraperson. Made clear by the closet in the background and bedroom-sized dimensions of the room, the viewer understands the setting of the video to be the home. The domestic fixtures and personal objects that adorn the space—items like a dresser for clothes, a rack on the wall that looks to hold hair bows, and a table and chairs made for a small child—ground such a reading. The impression of the home as the setting is underscored by the use of the hashtag #dancefromhome in the caption of the post.[33] Collectively, these features shape the meaning of the relationship between the cameraperson and the dancer. That is, it may be obvious that the two individuals are in close proximity at the moment of the video production; yet, the setting of the home articulates that they are *regularly* in close proximity, living and moving in the same space every day. With Gemma being a child, a minor who legally needs a guardian, this reading is especially potent. The viewer cannot help but take away the impression that it is a family member who is recording her—someone who watches over her both on camera and off camera, online and offline—a parent, perhaps.

Despite evidence that the producer of the video is the parent of Gemma, the caption is constructed from Gemma's perspective. The author thanks "Miss Chelsea," who appears to be Gemma's dance teacher, and uses the first-person voice to comment on the "amazing class."[34] Yet, the grammar and syntax in this caption demonstrate a maturity of language: "Thank you Miss @chelsebes for an amazing class. I had so much fun learning this combo." The proper prose, proper punctuation, and proper capitalization of letters indicate that the writer of the text may not have been a seven-year-old child but perhaps someone older, someone part of a different generation. The knowledge of new media mechanisms implied through the tagging of Gemma's dance teacher and the inclusion of several hashtags also indicates a seasoned user. Finally, the play on words in #socialdis-DANCING further conveys that the author of the post is not Gemma but rather an adult. This confusion of roles allows the parent-manager to curate the minor's public image, while giving their audience the impression that they are witnessing raw footage of a young dancer through her own eyes and worldview. Ultimately, the parent-manager can accrue social capital via the skills, interests, and work of their child.

The ambiguity of authorship evident in Gemma's post indicates a key feature of her minor choreography. Interestingly, the bio on Gemma's account states, as mentioned previously, "Dancer—Parent Run Act." This little blurb not only makes clear the involvement of Gemma's parent(s) in the production and management of the account but also gestures toward the obvious mechanisms of Gemma's minor choreography. The language defines the dancer as a "parent run act." There is no information about Gemma as a person, only that she is an *act* that is *run* by her parent(s). The language here is telling, as it places the action of the running with the parent and the dancer is made into the performance object—the former being active, the latter being passive.

Further complicating the already complex construction of authorship for Gemma's Instagram account are the subtle parent-child dynamics at play in the rehearsal video—dynamics that are evinced through Gemma's relationship to the camera. Gemma's gaze throughout the performance is of particular importance. As suggested in the caption, Gemma is apparently attending a dance class from home and is probably tuned into her teacher's instruction through a computer, tablet, or some other device. She seems to be watching and listening to the cues and feedback of the dance teacher, who seems to be known as Miss Chelsea. Whether Miss Chelsea's instructions are synchronous or asynchronous is secondary to Gemma's attention to the action unfolding on the screen. What is most notable is Gemma's redirection in gaze and attention toward the end of the video. Once she has finished with the phrase, whether by her own choice to stop or by the nature of the phrase's completion, she looks toward the camera/cameraperson and begins to move toward them. Gemma's expression at this moment is stoic and matter-of-fact. No words are spoken, but her eyes and comportment say, "There. Is that good?"

Despite its subtlety, this glimpse further shapes the dynamic at play between Gemma and the parent probably behind the camera. It underscores that (1) there is someone there to record the dance and (2) that person is part of a larger conversation with Gemma involving this at-home rehearsal. Through a complex mixture of both covert and overt strategies, Gemma's caretaker—whomever they may be—takes part in the minor choreography that defines Gemma's online persona, public image, and digital identity.

The shaping of Gemma's public persona, however covert or overt it may be, works to reproduce certain social and cultural values, namely, the alignment of dance with a middle- to upper-class normative gender ethic. Gemma's socioeconomic status is suggested through her participation in and commitment to a hobby that, in and of itself, is costly—especially at a competition dance studio like the one Gemma attends. Expenses for extracurricular dance include frequent rehearsals, costumes and makeup, flights and hotel bookings, and competition entry fees—amounting to, in some cases, $1,000 per month.[35] Alongside this fact, the viewer might also draw conclusions about Gemma's socioeconomic status from the space in which she performs. The setting for the video described above appears to be a bedroom that has been converted into a dance space. While this fact may be related to the COVID-19 pandemic and the need to move studio rehearsals and classes into the home, the adornments in the space suggest that its designation as a personal home dance studio precedes the pandemic. Trophies and awards sit here and there. Dancewear and hair accessories are organized on the walls. A small dance floor sits atop the hardwood flooring. These objects demonstrate a more long-standing purpose of the room as a space dedicated to Gemma and her dance training. Such information about Gemma's class status compounds with her normative expressions of girlhood through her dancing. That is to say, Gemma seems to be in pursuit of a contemporary ballet aesthetic and what Susan Foster calls an "industry body."[36] Her involvement in the competition dance circuit, evident through other posts on her profile, and her embodiment of competition dance tropes demonstrate this pursuit. Her large hair bows, bold makeup, and tight-fitting two-piece outfits further frame her public image as an aspiring industry dancer who foregrounds a virtuosic femininity. Approximating the style of girlhood displayed on shows like *Dance Moms*, Gemma's content presents a girl who fashions her identity within an environment that manufactures, promulgates, sensationalizes, and evaluates ideals of feminine beauty in young girls.[37] Not only is this version of femininity grounded in a binary logic of gender, but it also immerses that logic in a competitive, evaluation-based system concerning the dancing body.[38]

Gemma's display of a virtuosic feminine aesthetic and her adherence to normative femininity manifest through her body—not only in her attire and the movement tropes she embodies but also in her attentiveness and responsiveness to the screen in front of her. In following the cues from her dance teacher, Miss Chelsea, Gemma adjusts her body and movement to the instruction of her teacher. Gemma's competition ballet femininity is thus siphoned through her teacher and received through the body. This embodied transmission of values represents the minor choreography that she and her parent-manager perform.

Gemma's identity online is channeled through the efforts and labor of her parent(s), who may very well support Gemma's involvement in an atmosphere of competitive femininity. The degree to which a parent is involved in the reproduction of values, however, is not clear from the post on Instagram or from the larger account profile, due to the uncertainty of authorship. Similar to the ways in which the cameraperson-guardian obscures their presence in the caption, they also disguise their role of instilling values around Gemma's gender and other characteristics expressed through her dancing body. This approach, though it cannot reveal much information, is central to Gemma's minor choreography. The technique of obscuring the cameraperson-parent's role allows for the assumption that Gemma is the primary actor in the cultivation of her competitive ballerina femininity. Ultimately this approach conceals the mechanisms by which gender codes are reiterated through new media, making the promulgation of such values more effective.

Evident in the analysis of both Gemma's competition rehearsal and Declan's Nutcracker improvisation, children become the subjects through which codes and conventions are performed and reiterated on new media—they are both the recipients of those codes and the vessels through which the codes are circulated more broadly. The minor choreographies that appear through the children's posts, however, reflect different worldviews and mobilize a different set of cultural values. Declan, who wears feminine clothing and seems to take pleasure in embodying a ballerina aesthetic, tests the boundaries of boyhood. In this way, his performance and expression of gender seem internally motivated. Gemma, on the other hand, takes her cues from her teacher and studio, as she attunes herself to Miss Chelsea's feedback, thereby suggesting how her expression of gender is more externally motivated. Through her performance of a virtuosic femininity, Gemma seems to squarely represent the culture of both competition dance and narrative ballet, wherein the duality of gender and the standards of feminine beauty are reiterated and exaggerated. The mediatizations and public circulation of both children's gender work are nonetheless enabled by their parents/guardians through the uploading and circulating of the media on Instagram. Thus, while their minor choreographies may be cultivated through the familiality of domesticity, their online publicity embeds those choreographies in a wider social and cultural fabric.

Once a parent/guardian extends their minor choreography from their home and phone to a platform like Instagram, the image of that child gains a new social life and activates a new political dimension. The media are no longer part of a private family archive—a digital album of sorts—as may have been the case with home movies of the twentieth century. Instead, these images are subject to the whims of transmission, circulation, consumption, engagement, and dialogue, which are fraught with troubling implications surrounding the digital identity of minors and their inadvertent incorporation into a system of dataveillance, commercialization, and homophily. The following section thus attends to these issues to unpack the online life of minor choreography, articulating a shift in responsibility from the parent to the platform.

Part 3. Platform Orchestrations of Minors

The above analysis of home concerts and their minor choreographies opens out to a critique of the parents who create and manage accounts on behalf of their children. As is the case with the cultural antecedent of the show *Dance Moms*, these discussions tend to place the burden of responsibility on parents—they represent an easy, visible target of the deleterious effects of social media for children. To audiences of home concerts, parents who showcase their kids on Instagram may seem irresponsible for opting their children into a system that sensationalizes minors and eschews privacy boundaries. A broader perspective of the structures that enable such activity, however, demonstrates how the *system* is culpable for such a phenomenon rather than the *actors* within the system. After all, the technology and culture of Instagram—with its algorithms, data collection, and thrust of neoliberal branding—create the conditions from which parents make their decisions. Parents, then, become a red herring for the neoliberal malaise of social media, particularly as it concerns minors.

Considering this displacement of culpability, it becomes necessary to tease apart the ways in which Instagram enables, facilitates, and encourages phenomena like parent-managed accounts of children in the form of the home concerts intimaesthetic. Building upon techniques discussed in previous chapters, such as hashtagging and mentioning other users, these platform strategies include the privacy settings for an account, the ease of creating a new profile, and the encouragement of child-related content. While such features are ultimately employed by the users (i.e., the parent-managers), they are first and foremost enabled through the system that Instagram has developed. Not exhaustive of the techniques and approaches available to users, these three strategies together represent a sampling of how new media platforms enable the cultivation of public portraits and personae of, for, and on behalf of minors. A discussion of each one will reveal the social, political, and economic implications of family-oriented intimaesthetics as they appear on Instagram, while also gesturing toward the platform's own version of *control*. Parental control, that is, gives way to platform control; and minor choreographies open out to what I call *minor orchestrations*.

The difference between a public and private account is an important distinction in considering the net of exposure that a parent-managed account might cast on Instagram. Every account has this setting: a singular toggle to mark an account as private so that only accounts that a user approves can see the content of that user. It is arguably one of the few pieces of authority that a user has in determining who sees their content and is thus a critical component of any account, much less an account that features images and personal information of a minor. Yet, the privacy setting is *off* upon the creation of a new account, meaning that all accounts on Instagram are, by default, public. Thus, at the time of writing, any user who would like to see all of the content of someone with a public account can do so without that user's acknowledgment.[39]

The nature of the default publicity setting underscores the function of Instagram to encourage broad access to personal content and intimate data. On top of this default status is the difficulty of knowing about, accessing, and changing the setting. The platform does not point out through a setup wizard or pop-up notice when a user first creates an account what the default settings are and how that user might adjust them. If the user does know to look for them, they will have to dig into the Preferences panel and navigate through multiple clicks to locate the page with the privacy setting. While the percentage of users who have public versus private accounts is not publicly accessible information, the sheer difficulty of changing the default setting demonstrates Instagram's encouragement of an overabundance of public content. Through the subtle organization of its platform, Instagram thus cultivates a paradigm of mass self-exposure wherein users supposedly opt in to sharing their media widely; but in reality, the platform makes a user *work* to cling on to whatever threads of privacy might exist in such a space. Such "privacy work," as Alice Marwick terms it, captures the bait-and-switch logic of social media that is central to intimaesthetics.[40]

For content that features children, the paradigm of default publicity is especially troubling. Parents, when creating accounts that center their kids, do not always know to make their account private—and if they do know that it is possible, they might not know how to do it. Whether parents know about these settings or not, Instagram has cultivated a space for parent-managed public profiles to flourish. All of the Instagram accounts that were part of this analysis of intimaesthetics were, in fact, public profiles, which is the reason those profiles surfaced in the first place and therefore became available to study. Aside from critical analyses such as this one, anyone else on Instagram is able to see and engage with the content of both Declan's and Gemma's profiles. For the parent-managers of these accounts, the wide availability might mean that more people will like, view, and comment upon posts and that they might even accrue more followers (a major indicator of social capital on Instagram and other platforms). However, it might also mean that the children are made more susceptible to harmful remarks, data collection, scams, and commercialized interests. Thus, the openness of a public profile exacerbates the concerns that already lay bare with other types of intimaesthetics. That is to say, platforms like Instagram place personal data outside the realm of knowledge or authority of the user. Combined with the ambiguity of authorship for such accounts and the media on them, Instagram's system enacts its own mechanisms of control that disregard the needs of children and eschew the digital protections they require.

Indeed, the default public setting is merely one of Instagram's many orchestrations involving minors. Aside from this facet of Instagram use, the ease with which anyone might create a new profile in the first place plays into the problematic matrix of Instagram's trend of parent-managed accounts. As discussed in chapter 2, individuals create separate profiles so that they can cleave themselves into separate brands and capture distinct audiences. While this approach serves a purpose for individuals and their endeavors, it also suits parents who might want their children to have online visibility but want to be able to manage and monitor that visibility. Yet, again, this trend is enabled through Instagram's system, which has few guardrails in place to protect minors.

When a user creates a new profile on Instagram, the only information required is one's date of birth: an "age-gating" feature introduced in 2019 that is intended to ensure that users are old enough to own an account. Anyone under the age of thirteen is denied an account—or, more accurately, anyone who *claims* to be under the age of thirteen is denied an account. Of course, as the company has acknowledged, the age-gating feature is simple for users to circumvent.[41] All a child would need to do is input a date of birth that would make them at least thirteen years old—a possibility that became an active trend and an "open secret" at Meta, as the company not only understood that underage children were jumping the age gate in exorbitant numbers but also knowingly collected personal data about them.[42] Broader conversations around this feature are discussed in detail below, but its relevance here is to underscore how age-gating is the *only* precaution in place when creating a new account (at the time of writing). Especially for users who already have an account on Instagram, the process requires very few clicks. In such a case, the system automatically links the existing email address and other "private info" to the new account.[43] There is no system for verifying one's identity and no cap on how many different accounts may be linked to the same email address.[44] This systematic ease not only provides a breeding ground for fake accounts that deceive users, contributing to "click farms" that manipulate algorithms, but also enables children to have accounts by proxy, even if that proxy is their parents. It is just one way in which the age gate, put in place for security and privacy reasons, is able to be circumvented.

The existence of parent-managed accounts on Instagram is not surprising considering how the platform has built a user base that has grown into parenthood: users that were likely to have been active on Instagram for several years before they became parents, perhaps beginning before Instagram had any age-gating mechanisms in place. The movement, then, encourages its own circulation by way of networks of parents. That is, parents are exposed to the phenomenon when they access content belonging to their friends who have accounts of/about their own children. Then, by proxy, new parents are ushered into the movement, which encourages the cycle to continue, thereby initiating a sense of virality around the phenomenon. Ultimately this process, characteristic of a network society and its cultivation of homophilies, creates an opening for the children—the subjects of such a movement—to graduate to users themselves.[45]

Indeed, an existing base of parent-users helps to streamline a new generation onto the platform by initially creating profiles on their behalf. The fact of a child already being made the subject of content may prompt a parent to feel more comfortable with allowing that child to one day create and manage their own account. And then, on the child's end, they are likely to gain literacy about the platform after being the subject of its content, watching their parents engage on their behalf, and possibly even being informed about the engagement dynamics of the content (e.g., how many likes a post receives, who is commenting and what are they saying, and how many views a dance video gets). Of course, the child may end up directly managing aspects of their own proxy account, with or without their parents' supervision. Nonetheless, *any* engagement with the platform— either direct or indirect—introduces the child to the social, cultural, and economic rhythms of Instagram, while also allowing them to gain literacy of how to operate the app. Ultimately, these experiences prime children to one day manage their own accounts. As if Instagram were creating an assembly-line system, Instagram is able to inadvertently develop young users into adult users, thereby ensuring its future merely through enabling and circulating content about kids. The assembly begins when users grow into parents, parents get their children on the platform through proxy accounts, and eventually the children get their own profiles; and then one day, those children grow into parents, get their children on the platform, and so on.

This process of ushering in a new generation of users benefits Instagram, and its longevity, as both a platform and a subsidiary of a publicly traded corporation (i.e., Meta). While the company has not exposed any explicit plot to encourage the creation of parent-managed accounts, its system operates on algorithms that bolster the process described above. Content of and about kids, after all, tends to perform well on Instagram. The sheer volume and widespread use of child-related hashtags demonstrate this point. The two young dancers discussed in the previous section were not necessarily selected for their incorporation of hashtags, and yet both accounts heavily incorporate tags that suggest their status as children. For instance, Declan's Nutcracker post includes five hashtags, two of which reference his childhood: #boydancer and #childhoodunplugged. Gemma's post does not include child-specific tags, but many of her other posts do, some of which include #babyballerina, #dancerintraining, #minidancer, and #industrykids. Regardless of the degree to which Instagram's algorithms elevate child-related content—like those that appear in Declan's and Gemma's posts—the visibility and recurrence of such posts help sustain the home concerts intimaesthetic and subtly recruit new users into the Instagram ecosystem. Declan and Gemma are inadvertently part of this machine, regardless of whether they knowingly opted into it.

While we remain uncertain about the role that algorithms play in the social life of home concerts, we may turn toward Instagram's own business model to find more overt expressions of the company's interest in getting children onto their platform and keeping them there. Specifically, the company's attempt to launch a separate platform just for kids emphasizes its stake in content of, about, and for children. At the time of writing this book, Instagram Kids does not yet exist. However, in early 2021, the company announced plans to launch such a platform, built specifically for children under the age of thirteen. This development followed a change that the platform made in 2019 to add age gating. As noted above, the requirement for a user to enter their date of birth when creating an account is meant to ensure that they are over the age of thirteen. Instagram Kids was thus intended to capture users who were legally not allowed to have their own account on the regular Instagram app. However, those plans were derailed by criticism from a broad range of factions. In May 2021, for example, the National Association of Attorneys General wrote to Mark Zuckerberg expressing its displeasure with the possible new platform for children.[46] An influential article published in the *Wall Street Journal* later that year exposed a set of leaked internal research documents that Meta (then-Facebook) conducted on the impact that Instagram has on minors. The company found that for teenage girls, in particular, Instagram tends to negatively affect body image and self-confidence. Following the article's publication and the critiques it elicited among the public, Meta announced that it would pause the rollout of Instagram Kids.[47] Though these criticisms have temporarily forestalled the launch of this platform, the company claims it will continue its plan, because "kids are already online" and thus need "a version of Instagram that is designed for them."

Through both the recruitment of children on a possible separate platform and the algorithmic traction of content about kids on its original platform for users at least thirteen years old, Instagram works to sustain and expand its user base and thus the longevity of its brand. Of course, this longevity not only enables the maintenance of its user base but also gives way to the reproduction of dominant culture. As discussed in the introduction to the book, the connections between digital culture and hegemonic order manifest through the systematic properties of a network society: the capability to rapidly share content (both within and across platforms); the metrics of likes, views, and follower counts; the social linkages of tagging friends and families; the ways in which algorithmic predictions trigger real-life outcomes; the aggregating power of hashtags; and the homophilies that assemble and disperse groups of users, among other features and capabilities. The algorithms that drive these metrics and circulations might change, but the power that undergirds them remains. Since minors are immersed in this system, they inevitably become imbricated in the social, cultural, and economic realities of a network society. For Declan, his enthusiastic ballet improvisation became part of a larger performance of gender that works to both challenge and reiterate normative gender roles in dance. Notably, the family's white, upper-class status enables them to intervene in a dialogue around gender in a public way. For Gemma, her publicly broadcasted rehearsals demonstrate her embodiment of a competition dance ethic and the cultural values that undergird it: normative gender roles, ideals of beauty as white and thin, capitalism-steeped systems of ranking, movement tropes that privilege sensationalism, and a social standard that tends to disregard or denigrate difference. In both cases, the home dance productions become emblematic of larger cultural dynamics, thereby enveloping the children in those value systems. While offline spaces certainly enable similar maneuvers, doing so on a platform like Instagram further alienates the minor from the thing they made or did.[48] The proxy of a parent, as is the case with home concerts, intensifies that alienation. Then, the algorithmic circulation of the values presented through the media becomes enhanced or is completely transformed in the digital space. Instagram, that is, has the power to turn those mere images of everyday life for a child into modes and methods for the reproduction of hegemonic structures and values. The privacy settings, ease of creating a profile, and ways of establishing a user base are merely three strategies that the platform activates to reproduce hegemony.

The new social life of the media representing the home concerts type of intimaesthetic gestures toward changes in its minor choreographies. Though it is the parent/guardian who creates and uploads the media, the life of that media is determined by the technological systems of the platform. Thus, the techniques of the parent/guardian are now behind them: their way of framing the child in the home to capture the domestic performance, their on-camera dialogue (or lack thereof) with the child, their authoring of the caption that contextualizes the performance and elaborates its meaning, and, among others, the hashtags and mentions they include in the captions. With the media's upload to the platform, those minor choreographies give way to minor orchestrations. The strategies discussed above exemplify this change and allude to the ways in which the techniques and approaches of parents who produce content for and on behalf of their kids become engulfed in a larger mechanism of circulating systems of value. Indeed, their media becomes orchestrated by invisible strings, unknown instruments, and covert notes of discord.

Conclusion

The phenomenon of parent-managed accounts on Instagram is imbued with layers of meaning, while also articulating the home concerts type of intimaesthetics. By highlighting the relationship between performer and camera, the home concert mode reveals the presence and role of another person in the recording, alongside the relational dynamics at play in the domestic scene. Through this lens, one may train their eyes to the mechanisms by which parents record and upload home dance videos of their children. Those techniques, defining minor choreographies, gesture toward certain social, cultural, economic, and political intricacies regarding children on new media. The cases of Declan and Gemma illuminate some of these intricacies by revealing variations in the performativity of gender through home dance videos of kids. Of course, when situated within a landscape of digital culture, those expressions become imbricated in complex systems of value.

Indeed, home concerts media on Instagram not only reveals information about its dynamics of production but also opens out to wider discourses surrounding youth culture online. Aside from the expanding offering of media platforms, this subset of content reflects Instagram's grab for profitable segments of the population and its maneuvers to subtly recruit its future user base. In other words, youth culture on new media—including content recorded by parents—represents both the profitability of cultural trends across all demographics, including minors, and the possibility for young users to grow with the platform and establish greater security of the company's future profits. Meta's efforts to develop a separate platform for children may be stalled for now, but this initiative reflects the company's continued interest in minors as a target population—an interest that will likely develop and manifest in new ways over time.

Conclusion

I began this study four years before the COVID-19 pandemic upended and rerouted the lives of people around the globe. And then, when beginning the final chapter of this text in 2020, I witnessed (and personally experienced) the mass sequestration of bodies into the homespace and the significant rise in the amount of time spent online due to lockdowns. This abrupt pivot toward interiority and domesticity prompted a remarkable surge in home dance videos on new media platforms. Dancers turned toward their devices to continue their training when studios closed, to express their state of despair in a trying time, to find some sense of belonging with others online, and to document their at-home workouts. They ultimately created videos that aestheticized intimacy, particularly at a time when in-person *closeness* was hampered, if not altogether foreclosed. The cultivation of a *different sort of closeness* then became a relief channel for individuals in home quarantine and isolation, or under mandated lockdowns. While this increase of media did not affect the structure of my analysis, it does underscore the criticality embedded in home dance videos—a criticality that was present before the pandemic but became more palpable during it. Thus, while the pandemic plays only a minimal role in *Homebodies*, the lessons from intimaesthetics critically resonate with cultural productions that occurred during that period.

Now imbricated in a historical moment when at-home performances surged, this study of home dance videos on Instagram reveals the mechanisms through which intimacy is aestheticized in and through new media, particularly from 2010 to 2020. A performer's choreographies of body, space, and media—cultivated through their relationship to the camera and cameraperson—produce the four intimaesthetics described in the book. Candid dancing, constructed through the dancer's unknowingness of both the camera and person recording the action, articulates a fascination with the unseen and unseeing dancing body. The desire to both fetishize and discipline that body is embedded in the fact of its recording. The moving selfie, created through the dancer's recognition of the camera and the obviousness of their self-recording, articulates the many layers of fashioning one's digital persona. The nonchalant gestures intimaesthetic, produced via the dancer's performed obliviousness toward the camera yet obvious self-recording, constructs a sense of oblivion through their modeling of privacy. Finally, the home concerts intimaesthetic, cultivated through the cameraperson's coordinated capturing of the dancer, who acknowledges the camera, reveals the complications of authority and rights over one's image, particularly for minors who, at times, become the subjects of those images. These four intimaesthetics illustrate the mechanisms through which new media users cultivate a sense of closeness with their viewers. They result in media objects that present as seemingly familiar and authentic, however contrived those categories may be.

While the four types of intimaesthetics revolve around the subject's relationship to the camera, their online circulation catapults them into a new environment with particular systems of power. A platform like Instagram, for instance, is commanded by a neoliberalist marketization of self and life, by a post-panoptic sense of surveillance, and by a structure of algorithmic determination—among other facets of the platform and digital culture at large.[1] Thus, each of the intimaesthetics becomes complicated by its encounter with an online audience. Home dance videos in this space become aggregated, tracked, archived, and fed through pathways of capture—all while distributing illusions of intimacy, privacy, and authenticity. In this sense, candid dancing, moving selfies, nonchalant gestures, and home concerts become imbricated in a system that encourages the offering of personal, private, intimate, and interior data and then subsequently utilizes, taxonomizes, and capitalizes upon that data—in ways that are both unknown and unfavorable to the user.

Each chapter draws out the tensions between these two aspects of intimaesthetics—between, on the one hand, the dancer's choreographies of body, space, and media and, on the other hand, the platform's systematic work on individual posts, as well as on the user's digital identity. The former suggests the performer's seeming agency over the production of their image, while the latter indicates social media's undercutting of that agency. Of course, the performer's choices during production are often *already influenced* by the culture of the platform: by the trends in music, fashion, and ways of moving; by the latest news, memes, and viral movements; and, among other factors, by the popularity (or lack thereof) of their previous posts. In other words, just as the homebody is shaped by the world beyond its walls, it is also determined by the digital culture in which it already engages. Before it works to aestheticize intimacy, the homebody has already seen, known, and felt intimaesthetics through its online participation.

An understanding of intimaesthetics thus gestures to both the *culture of consent* on new media, via the performer's production of intimaesthetics, and the system's obfuscation of that which the performer is *consenting to*.[2] As expressed through each type of intimaesthetic, the space of the home is integral to both sides of this pattern: to the performer's construction of intimacy and to the circulation of that material and the personal data it might offer. For the candid dancer, the homespace structures their choreography of abandon, which invites them to "dance like nobody's watching" but ultimately houses the recapturing of the dancer's movements back into a visual economy. For the selfie dancer, the homespace provides a vessel for personal history and the private cultivation of self so that their autochoreography might more easily fold into the fabric of Instagram's selfie culture. For the nonchalant dancer, the home cultivates a sense of the forgotten, marginal, and rogue so that they more readily emphasize the stretch between public discourse and their space of oblivion. And, finally, for the home concert performer, the domestic situation cultivates a sense of familiarity and familiality that leads to the platform's minor orchestrations of content about, featuring, and for children. While this typology does not exhaust how domestic space is utilized toward productions of authenticity and intimacy, it effectively captures a dynamic range of choreographic utilizations. That very range demonstrates how the home is not a semiotic monolith. Though this space harbors a universalist sensibility of interiority in the public imagination, its choreographic deployments are intricate, situational, and semiotically rich.

While the homespace might appear on and across new media platforms, Instagram serves as an appropriate platform through which to consider the production of intimaesthetics within the home, as it foregrounds images, allows for the shaping of public personae through the personal profile, and enables the further entanglement of quotidian performance and commercial agendas. Following the premises of platform specificity and platform affordances, the technological features of Instagram enable particular pathways for the circulation of intimaesthetics. In *Homebodies*, I examine Instagram's default privacy settings, its change from a chronological to a "relevant" feed, its addition of "sponsored" posts, and its ease of managing multiple accounts, among other features. Users then respond to those specificities when creating their home dance videos, when editing those media, when uploading them to the platform, and when engaging with others through the posts. Ultimately, the systematic qualities of the platform enable the cultivation of closeness with the dancer's audience.

Though Instagram is the locus of analysis of *Homebodies*, it is only a sliver of how intimaesthetics might operate across new media more broadly. Indeed, many other platforms encourage and host the aestheticization of intimacy—TikTok, Snapchat, Tumblr, and YouTube, to name a few. Of course, these platforms also have their own technological specificities, histories of development, and neoliberal tentacles. For instance, while TikTok is home to countless home dance videos, its technical and cultural specificities undoubtedly engender a distinct sensibility to the intimaesthetics that appear through those videos. Since its parent company, ByteDance, acquired Musical.ly, a platform for dubbing songs and sound clips, TikTok has more obviously foregrounded previously produced and previously circulated audio in the content on its platform. Moreover, considering that ByteDance is based out of Beijing (at the time of writing), its politics and economics of circulation undoubtedly shape the platform in particular ways. Intricacies such as these are beyond the scope of *Homebodies*; nonetheless, the investigation of intimaesthetics on Instagram calls for the in-depth study of how other platforms might aestheticize intimacy. How do performers on TikTok engage in choreographies of body, space, and media to cultivate a sense of closeness with their audience? Then, how might the platform incorporate, leverage, and circulate the products of those choreographies? How do geopolitics figure into the circulation of intimate, everyday media? While these questions remain largely unanswered for now, subsequent studies may reveal new insights about the life of intimaesthetics outside of Instagram.

Indeed, the theory of intimaesthetics harbors the potential for further examinations. The methodology that resulted in this theory might also serve well in other investigations of performance in digital culture. Namely, the media I studied emerged from two divergent yet interdependent dimensions of new media: on the one hand, the social life and pathways of circulation of a particular media object and, on the other hand, the place where it "resides" with other objects. In other words, I followed media across tags and nodes of engagement, and I also studied the longitudinal release of media through profile analysis. I engaged this approach in the particular environment of Instagram, but it could also be used for cross-platform investigations or for investigations within a particular platform other than Instagram. For instance, we might imagine how this dual lens might shed light on the circulation of media objects on and beyond You-Tube. Indeed, considering the ability of YouTube videos to be embedded on most any website yet also to reside on a YouTube channel, playlist, and account, the *Homebodies* research method would illuminate the pathways of circulation for media on that platform.

While the methodology undergirding *Homebodies* contributes to areas wherein new media artifacts are the objects of study, it also possesses technical caveats. Namely, the process of searching a platform yields only posts by users with *public profiles*. In other words, the locatability of *individual home dance videos* and the study of the *profiles* on which they appear are contingent upon the owners of those accounts maintaining the default *public* setting on their accounts. For this study, the public nature of the home dance videos is integral to the analysis of intimaesthetics, as it underscores the *leaping scales* that occur from the home to the public sphere of social media and the contradictions suggested in that maneuver.[3] However, for instances that do not concern the publicization of privacy, the aestheticization of intimacy, or the picturing of authenticity, researchers would need to consider how a pool of publicly accessible videos might skew the meaning of that content. They might ask, for instance, whether users who set their profiles to a public status might produce a certain *type* of content. This confounding variable would then skew any reading of that content. The researcher might attempt to avoid this conundrum by investigating content from a mixed pool of public and private profiles. However, such a path introduces a separate dilemma: in order to gather data from a private profile, the researcher would need to follow such an account, which is contingent upon the user of the private profile accepting the researcher's follow request. Even if the private-profile user were to accept the follow request, the question remains whether that method would skew the sampling of data. It is, after all, possible for users to engage in Instagram as a mere storage bank of images solely for their own recordkeeping, in which case they would ensure their profile is private and would also refuse any follow requests. Such a case would make for a provocative study of intimaesthetics; yet, the privacy factor of this phantom user's account is a self-fulfilling prophecy. The uber-private user might aestheticize intimacy, but we will never know it because of their commitment to privacy.[4]

Of course, research in a landscape as fluid as new media begets its share of quandaries and caveats. Such considerations are important to acknowledge, particularly as this landscape continues to shift over time. The theories and methods that *Homebodies* offers stand to benefit from future investigations of neoliberalism-tinged cultural production online. However, even more so than the current state of Web 2.0—dominated by user-generated content, electronic communication, and mechanisms for managing big data—intimaesthetics may prove to be a useful framework for the world of Web 3.0, a paradigm characterized by the imbrication of humans, computers, and AI systems. Developments in the realm of extended reality and blockchain technology may shift how new media users not only produce, circulate, and consume media but also how they author, archive, and exchange it. These developments have already allowed performers to distribute their choreographies in ways that not even Web 2.0 platforms like Instagram have allowed. Interestingly, the parent company of Instagram has marked its move into the "metaverse" of Web 3.0 by changing its name from Facebook to Meta and venturing into the field of virtual reality. With this increased exposure through both virtual reality and gallerylike new media platforms, home dance choreographies become further inculcated in the capitalist marketplace. Thus, the future of intimaesthetics may see a shift from covert to more overt orientations toward capitalism. It might also see changes in the respective logics of the choreography of abandon, autochoreography, choreography of oblivion, and minor choreography, particularly as orientations toward agency, identity, and authorship change. Intimacy is already being aestheticized, but will it also be tokenized?

Notes

INTRODUCTION

1. This range in orientations toward intimacy and the internet may be seen through the following texts: Lauren Rosewarne, *Intimacy on the Internet: Media Representations of Online Connections* (London: Routledge, 2016); Anna M. Lomanowska and Matthieu J. Guitton, "Online Intimacy and Well-Being in the Digital Age," *Internet Interventions* 4 (2016): 138–44; Valerie Francisco, "'The Internet Is Magic': Technology, Intimacy and Transnational Families," *Critical Sociology* 41, no. 1 (2015): 173–90; and Ya-Rong Huang, "Identity and Intimacy Crises and Their Relationship to Internet Dependence among College Students," *CyberPsychology & Behavior* 9, no. 5 (2006): 571–76.

2. For notions of intimacy as a spatial concept, see Gaston Bachelard, *The Poetics of Space: The Classic Look at How We Experience Intimate Places* (Boston: Beacon Press, 1994); for a sense of how it is psychoanalytical register, see Jacques-Alain Miller, "Extimité," in *Lacanian Theory of Discourse: Subject, Structure, and Society*, ed. Mark Bracher et al., 74–87 (New York: NYU Press, 1994); and for a sense of its sociocultural dimension, see Staci Newmahr, *Playing on the Edge: Sadomasochism, Risk, and Intimacy* (Bloomington: Indiana University Press, 2011), and Alex Lambert, *Intimacy and Friendship on Facebook* (London: Palgrave MacMillan, 2013). Moreover, intimacy's relation to performance has been discussed with varying scopes and lenses by Susan Kozel, *Closer: Performance, Technologies, Phenomenology* (Cambridge, MA: MIT Press, 2008); Josephine Machon, *Immersive Theatres Intimacy and Immediacy in Contemporary Performance* (London: Palgrave MacMillan, 2013); and Maria Chatzichristodoulou and Rachel Zerihan, eds. *Intimacy Across Visceral and Digital Performance* (London: Palgrave Macmillan, 2014).

3. Sherry Ortner, "Is Female to Male as Nature Is to Culture?" *Feminist Studies* 1, no. 2 (1972): 5–31.

4. David Roche and Isabelle Schmitt-Pitiot, *Intimacy in Cinema: Critical Essays on English Language Films* (Jefferson: McFarland, 2014), 2.

5. Here, Thomas Leddy draws on Hans Gumbrecht to situate everyday aesthetics within and against a more dominant aesthetics, particularly that of Western contemporary art. *The Extraordinary in the Ordinary: Aesthetics of Everyday Life* (Toronto: Broadview Press, 2012), 108.

6. Yuriko Saito, *Everyday Aesthetics* (Oxford: Oxford University Press, 2007), 4.

7. In particular, Ngai writes that the categories of the beautiful and sublime "make insistent if not necessarily indirect claims for their extra-aesthetic power (moral, religious, epistemological, political), asserting not just a specifically aesthetic agency but agency in realms extending far beyond art and culture." By contrast, everyday aesthetic categories—which for Ngai are the zany, cute, and interesting—enable a more "direct reflection on art and society, and more specifically on how 'that very distance of art from its social context which allows it to function as a critique and indictment of the latter also dooms its interventions to ineffectuality and relegates art and culture to a frivolous, trivialized space in which such intersections are neutralized in advance.'" Sianne Ngai, *Our Aesthetic Categories: Zany, Cute, Interesting* (Cambridge, MA: Harvard University Press, 2012), 22–23.

8. Ngai, *Our Aesthetic Categories*, 18.

9. Pierre Bourdieu, "Structures and the Habitus," in *Outline of a Theory of Practice* (Cambridge: Cambridge University Press, 1977), 72.

10. Most notably, Laura Mulvey's "male gaze," Michel Foucault's "clinical gaze," and Franz Fanon's "white gaze." Laura Mulvey, *Visual and Other Pleasures* (Bloomington: Indiana University Press, 1989); Michel Foucault, *The Birth of the Clinic* (New York: Vintage Press, 1994 [1963]); and Franz Fanon, *Black Skin, White Masks*, trans. R. Philcox (New York: Grove Press, 2008), 90.

11. The camera's lens as that which both represents and enables the consuming, objectifying gaze.

12. This technique resembles Susan Foster's mentioning of the "inward gaze" that the dancers in Merce Cunningham's works tend to employ. Foster writes that this gaze "encourages audiences to apprehend the kinaesthetic sensations of the act of moving." *Reading Dancing: Bodies and Subjects in Contemporary American Dance* (Berkeley: University of California Press, 1986), 64.

13. This technique perhaps aligns with Foster's discussion of the predominant countenance of the dancers in Martha Graham's works. Foster characterizes this gaze as one that is "absorbed in the world of the dance to the exclusion of any other world." The effect on the viewer is that "by declining to acknowledge the presence of the audience, [the dancers] ask the audience to look in on the action." Foster, *Reading Dancing*, 64.

14. Sherril Dodds and Colleen Hooper, "Faces, Close-Ups and Choreography: A Deleuzian Critique of *So You Think You Can Dance*," *International Journal of Screendance* 4, no. 1 (2014): 94.

15. Mary Douglas, "The Idea of a Home: A Kind of Space," *Social Research* (1991): 289 (emphasis added).

16. Linda McDowell, "Rethinking Place: Thoughts on Spaces of the Home, Absence, Presence, New Connections and New Anxieties," in *The Domestic Space Reader*, ed. Chiara Briganti and Kathy Mezei, 54–58 (Toronto: University of Toronto Press, 2012), 56.

17. This position relies on Henri Lefebrve's arguments around the social production of space in *The Production of Space*, trans. Donald Nicholson-Smith (Oxford: Blackwell, 1991).

18. Defining the notion of dwelling, Heidegger writes, "To say that mortals *are*, is to say that *in dwelling* they persist through spaces by virtue of their stay among things and locations." Heidegger continues, claiming that "dwelling . . . is the basic character of Being, in keeping with which mortals exist."

This idea that dwelling is a static experience suggests its resistance to being constructed through social, cultural, economic, and political contingencies. Martin Heidegger, *Basic Writings: Revised and Expanded Edition* (New York: Harper Collins, 1993), 362.

Notably, Sara Ahmed critiques Heidegger's conceptualization of dwelling and its impact on human perception, and in particular, the ways in which subjects are "oriented" in space to perceive particular objects, working to reproduce a dominant value system. *Queer Phenomenology: Orientations, Objects, Others* (Durham: Duke University Press, 2008).

19. As Gaston Bachelard writes, "The house shelters daydreaming, the house protects the dream, the house allows one to dream in peace." *The Poetics of Space*, trans. Maris Jolas (New York: Penguin Books, 2014), 6.

The subtext of Bachelard's statement here is that the public *does not* protect one's imagination and the public does not promote daydreaming. Instead, the world outside the home betrays the subject's natural inclination to dream, create, and express.

20. Susan Sontag, *Regarding the Pain of Others* (New York: Farrar, Straus and Giroux, 2003), 46.

21. These ideas of "capture" reflect the ways in which Walter Benjamin characterizes the photographic image. For Benjamin, because photography can be so easily reproduced, it robs the image of a sense of aura. "The Work of Art in the Age of Mechanical Reproduction," in *Aesthetics*, 66–69 (London: Routledge, 2017).

22. Luc Boltanski and Eve Chiapello, *The New Spirit of Capitalism* (London: Verso, 2005), 465–66.

23. Sarah Banet-Weiser, *Authentic™: The Politics of Ambivalence in a Brand Culture* (New York: NYU Press, 2012).

24. David Harvey most thoroughly details the economic and political conditions in which neoliberalism emerged, among which include policies that enabled widespread deregulation, privatization, and free market competition. See *A Brief History of Neoliberalism* (Oxford: Oxford University Press, 2007). In addition to this text, notable contributions to the discourse on neoliberalism include Noam Chomsky, *Profit over People: Neoliberalism and Global Order* (New York: Seven Stories Press, 1999); Slavoj Žižek, *The Courage of Hopelessness: Chronicles of a Year of Acting Dangerously* (London: Allen Lane, 2017); and Richard Wolff, *Democracy at Work: A Cure for Capitalism* (Chicago: Haymarket Books, 2012).

25. Nick Couldry, *Why Voice Matters: Culture and Politics after Neoliberalism* (London: Sage, 2010), 73–90.

26. Wendy Hui Kyong Chun, *Programmed Visions: Software and Memory* (Cambridge, MA: MIT Press, 2011), 8.

27. Wendy Hui Kyong Chun, *Updating to Remain the Same: Habitual New Media* (Cambridge, MA: MIT Press, 2016).

28. This position is also informed by Amy Dobson, Nicholas Carah, and Brady Robarbs's discussion of "digital intimate publics." Dobson, Carah, and Robarbs draw on Lauren Berlant's notion of "intimate publics" to "think about how contestations over power play out in the generative, liminal space where the public and the private intermingle." Focused specifically on social media, the concept of digital intimate publics enables one to "critically [examine] the relationship between the political valence of public performances of all kinds of intimacy on platforms that privatise, *as in commercialise and take ownership of,* that intimacy." "Digital Intimate Publics and Social Media: Towards Theorising Public Lives on Private Platforms," in *Digital Intimate Publics and Social Media,* ed. Amy Dobson, Brady Robarbs, and Nicholas Carah (Cham: Springer, 2018), 6–8.

29. Jeremiah Morelock and Felipe Ziotti Narita, "Introduction: Information Technology and Authoritarian Populism," in *The Society of the Selfie: Social Media and Liberal Democracy* (London: University of Westminster Press), 3

30. Couldry, *Why Voice Matters,* 6.

31. See Roy Boyne, "Post-Panopticism," *Economy and Society* 29, no. 2 (2000): 285–307; and David Lyon, *Surveillance Society: Monitoring Everyday Life* (Buckingham: Open University Press, 2001). This theory, though novel in its own right, relies heavily on Michel Foucault's conceptualization of "panopticism," as outlined in *Discipline and Punish: The Birth of the Prison,* trans. Alan Sheridan (New York: Vintage Books, 1995).

32. See note 28 for a definition of "digital intimate publics." Two primary features of this concept are that digital intimacy is both social capital and labor. Dobson, Carah, and Robarbs, "Digital Intimate Publics," 9.

33. The notion of "algorithmic surveillance" captures the phenomenon of surveillance through step-by-step computational instructions. The term was coined by Gary Armstrong and Clive Norris in their foundational text, *The Maximum Surveillance Society: The Rise of CCTV* (Oxford: Berg, 1999).

The notion of the black box captures the fact that users are not aware of the mechanisms through which their data is collected, circulated, and profiled. See, for instance, Taina Bucher, *If . . . Then: Algorithmic Power and Politics* (New York: Oxford, 2018).

34. Rita Raley, "Dataveillance and Countervailance," in *Raw Data Is an Oxymoron,* ed. Lisa Gitelman, 121–45 (Cambridge, MA: MIT Press, 2013); Jan Van Dijck, "Datafication, Dataism and Dataveillance: Big Data Between Scientific Paradigm and Ideology," *Surveillance & Society* 12, no. 2 (2014): 197–208.

35. This notion appeals to David Harvey's claim that neoliberalism creates a "culture of consent," meaning that neoliberalism is activated by individuals who inadvertently agree to its terms, even though those terms might ultimately disadvantage the individuals who consent to them. For more, see *A Brief History of Neoliberalism.*

36. Sarah Banet-Weiser, *Authentic™: The Politics of Ambivalence in a Brand Culture* (New York: NYU Press, 2012), 221.

37. Instagram's origins must be nuanced a bit here. While it rolled out to users as a photography platform, its earliest iteration was a "check-in" application called Burbn, where users would announce their location to friends on the platform and be able to also see where their friends had checked in. As founders Kevin Systrom and Mike

Krieger recount, once they added the ability for users to attach photos to their check-in, they realized they had tapped into a market gap in social media. From there, they decided to solely focus on photography and changed the name of the platform to reflect that focus. The "gram" in Instagram thus refers to the ability to take a snapshot, add a filter to it, and share it out to followers; the "insta" suggests that users can accomplish that task with little time and effort. Kevin Systrom and Mike Krieger, interview with Guy Raz, *How I Built This*, podcast audio, September 18, 2016.

38. While YouTube is also oriented around images—moving images, specifically—its function as a video player that works well with other platforms, such as the ability to embed its content on myriad other sites, defines its elasticity beyond the purpose of aestheticizing intimacy. In other words, while content on YouTube might offer intimaesthetics, the transitory nature of its videos allows its media to circulate and "live" beyond the confines of the platform.

39. Indeed, TikTok launched in 2016. The platform entered the scene as a direct competitor of Instagram, as it imitated much of its functionality. In this way, it largely extended/repackaged the intimaesthetics that Instagram instituted since its launch in 2010.

After TikTok's acquisition of Musical.ly, the platform arguably came to foreground audio over video, sound over movement. TikTok nonetheless has proven to be a global cultural phenomenon. More scholarly research on home dance videos circulating on TikTok is thus necessary in order to capture the platform's wide and ever-shifting field of cultural production.

40. Roger Fidler, *Mediamorphosis: Understanding New Media* (Thousand Oaks, CA: Pine Forge Press, 1997).

41. While intimaesthetics may be applied to studies of media on TikTok, there are certainly distinctions worth exploring. Further study of TikTok's specificities in aestheticizing intimacy is warranted but beyond the scope of this book.

42. Lev Manovich, *The Language of New Media* (Cambridge, MA: MIT Press, 2002).

Of course, as Jay Bolter and Richard Grusin argue, new media extends and relies on old media, thus that separation between the two proves unproductive in articulating a nuanced landscape of technological and media development. Bolter and Grusin propose the notion of "remediation" in place of new media. *Remediation: Understanding New Media* (Cambridge, MA: MIT Press, 1999).

43. Lev Manovich, for instance, discusses technologies like computer games and CD-ROMs as new media. Lev Manovich, *The Language of New Media*.

44. Boyne, "Post-Panopticism."

CHAPTER 1

1. My employment of the natural body draws on Doran George's study of the cultivation of a body that is perceived to be entwined with nature. George traces this body through the training regimes of Somatics and the culture surrounding its study. The regimes through which the natural body is constructed "[establish] unimpeachable bodily truth by virtue of its discovery in such distinct contexts as Zen Buddhism and martial arts, which each supposedly exhibited truths similar to Western physiology and evolutionary theory. . . . By the new millennium, Somatics still manifested a canonical

universal body as an ostensibly invisible category of nature." Doran George, *The Natural Body in Somatics Dance Training*, ed. Susan Foster (Oxford: Oxford University Press, 2020), 4.

Borrowing George's approach to the constructed natural body, we might consider how the phrase "dance like nobody's watching" similarly relies on a cultural regimen that promulgates conceptions of the natural body.

2. Kiri Miller makes a subtle reference to this phrase when she writes that "dancing to club hits like no one is watching is a high-risk guilty pleasure." *Playable Bodies: Dance Games and Intimate Media* (New York: Oxford University Press), 27. Miller's qualification of this activity as both "high-risk" and a "guilty pleasure" is revealing of the affective dissonance that this event elicits.

3. This range in dates is based on the show that was hosted by Allen Funt, who created the show and became its public face. Subsequent versions of the show continued beyond 1992 and included hosts Peter Funt (Allen Funt's son), actor Suzanne Somers, and reporter/TV personality Dina Eastwood. These later iterations were not as wildly popular as the show was under Allen Funt's direction.

4. Funt launched a laughter therapy program in which he would send episodes of the show to individuals recovering from an injury or illness. In his memoir, Funt discusses the role of the show and its humor in his father's own recovery from a stroke. Allen Funt and Philip Reed, *Candidly, Allen Funt: A Million Smiles Later* (Fort Lee, NJ: Barricade Books, 1994).

5. Stanley Milgram and John Sabini, "Candid Camera," *Society* (New Brunswick) 16, no. 6 (1979): 72–75.

6. Fred Nadis, "Citizen Funt: Surveillance as Cold War Entertainment," *Film & History* 37, no. 2 (2007): 18–19.

7. *Candid Camera*'s play with surveillance is not isolated from its cultural and historical contexts. Airing from 1948 to 1992, *Candid Camera* almost precisely coincides with the span of the Cold War: a period when heightened fears of espionage mingled with domestic surveillance campaigns on the part of the US government. Bradley Clissold notes these connections in "Candid Camera and the Origins of Reality TV: Contextualizing a Historical Precedent," in *Understanding Reality Television*, ed. Su Holmes and Deborah Jermyn (New York: Routledge, 2004).

8. Clay Calvert goes so far as to claim that *Candid Camera* marked the beginning of screenic voyeurism altogether, in *Voyeur Nation: Media, Privacy, and Peering in Modern Culture* (Boulder, CO: Westview Press), 42.

9. Jonathan Finn, "Seeing Surveillantly: Surveillance as Social Practice," in *Eyes Everywhere*, ed. Randy Lippert, Aaron Doyle, and David Lyon (London: Routledge, 2012), 77–78.

10. Susan Foster, *Choreographing Empathy: Kinesthesia in Performance* (New York: Routledge, 2010), 5.

11. Michel Foucault, *Discipline and Punish: The Birth of the Prison* (New York: Vintage Books, 1995), 201.

12. Foucault defines docile bodies as those that are rendered obedient by the simultaneous optimization of their utility and the minimization of their political agency. *Discipline and Punish*, 138.

13. David Lyon, *Surveillance Studies: An Overview* (Cambridge: Polity, 2007), 59.

14. In particular, Lyon draws on Deleuze's concept of a "control society," wherein "[government] surveillance has been superseded by other forms of power than discipline, mediated by electronic technologies." *Surveillance Studies*, 60.

15. Roy Boyne, "Post-Panopticism," *Economy and Society* 29, no. 2 (2000): 285–307.

16. My use of exhausted bodies is informed by, but ultimately departs from, André Lepecki's sense of exhaustion. For Lepecki, it is the dance that is exhausted (due to economic conditions of the world and a number of geopolitical events). However, here I articulate dance as a *response* to exhaustion. *Exhausting Dance Performance and the Politics of Movement* (New York: Routledge, 2006).

17. Susan Sontag, *On Photography* (New York: Farrar, Straus, and Giroux, 1973), 140.

18. The activity of dancing-while may also be a slight break from a given activity. If a dancer is dancing while eating, for instance, they might not be taking bites of their food at the exact same time of breaking out into a groove. Instead, keeping with this example, they might be dancing *between* bites. Thus, the preposition of "while" is to be conceived broadly. This perspective carries through to the examples analyzed in part 2.

19. The power of the camera's gaze as a force of power over the subject has been well documented in cinema and media studies and feminist film theory. See, for instance, Laura Mulvey, "Visual Pleasure and Narrative Cinema," in *Visual and Other Pleasures*, 14–26 (London: Palgrave Macmillan, 1989); Morna Laing and Jacki Willson, *Revisiting the Gaze: The Fashioned Body and the Politics of Looking* (London: Bloomsbury, 2020); Lisa French, "The 'Female Gaze,'" in *The Female Gaze in Documentary Film*, 53–70 (Cham: Springer International Publishing, 2021); and E. Ann Kaplan, *Looking for the Other: Feminism, Film, and the Imperial Gaze* (New York: Routledge, 1997).

20. When introspection *is* a sensibility present in a dancer's performance, it may be presumed to be part of the choreography: a stylistic choice that was prepared and rehearsed or an aspect of the performer's character. Exceptions include somatic training techniques, as elucidated in George, *The Natural Body in Somatics Dance Training*.

21. Kobena Mercer, "Unburying the Dismembered," in *New Histories* (Boston: Institute of Contemporary Art, 1996), 165. This very quote also appears in Rebecca Schneider, *Performing Remains: Art and War in Times of Theatrical Reenactment* (Abingdon, Oxon: Routledge, 2011), 98.

22. The notion of desire referenced here is grounded in Lacanian psychoanalysis, which is based on a theory of *lack*. Based on this premise, Lacan might argue the candid dancer is ridiculed precisely because they are the object of the viewer's desires.

23. The linkage between dance and femininity is thoroughly researched. For a discussion of dance and gender through multiple perspectives and in a range of contexts, see Helen Thomas, ed., *Dance, Gender, and Culture* (Basingstoke: MacMillan, 1993). For a consideration of the feminine gendering of dance from the perspective of boys and men, see Dough Risner, *Stigma and Perseverance in the Lives of Boys Who Dance* (Lewiston, NY: Edwin Mellen Press, 2009).

Of course, any constructions of dance as feminine are culturally constituted and thus differ across contexts. In each context in which representations of femininity appear in dance, gender is intersected with race, ethnicity, class, nationality, age, and ableness.

24. For an impressive history of the role of dance and gender in pre- and postrevo-

lutionary Iran, see Ida Meftahi, *Gender and Dance in Modern Iran: Biopolitics on Stage* (New York: Routledge, 2016).

25. Afsaneh Najmabadi, *Professing Selves: Transsexuality and Same-Sex Desire in Contemporary Iran* (Durham: Duke University Press, 2014).

26. According to Haleh Esfandiari, the moment of revolution was an "earthquake" in women's professional lives and public roles, wherein they had to change occupations to adapt to the pressures of a new regime, recede from public life, and find new ways of existing in a system with strict boundaries for women. *Restructured Lives: Women and Iran's Islamic Revolution* (Washington, DC: Woodrow Wilson Center Press, 1997), 105–32.

27. Elahi Babak and Persis M. Karim, "Introduction: Iranian Diaspora," *Comparative Studies of South Asia, Africa and the Middle East* 31, no. 2 (2011): 381–87.

28. The evidence of this relationship rests with where the video lives in new media. That is, it was posted to a personal profile of a then-high-school girl. Other images on the profile show the girl with her friends, especially one in which they were celebrating their high school graduation. The girl's nicely pressed school uniform and her later enrollment in an out-of-town university suggest an upper-class status. She is also white, while the dancer is black. Considering this information, the analysis here is based on the possibility that the cameraperson is the daughter of the dancer's employer. Other possibilities for this relational dynamic certainly exist, but the dancer's choreography of abandon is not compromised by those possibilities. Instead, what is most critical to the dancer's abandonment of class is the notion that the dancer and cameraperson appear to know each other well and have a playful relationship. Nonetheless, there are nuances to that relationship that are the subject of discussion in this analysis.

29. The prospect of the scene's two different moments of discovery reveals a trope in smartphone use: it is not always obvious when someone is recording a scene, as there are a number of other engagements with such a device that would, to an outsider, resemble how someone might hold a smartphone to record. From the dancer's perspective, for instance, the camera operator may be merely checking her text messages, scrolling through her social media feed, reading an email, or consuming some other media

30. Ena Jansen, *Like Family: Domestic Workers in South African History and Literature* (Johannesburg: Wits University Press), 2–3.

31. Jacklyn Cock, *Maids and Madams: A Study in the Politics of Exploitation* (Johannesburg: Raven Press, 1980).

32. Tamara Shefer, "Fraught Tenderness: Narratives on Domestic Workers in Memories of Apartheid," *Peace and Conflict: Journal of Peace Psychology* 18, no. 3 (2012): 307–17.

33. Jansen, *Like Family*, 4.

34. Shefer, "Fraught Tenderness," 311.

35. For an example of eventicization being employed in education, see Liselott Olsson, "Eventicizing Curriculum: Learning to Read and Write Through Becoming a Citizen of the World," *Journal of Curriculum Theorizing* 28 (2012): 88–107; for an example in cinema media studies, see Reema Fadda, "Playing Against Invisibility: Negotiating the Institutional Politics of Cultural Production in Palestine," *Future Imperfect: Contemporary Art Practices and Cultural Institutions in the Middle East*, 149–66 (Berlin:

Sternberg Press, 2016); for an example in tourism studies, see Maria Gravari-Barbas and Sébastien Jacquot, "Mechanisms, Actors and Impacts of the Touristification of a Tourism Periphery: The Saint-Ouen Flea Market, Paris," *International Journal of Tourism Cities* 5, no. 3 (1AD): 370–91.

Of course, discourses on metaphysics and philosophy have produced most of the literature on the event—namely, through the work of Jacques Derrida, Maurice Blanchot, Alain Badiou, Giles Deleuze, and Martin Heidegger. For a helpful summary of these theories and the conversation among them, see Ilai Rowner, *The Event: Literature and Theory* (Lincoln: University of Nebraska Press, 2015).

36. Much of the theory surrounding the event is steeped in linguistics. For instance, Deleuze claims that philosophers typically understand the event's relation to language in three ways: denotation, manifestation, and signification. Interestingly, Deleuze claims that this alignment with language forecloses the sensorial possibilities of the event; thus, he attributes a fourth characteristic to the event: sense. Gilles Deleuze, *The Logic of Sense*, trans. Mark Lester and Charles Stivale, ed. Constantin V. Boundas (New York: Columbia University Press, 1990).

37. Heidegger, perhaps most notably, connects the event to human perception—primarily visibility, employing the term *Ereignis* to capture the ways an event occurs through one's perceptual appropriation of the world. As David Kleinberg-Levin notes, "Understood as an ontological 'event,' an event bearing on the meaning of being, Heidegger's keyword 'Ereignis' functions as an adumbration of the possibility of a fundamental transformation of the world" (44). Kleinberg-Levin later elaborates: "Drawing on the etymological association of Ereignis (event of appropriation) and er-aügen, which originally meant 'to bring something into view, that is, to catch sight of something, call something into view, hence to appropriate it' Heidegger turns to vision to explain our essential nature in its role as opening clearings for the visible presence of the world" (86). While Heidegger's approach to an essential human experience has been thoroughly critiqued in a wide range of disciplines, the connection he suggests between the event and visibility is profound in how it applies to the candid dancing phenomenon. David Kleinberg-Levin, *Heidegger's Phenomenology of Perception* (London: Rowman and Littlefield International, 2020).

38. The use of "particular" here is a nod to the discourse on the event and the debates around its ontology. In philosophical discourses, that is, debates ensue regarding the extent to which an event is a "particular" or a "universal." While this debate is largely beyond the concerns of this book, it informs how we might conceptualize a candid dance scene. We might envision, for instance, how the particularities of the scene help viewers to understand the dance as an event. Interestingly, the video itself engages in a politics of mass reproduction that suggests that the dance may have qualities of a universal. For more on the ways in which an event might be both particular and universal, see Donald Davidson, "Events as Particulars," *Noûs* 4, no. 1 (1970): 25–32.

39. James Durham Peters, "Calendar, Clock, Tower," in *Deus in Machina: Religion and Technology in Historical Perspective*, ed. Jeremy Stolow (New York: Fordham University Press, 2013), 42.

40. This mode of temporality reflects what Andrew Hoskins calls "digital network memory," which captures how memory is "increasingly networked, but also actively and re-actively constructed on-the-fly" and "characterized by its mediated or mediatized

emergence through a range of everyday digital media." "Digital Network Memory," in *Mediation, Remediation, and the Dynamics of Cultural Memory*, ed. Astrid Erll and Ansgar Nünning (Berlin: Walter de Gruyter, 2009), 92.

41. Christian Fuchs, "Digital Prosumption Labour on Social Media in the Context of the Capitalist Regime of Time," *Time & Society* 23, no. 1 (2014): 97–123.

42. Relevance sorting and its associated power dynamics produce both algorithmic bias and algorithmic visibility. These concepts are discussed widely in critical internet studies and media studies. The discourse on algorithmic bias may be gleaned in the works of Cathy O'Neil, Megan Garcia, and Safiya Noble, among others. The discourse on algorithmic visibility may be understood through the works of Taina Bucher and Crystal Abidin. See, for instance, Cathy O'Neil, *Weapons of Math Destruction: How Big Data Increases Inequality and Threatens Democracy* (New York: Crown, 2017); Megan Garcia, "Racist in the Machine: The Disturbing Implications of Algorithmic Bias," *World Policy Journal* 33, no. 4 (2016): 111–17; Safiya Noble, *Algorithms of Oppression: How Search Engines Reinforce Racism* (New York: NYU Press, 2018); Taina Bucher, "Want to Be on the Top? Algorithmic Power and the Threat of Invisibility on Facebook," *New Media & Society* 14, no. 7 (November 2012): 1164–80; Crystal Abidin, "#In$tagLam: Instagram as a Repository of Taste, a Brimming Marketplace, a War of Eyeballs," in *Mobile Media Making in the Age of Smartphones*, ed. M. Berry and M. Schleser (New York: Palgrave Pivot, 2014), 119–28; and Caitlin Petre, Brooke Erin Duffy, and Emily Hund, "'Gaming the System': Platform Paternalism and the Politics of Algorithmic Visibility," *Social Media + Society* (October 2019).

43. This battle against the timestamp supports what Taina Bucher proposes in the discussion of the algorithmic "threat of invisibility." "Want to Be on the Top?"

44. For a review of how the timestamp is used to mine data on new media, see Gabor Szabo et al., "Temporal Processes: The When of Social Media," in *Social Media Data Mining and Analytics* (Indianapolis: Wiley, 2019), 77–121; and Lam Thuy Vo, *Mining Social Media: Finding Stories in Internet Data* (San Francisco: No Starch Press, 2019).

45. For a demonstration of the democratic promise of the internet, see Douglas Rushkoff, *Open Source Democracy: How Online Communication Is Changing Offline Politics* (London: Demos, 2003). For a study of how the internet fell short of its political and economic opportunities, see Robert McChesney, *Digital Disconnect: How Capitalism Is Turning the Internet Against Democracy* (New York: New Press, 2013).

46. There are notable exceptions to this statement, including examples of "tactical media" discussed in Rita Raley, *Tactical Media* (Minneapolis: University of Minnesota Press, 2009); and discussions of the work of the activist duo The Yes Men, as detailed in Ian Reilly, *Media Hoaxing: The Yes Men and Utopian Politics* (Lanham, MD: Lexington Books, 2018).

47. This process is not far from what Shoshana Zuboff describes as "kidnap, corner, compete," which Zuboff argues is part of the strategies of surveillance capitalism. *Surveillance Capitalism: The Fight for a Human Future at the New Frontier of Power* (New York: Public Affairs, 2019).

CHAPTER 2

1. This position may be complicated by the arguments of Paul Frosh in "The Gestural Image: The Selfie, Photography Theory, and Kinesthetic Sociability," *International*

Journal of Communication 9 (2015): 1607–28. In this article, Frosh examines the power of the photographic selfie to capture "embodied technicity" (1614).

2. Video selfies appear as examples in a range of texts but are not thoroughly theorized in relation to medium and genre. One notable exception is Florian Krautkrämer and Matthias Thiele, "The Video Selfie as Act and Artifact of Recording," in *Exploring the Selfie*, ed. Julia Eckel, Jens Ruchatz, and Sabine Wirth, 239–59 (Cham: Palgrave Macmillan, 2018). While the authors focus on the aesthetic and semiotic characteristics of a video selfie, the article revolves around how the style appears in documentary and amateur filmmaking, primarily within the Hollywood film industry.

Of course, there are other concepts beyond the "video selfie" that articulate a *type* of selfie that might use video. An especially apt example is that of the *musical selfie*, which, as proposed by Sumanth Gopinath and Jason Stanyek, describes the trend of amateur musical performances, as well as self-representation through the development and circulation of musical playlists. This concept is articulated through examples where performers listen to music on their headphones while recording themselves. Though the theory is tethered to the particularities of music and sound, it nonetheless attends to the performance-based mode of self-representation through video. Sumanth Gopinath and Jason Stanyek, "Technologies of the Musical Selfie," in *The Cambridge Companion to Music in Digital Culture*, ed. David Trippett, Monique M. Ingalls, and Nicholas Cook, 89–118 (Cambridge: Cambridge University Press, 2019). Also see Muriel Tinel-Temple, Laura Busetta, and Marlène Monteiro, eds., *From Self-Portrait to Selfie: Representing the Self in Moving Image* (Oxford: Peter Lang, 2019).

3. Notably, definitions of the selfie beyond that of the dictionary are truer to a relationship-based orientation (that is, the relationship between the subject and the camera). For instance, Ace Lehnur in his edited volume exclaims: "Defined as a self-image made with a hand-held mobile device and shared via social media platforms, the selfie has facilitated self-imaging." *Self-Representation in an Expanded Field: From Self-Portraiture to Selfie, Contemporary Art in the Social Media Age*, ed. Ace Lehnur (Basel: MDPI, 2021), n.p.

4. Hagi Kenaan underscores this point when writing, "The selfie is clearly grounded in important technological developments that photography and communication have undergone in the last 20 years, but these developments are in themselves insufficient for assessing the new kind of image-ness that the selfie brings about." "The Selfie and the Face," in *Exploring the Selfie*, ed. Julia Eckel, Jens Ruchatz, and Sabine Wirth (Cham: Palgrave Macmillan, 2018), 14.

5. Some scholars would even argue that the category of selfie requires genres in and of itself. See, for instance, Bernd Leiendecker, "Of Duck Faces and Cat Beards: Why Do Selfies Need Genres?" in *Exploring the Selfie*, ed. Julia Eckel, Jens Ruchatz, and Sabine Wirth, 189–209 (Cham: Palgrave Macmillan, 2018).

6. My use of pact here references one of the most foundational theories for the study of autobiography: Philippe Lejeune's "autobiographical pact," or the reading contract between author and reader wherein the text articulates a unity of author, narrator, and protagonist. "The Autobiographical Pact," in *On Autobiography*, ed. P. J. Eakin, 3–30 (Minneapolis: University of Minnesota Press, 1989).

7. Crystal Abidin, "'Aren't These Just Young, Rich Women Doing Vain Things Online?': Influencer Selfies as Subversive Frivolity," *Social Media + Society* 2, no. 2 (2016): 1–17.

8. Brian Droitcour, "A Selfie Is Not a Portrait," Culturetwo.wordpress.com, October 24, 2013, accessed July 1, 2020, https://culturetwo.wordpress.com/2013/10/24/a-selfie-is-not-a-portrait.

9. For Julia Eckel, this understanding produces "degrees of selfieness," or "the purely visual and conventionalized traits of the pictures pointing to their selfie status and not the maybe/maybe-not factual contexts of production they originated from." "Selfies and Authorship: On the Displayed Authorship and the Author Function of the Selfie," in *Exploring the Selfie: Historical, Theoretical, and Analytical Approaches to Digital Self-Photography*, ed. Julia Eckel, Jens Ruchatz, and Sabine Wirth (Cham: Palgrave Macmillan, 2018), 142.

10. According to Laura Marks, "Haptic images invite the viewer to dissolve his or her subjectivity in the close and bodily contact with the image." In addition, these media "[involve] giving up visual control." *Touch: Sensuous Theory and Multisensory Media* (Minneapolis: University of Minnesota Press, 2002), 13.

11. These three facets of the dancer and their image revolve around the objectification of the dancing body, which has been written about extensively. Susan Leigh Foster puts various threads of the dancing body's objectification into conversation with one another in "The Ballerina's Phallic Pointe," in *Corporealities: Dancing Knowledge, Culture, and Power*, ed. Susan Leigh Foster, 1–25 (London: Routledge, 2004).

12. Sarah Pink, *Home Truths: Gender, Domestic Objects and Everyday Life* (London: Taylor and Francis, 2020).

13. My use of signature draws from Jacques Derrida's understanding of it as linked to a particular place and time. In the home dance selfie, the signature indicates authorship, and its linking to the home at a particular moment in the dancer's day and life contributes to her autochoreography. "Signature, Event, Context," in *Limited, Inc.*, 1–23 (Evanston: Northwestern University Press, 1988). The notion of signature is also used frequently in discourses on autobiography.

14. The direct address has been studied extensively across a range of scholarly disciplines. My use of it here may be located at the intersection of cinema media studies and performance studies. For instance, see Oliver Double, "Introduction," in *Popular Performance*, ed. Adam Ainsworth, Oliver Double, and Louise Peacock (London: Bloomsbury, 2017), 1–29; and Colleen Dunagan, *Consuming Dance: Choreography and Advertising* (New York: Oxford University Press, 2018), 54–61.

15. This choreography of the face draws from dance vocabularies, as well as everyday codes and conventions, but is ultimately produced through the screen apparatus. In an article detailing the concept of facial choreography, Dodds and Hooper recall Deleuze's notion of the abstract machine of faciality, which they characterize as a force that produces "legible messages that resist ambiguity, polyvocality, and heterogeneity." In this way, facial choreography, they argue, becomes incorporated into hegemonic structures of capture. "Faces, Close-Ups and Choreography: A Deleuzian Critique of *So You Think You Can Dance*," *International Journal of Screendance* 4, no. 1 (2014): 93–113.

Notably, Hagi Kenaan analyzes and deconstructs the centrality of the face in the selfie image. "The Selfie and the Face."

16. My use of "anchor" borrows from Roland Barthes's distinction of *relay* and *anchor* in how a caption adds meaning to the image (which, in Barthes's case, is the comic strip). *Image-Music-Text*, trans. Stephen Heath (New York: Hill and Wang, 1978).

17. Mar's transition to a nonbinary gender is evident in their post-2020 Instagram posts. However, since the historical parameters of this analysis are confined to 2010–20, the narrative around that transition is beyond the limits of this book. Nonetheless, Mar's performance of self throughout their transition, including posts about their "top surgery" in 2022, is exemplary of their autochoreography.

18. The handle for Mar's account is @personalpractice, which is fitting, as much of the content on her account is sited in the home and has an autobiographical thrust. Siobhan Burke discusses the personal dimension to Mar's practice in "A Graveyard? She's Danced There. Just Check Instagram," *New York Times*, August 1, 2017, https://www.nytimes.com/2017/08/01/arts/dance/Mar-Mar-instagram-project-personal-practice.html.

Mar's sense of personal practice captured in her handle and running throughout her videos also speaks to a wider phenomenon of solo performance in new media. In their editorial, Harmony Bench and Simon Ellis reflect on what the singular dancing body means in the discourse of screendance: "Does solo performance reflect an impulse to withdraw from the world and amplify the self? Or conversely, does solo performance offer a space from which to critique such withdrawal?" "Editorial: Solo/Screen," *International Journal of Screendance* 8 (2017).

19. Catherine Hakim, *Erotic Capital: The Power of Attraction in the Boardroom and the Bedroom* (New York: Basic Books, 2011).

20. Harmony Bench, "Media and the No-Place of Dance," *Forum Modernes Theater* 23, no. 1 (2008): 37–47; Philip Auslander, *Liveness: Performance in a Mediatized Culture* (London: Routledge, 1999).

21. Leaping scales borrows from and reimagines Neil Smith's concept of "jumping scales." For Smith, spatial boundaries tend to restrict rather than facilitate everyday life. Of course, Smith develops this concept in relation to the transgressive maneuvers of homeless individuals in urban centers, who might move in and out of body, home, community, urban, region, nation, and global spaces. Leaping scales takes this notion and applies it to the movements of the mediatized home dancing body. Neil Smith, "Contours of a Spacialized Politics: Homeless Vehicles and the Production of Geographical Scales," *Social Text* 33 (1992): 55–81.

22. My use of "social life" borrows from Arjun Appadurai's generative work on the "social life of things" in "Introduction," in *The Social Life of Things: Commodities in Cultural Perspective*, ed. Arjun Appadurai, 3–63 (Cambridge: Cambridge University Press, 1986). Notably, scholars Anthea Kraut and Susan Leigh Foster apply Appadurai's thinking to the circulation of dance in and out of the commodity state. Most relevant to my concerns here, Harmony Bench conceptualizes *digital dance* in terms of its circulation through new media. In *Perpetual Motion*, Bench addresses how digital dance "[becomes] positioned within a corporeal common that ostensibly can be mined by anyone." This notion of the commons qualifies my understanding of dance's "social life on new media," as it emphasizes how dance on new media is susceptible to commodification and what Bench terms "infelicitous acts of transfer." *Perpetual Motion: Dance, Digital Cultures, and the Common* (Minneapolis: University of Minnesota Press, 2020), 142–56. Also, as mentioned above, see Anthea Kraut, *Choreographing Copyright: Race, Gender, and Intellectual Property Rights in American Dance* (New York: Oxford University Press,

2016); and Susan Leigh Foster, *Valuing Dance: Commodities and Gifts in Motion* (New York: Oxford University Press, 2019).

23. This use of teaching and learning refers to a class of algorithms known as "machine learning," which identifies patterns in user behavior and automatically adjusts itself to better respond to future behavior. For a review of machine learning on new media in particular, see Taina Bucher, "Nothing to Disconnect from? Being Singular Plural in an Age of Machine Learning," *Media, Culture & Society* 42, no. 4 (2020): 610–17; and Nicholas Carah and Daniel Angus, "Algorithmic Brand Culture: Participatory Labour, Machine Learning and Branding on Social Media," *Media, Culture & Society* 40, no. 2 (2018): 178–94.

24. Jansson and Fast define a click economy as when "the accumulation of friends, followers, likes, and so forth is turned into a currency that measures and classifies the social status of individuals, and thus legitimizes new ways of relating to others." "Transmedia Identities: From Fan Cultures to Liquid Lives," in *The Routledge Companion to Transmedia Studies*, ed. Matthew Freeman and Renira Rampazzo Gambarato, 340–49 (London: Routledge, 2019), n.p.

25. Instagram, "See Posts You Care about First in Your Feed," March 15, 2016, https://about.instagram.com/blog/announcements/see-posts-you-care-about-first-in-your-feed#:~:text=The%20order%20of%20photos%20and,just%20in%20a%20different%20order.

26. For an in-depth analysis of the social, political, and economic impacts of black boxes in network society, see Frank Pasquale, *The Black Box Society: The Secret Algorithms That Control Money and Information* (Cambridge, MA: Harvard University Press, 2015).

27. Josh Constine, "How Instagram's Algorithms Work," *Tech Crunch*, June 1, 2018, https://tcrn.ch/2LN5kDX.

28. Abbas Razaghpanah et al., "Apps, Trackers, Privacy, and Regulators: A Global Study of the Mobile Tracking Ecosystem," paper presented at the 25th Annual Network and Distributed System Security Symposium (NDSS 2018).

29. Taina Bucher, *If . . . Then: Algorithmic Power and Politics* (New York: Oxford University Press, 2018).

30. Bucher, *If . . . Then*, 113–17.

31. An example may be found in Mary Keutelian, "The Best Times to Post on Social Media in 2022," *SproutSocial*, April 13, 2022, accessed April 15, 2022, https://sproutsocial.com/insights/best-times-to-post-on-social-media/.

32. According to Mary V. Wrenn, agency that exists only in one's perception, which she calls "inauthentic agency," is a hallmark of neoliberalism. "Agency and Neoliberalism," *Cambridge Journal of Economics* 39, no. 5 (2015): 1231–43.

Regarding the prospect of agency with algorithms, Urbano Reviglio and Claudio Agosti claim that such "algorithmic sovereignty" has not yet been realized but has potential to infuse greater user agency into a problematic system of power. "Thinking Outside the Black-Box: The Case for 'Algorithmic Sovereignty' in Social Media," *Social Media + Society* 6, no. 2 (2020): 1–12.

33. Theresa Senft, "Microcelebrity and the Branded Self," *A Companion to New Media Dynamics* 11 (2013): 346–54.

34. A "story" on Instagram is distinct from a post in that it disappears after twenty-

four hours of posting. Posts, on the other hand, remain on the user's personal profile indefinitely. It is worth noting that Instagram added this feature in 2016, primarily to compete with Snapchat.

35. This facet of new media is the central argument of Wendy Chun's *Habitual New Media: Updating to Remain the Same* (Cambridge, MA: MIT Press, 2018).

36. "#Funeral and Instagram: Death, Social Media, and Platform Vernacular," Information, Communication & Society 18, no. 3 (2015): 257.

37. In his treatise, Peters writes: "We are CEOs of our own companies: Me Inc. To be in business today, our most important job is to be head marketer for the brand called You." "The Brand Called You," *Fast Company* 10, no. 10 (1997): 83.

Notably, Sarah Banet-Weiser details neoliberalism's promulgation of brand culture, particularly through the appeal to/of "authenticity." *Authentic™: The Politics of Ambivalence in a Brand Culture* (New York: NYU Press, 2012).

38. Couldry, *Why Voice Matters*, 73–90.

39. Luc Boltanski and Eve Chiapello, *The New Spirit of Capitalism*, trans. Gregory Elliott (New York: Verso, 2005), 466.

40. Banet-Weiser, *Authentic™*, 3.

41. Boltanski and Chiapello, *The New Spirit of Capitalism*, 182.

42. The marketing perspective of personal branding is represented through Peter Montoya, *The Personal Branding Phenomenon: Realize Greater Influence, Explosive Income Growth and Rapid Career Advancement by Applying the Branding Techniques of Michael, Martha, and Oprah* (Santa Ana, CA: Peter Montoya, 2002). In this guide, Montoya outlines the "Eight Unbreakable Laws of Personal Branding," consisting of specialization, leadership, personality, distinctiveness, visibility, unity, persistence, and goodwill. The "Law of Unity" speaks to the consistency factor of one's personal brand on new media.

The cultural studies perspective is represented through Alison Hearn, "Meat, Mask, Burden: Probing the Contours of the Branded 'Self,'" *Journal of Consumer Culture* 8, no. 2 (2008): 197–217.

43. This approach of flattening and reproducing reflects the nature of capitalism at large. It reflects the application of a Taylorist model of production to the individual subject. Wendy Chun connects the Taylorist logic to new media practices. *Habitual New Media*, 8.

44. This position slightly differs from that of Julia Eckel, who writes of the selfie that "it is not the single photograph that is intended to capture all of the individual in one shot but the outcome of a series of images that stands for the multifacetedness of the single, unseizable individual as well as for a multiplied individuation of the masses." While, yes, an individual image never represents the whole of the person, it might be consistent with the subject's brand as a whole, which may be understood through the individual image. "Selfies and Authorship," 148.

45. Lionel Wee and Ann Brooks, "Personal Branding and the Commodification of Reflexivity," *Cultural Sociology* 4, no. 1 (2010), 56. Also see Jennifer Whitmer, "You Are Your Brand: Self-Branding and the Marketization of Self," *Sociology Compass* 13, no. 3 (2019): 1–10.

46. Donté's expression of these political views is consistent with the trends on new media in 2020, an exceptional year for its attention on the homebody, its amplification of new media practices, and its exacerbations of online political dialogue. While these

points all implicate concepts discussed in this chapter, they reflect a larger social, cultural, and economic shift that is beyond the scope of this book.

47. At the time of posting, Mar used she/her pronouns and would describe herself as a lesbian with "soft butch" leanings. It wasn't until 2022 that Mar came out as nonbinary with they/them pronouns. As the subjects of analysis, the posts where Mar describes themselves as a "woman" remain unchanged throughout this book, as they do on Instagram.

48. For more on postfeminism, particularly in relation to media, see Angela McRobbie, "Post-Feminism and Popular Culture," *Feminist Media Studies* 4, no. 3 (2004): 255–64; Rosalind Gill, "Post-Postfeminism? New Feminist Visibilities in Postfeminist Times," *Feminist Media Studies* 16, no. 4 (2016): 610–30; and Sarah Banet-Weiser, "Postfeminism and Popular Feminism," *Feminist Media Histories* 4, no. 2 (2018): 152–56.

49. This analysis of Mar's online life/work gestures toward the ambiguousness of gift and commodity transactions on new media. Notably, Harmony Bench conceptualizes the transfer of movement on new media through the framework of the gift and commodity. *Perpetual Motion.*

50. Susan Foster, *Valuing Dance: Commodities and Gifts in Motion* (New York: Oxford, 2019).

51. Colleen Dunagan cleverly applies the concept of capitalistic "incorporation" to the ways in which the dancing body is utilized in marketing and advertising. *Consuming Dance.*

52. While the precise payment that Donté receives for his ambassadorship is not public information, job postings on sites like promo.work show that a Starbucks Brand Ambassadorship is a temporary, part-time, paid position in which the employee works between three and eight hours per week.

CHAPTER 3

1. Henry Jenkins, *Textual Poachers: Television Fans and Participatory Culture* (New York: Routledge, 1992), 152–84.

2. Of course, beyond the techniques of early cinema, the notion of "breaking the fourth wall" developed as what Tom Brown calls a "counter cinema": a way to intentionally subvert the power of the camera, break the narrative, and call the relationship between spectator and performer into question. Nonetheless, as both Bordwell and Brown note, the technique was also utilized in comedy and musical performances to build a connection with the audience. Tom Brown, *Breaking the Fourth Wall: Direct Address in Cinema* (Edinburgh: Edinburgh University Press, 2012).

3. Bordwell's *Figures Traced in Light*, in particular, focuses on the director's work with performers: how their bodies are framed and staged in order to construe a particular sentiment or cultivate the narrative. Bordwell captures this consideration by mapping the stylistic techniques of Feuillade, Mizoguchi, Angelopoulos, and Hou. Repeatedly, Bordwell refers to this work as "choreography," a word choice that is telling of the centrality of the body in techniques of filmmaking and storytelling. *Figures Traced in Light: On Cinematic Staging* (Berkeley: University of California Press, 2005).

4. In an earlier work, Bordwell draws on the work of Tom Gunning to illustrate how the direct address is part of the techniques of early filmmakers, before narrative

cinema had fully developed. Bordwell writes that "this technique [of acknowledging the camera] suited the 'exhibitionist' side of early film. With the rise of a narrative cinema, though, such asides disrupted the illusion of a self-contained story world, and so they largely disappeared. Direct address would resurface at moments of comedy or musical performance—exactly those occasions that could constitute 'attractions' even in a well-developed narrative context." *Figures Traced in Light*, 127.

5. For an apt discussion of the use of the direct address in reality television and other documentary forms, see Leigh Edwards, "Chasing the Real: Reality Television and Documentary Forms," in *Docufictions: Essays on the Intersection of Documentary and Fictional Filmmaking*, ed. Gary D. Rhodes and John Parris Springer (Jefferson, NC: McFarland, 2006).

6. Lev Manovich, *The Language of New Media* (Cambridge, MA: MIT Press, 2001).

7. The discourse on amateurs in media production is robust. For the purposes here, I specifically draw on the role of the amateur in participatory culture. For a re-view of this figure, see Kiri Miller, *Playing Along: Digital Games, YouTube, and Virtual Performance* (Oxford: Oxford University Press, 2012); Annamaria Motrescu-Mayes and Susan Aasman, *Amateur Media and Participatory Cultures: Film, Video, and Digital Media* (Abingdon: Routledge, 2019); and Henry Jenkins, *Convergence Culture: Where Old and New Media Collide* (New York: NYU Press, 2006).

8. While we might tend to associate technological surveillance with video, Jeff Hey-don acknowledges that the device of the camera obscura had been used before video for surveillance purposes. Heydon provides the example of one such device being used in Glasgow in 1824 to apprehend a thief. *Visibility and Control: Cameras and Certainty in Governing* (Washington, DC: Lexington Books, 2021), 9.

9. Jon Coaffee, David Murakami Wood, and Peter Rogers, "Controlling the Risky City," in *The Everyday Resilience of the City: How Cities Respond to Terrorism and Disaster* (Basingstoke: Palgrave Macmillan, 2009), 80.

10. Prominent in that discussion is the notion of surveillance as social practice, elaborated in Jonathan Finn, "Seeing Surveillantly: Surveillance as Social Practice," in *Eyes Everywhere*, ed. Randy Lippert and Aaron Doyle; also see David Lyon, *The Elec-tronic Eye: The Rise of Surveillance Society* (Cambridge: Polity Press, 1994).

11. The public understanding of CCTV as a crime prevention tool appears across literature on the subject. See, for instance, Clive Norris and Michael McCahill, "CCTV: Beyond Penal Modernism?" *British Journal of Criminology* 46, no. 1 (2006): 97–118; and Sean Hier, "Risky Spaces and Dangerous Faces: Urban Surveillance, Social Disorder, and CCTV," *Social & Legal Studies* 13, no. 4 (2004): 541–54.

Studies describing resistance against surveillance are also numerous. As David Lyon aptly points out, resistance to surveillance may be as minor as closing your blinds at home or as involved as joining an anti-surveillance movement.

12. Deborah Jermyn, "Video Technologies, Actuality and Affect in the Television Crime Appeal," in *Understanding Reality Television*, ed. Su Holmes and Deborah Jermyn, 71–90 (London: Routledge, 2004).

13. Steve Mann, "'Sousveillance': Inverse Surveillance in Multimedia Imaging," in *Proceedings of the 12th Annual ACM International Conference on Multimedia*, 620–27.

Relevant to our purposes, this technique is applied to new media in Steve Mann and Joseph Ferenbok, "New Media and the Power Politics of Sousveillance in a Surveillance-Dominated World," *Surveillance & Society* 11, no. 1/2 (2013): 18–34.

14. For a review of the notion of apathy toward surveillance and the "privacy paradox," see Eszter Hargittai and Alice E. Marwick, "'What Can I Really Do?' Explaining the Privacy Paradox with Online Apathy," *International Journal of Communication* 10 (2016): 3737–57.

15. Duke claims that nontargets "do not effectively fear certain specific forms of surveillance and thus are very likely to present behavioral passivity towards them." "Nontargets: Understanding the Apathy Towards the Israeli Security Agency's COVID-19 Surveillance," *Surveillance & Society* 19, no. 1 (2021): 117. While Duke does not extensively trouble the notion of a nontarget, considering its antithesis (the target) gestures toward the privileged position of the nontarget to *not* feel that they are the focus of surveillance, source of suspicion, or persona non grata. Depending on the context, factors like race, ethnicity, class, gender, sexual orientation, age, or ability may play into who is a target and who is a nontarget. Duke's analysis would benefit from complicating the notion of the nontarget to account for identity and privilege.

16. Daniel J. Solove, *Nothing to Hide: The False Tradeoff Between Privacy and Security* (New Haven: Yale University Press, 2011). For a comprehensive review of the privacy paradox in general, see Robert Carey and Jacquelyn Ann Burkell, "A Heuristics Approach to Understanding Privacy-Protecting Behaviors in Digital Social Environments," in *In Lessons from the Identity Trail: Anonymity, Privacy and Identity in a Networked Society*, ed. Ian Kerr, Valerie Steeves, and Carole Lucock, 65–82 (Oxford: Oxford University Press, 2009); Nina Gerber, Paul Gerber, and Melanie Volkamer, "Explaining the Privacy Paradox: A Systematic Review of Literature Investigating Privacy Attitude and Behavior," *Computers & Security* 77 (2018): 226–61.

17. Surveillance society, as discussed in greater depth in chapter 1, describes a distributed network of surveillance into cultural systems, legal structures, government institutions, corporate enterprise, and everyday life. See Clive Norris and Gary Armstrong, *The Maximum Surveillance Society: The Rise of CCTV* (Oxford: Berg, 1999); David Lyon, *The Electronic Eye: The Rise of Surveillance Society* (Cambridge: Polity Press, 1994); and David Lyon, *Surveillance Society: Monitoring Everyday Life* (Buckingham: Open University, 2001).

18. Here, I borrow Henri Lefebvre's concept of social space to work against any sense that the home is *not* socially constructed and determined. Indeed, it is just as socially constructed and culturally contingent as any other space outside its walls. *The Production of Space,* trans. Donald Nicholson-Smith (Blackwell: Oxford, 1991).

19. This idea that a dwelling is static suggests its resistance to being constructed through social, cultural, economic, and political contingencies. Notably, Sara Ahmed critiques Heidegger's conceptualization of dwelling and its impact on human perception. Specifically, Ahmed takes issue with the prospect that subjects are "oriented" in space to perceive particular objects, which she argues works to reproduce a dominant value system. Sara Ahmed, *Queer Phenomenology: Orientations, Objects, Others* (Durham: Duke University Press, 2008).

20. Leap in scales is an allusion to Neil Smith's "jumping scales." "Contours of a

Spacialized Politics: Homeless Vehicles and the Production of Geographical Scales," *Social Text* 33 (1992): 55–81.

21. Marc Auge, *Oblivion* (Minneapolis: University of Minnesota Press, 2004), 21.

22. Joseph Roach, *Cities of the Dead: Circum-Atlantic Performance* (New York: Columbia University Press, 1996).

23. Schneider, *Performance Remains*, 22.

24. Schneider, *Performance Remains*, 100.

25. J. L. Austin, *How to Do Things with Words* (Oxford: Clarendon Press, 1962); Judith Butler, *Gender Trouble: Feminism and the Subversion of Identity* (New York: Routledge, 2006).

26. See, for instance, Julie Reiss, *From Margin to Center: The Spaces of Installation Art* (Cambridge, MA: MIT Press, 1999); and Joana Antunes, Maria de Lurdes Craveiro, and Carla Alexandra Gonçalves, eds., *The Centre as Margin: Eccentric Perspectives on Art* (Wilmington, DE: Vernon Press, 2019).

Of course, as Donald Kuspit argues, the term is "virtually indefinable" when used to describe artistic practice. For Kuspit, marginality is "social construction" that is used in a relative sense (*this* over *that*). "The Appropriation of Modern Art in the 1980s," *American Art* 5 no. ½ (1991): 132.

27. Joana Antunes, Maria de Lurdes Craveiro, and Carla Alexandra Gonçalves, eds., *The Centre as Margin: Eccentric Perspectives on Art* (Wilmington, DE: Vernon Press, 2019), xvii–xviii.

28. José Esteban Muñoz, *Disidentifications: Queers of Color and the Performance of Politics* (Minneapolis: University of Minnesota Press, 1999).

29. This understanding of the rogue as an individual may be elaborated through a consideration of the Kantian "rogue object," which Robert Hanna, in reading Kant's transcendental idealism, considers to be certain entities of "intuitional experience" that resist conceptual and judgmental experience and "turn out to be causally deviant and nomologically ill-behaved, thereby falling outside the Categories." It must be noted, however, that the context from which this quote is excerpted is much denser than its invocation here might suggest, specifically in regards to the two notions of conceptualism and categories, which are key concepts in Kant's transcendental idealism. Robert Hanna, "Kant's Non-Conceptualism, Rogue Objects, and the Gap in the B Deduction," *International Journal of Philosophical Studies* 19, no. 3 (2011): 399–415.

30. De Kosnik, *Rogue Archives*, 3.

31. De Kosnik, *Rogue Archives*, 135.

32. "The Top Feel-Good Viral Moments of 2018," *Vogue*, December 25, 2018, accessed May 19, 2019, https://www.vogue.com/article/best-memes-of-2018-feel-good-viral-moments; "The Most Talked about Cultural Moments That Defined 2018," *CNN*, December 20, 2018, accessed May 19, 2019, https://www.cnn.com/style/article/cultural-moments-that-defined-2018/index.html.

33. Gunther Kress, *Literacy in the New Media Age* (London: Routledge, 2003), 173.

34. Such a view relies, in a more fundamental way, on Susan Foster's premise that dance is a text to be read within a system of signs and codes. Thus, Danko's video can only "write back" to Beyoncé because his body is imbricated in a semiotic network, distinct from but drawing into the system of codes through which Beyoncé's performance

may be read. *Reading Dancing: Bodies and Subjects in Contemporary American Dance* (Berkeley: University of California Press, 1986).

35. Some scholars might also consider this concept characteristic of "prosumerism": a term coined by Alvin and Heidi Toffler that may be described as a phenomenon in which "a consumer . . . takes part in the production or distribution process, without being paid for it in wages." Olivier Frayssé and Mathieu O'Neil, eds., *Digital Labour and Prosumer Capitalism: the US Matrix* (Basingstoke: Palgrave Macmillan, 2015), n.p. See also Alvin Toffler, *The Third Wave* (New York: Morrow, 1980).

36. Jenkins, *Textual Poachers*, 155.

37. Jenkins argues against Michel de Certeau's proposition that "reading is poaching" to articulate how writing is reading, and reading is writing. For Jenkins, fan fiction is the quintessential case that helps deconstruct de Certeau's position. Jenkins, *Textual Poachers*.

38. De Kosnik, *Rogue Archives*, 141.

39. My use of "aspirational capital" draws from Yosso's model of six types of capital that people of color might cultivate to navigate difficult circumstances of dominant culture. Aspirational capital in particular refers to one's ability to activate resiliency in response to adversity. Though Danko's home dance video does not necessarily demonstrate any situation of adversity, his awestruck comportment toward Beyoncé suggests a desire to move "upward" toward her. Thus, my use of aspirational capital also cues a media industry studies sense of the "aspirant": a "below the line" worker who engages in an exhaustive degree of creative labor to activate mobility in some hierarchical ecosystem.

40. Sally Banes, *Terpsichore in Sneakers: Post-Modern Dance* (Boston: Houghton Mifflin, 1980), 77–91.

41. While the theory of necropolitics is primarily discussed in relation to contemporary geopolitics and war, it also has many implications for the body and how the body of the living relates to that of the no longer living. See Achille Mbembe, *Necropolitics*, trans. Steven Corcoran (Durham: Duke University Press, 2019). Thanks to Melissa Melpignano for her insights on this matter.

42. The act of mourning, grieving, or lamenting the loss of an icon or a beloved person in and through new media is no new phenomenon. Of course, it is worth noting here how the performance of grief or mourning on the new media platform tends to acquire a particular character, considering the prospects of mass circulation and viewership, algorithmic patterning, and digital archiving that such an expression undergoes. Gillian Terzis, for instance, notes how the performance of grief on new media, particularly around a public figure, incites "emotional contagion," cultivated by the viral accumulation of content around the death of a particular individual. Though we might critique the subtle denigrations of "emotion" that color Terzis's analysis, we may also take note of how this theory illustrates a new-media-specific rapidity of expressions and discourses surrounding grief. "Death Trends: Hashtag Activism and the Rise of Online Grief," *Kill Your Darlings* 22 (2015): 9–24.

43. For a discussion of reputational capital, see Philip Drake, "Reputational Capital, Creative Conflict and Hollywood Independence: The Case of Hal Ashby," in *American Independent Cinema: Indie, Indiewood and Beyond*, ed. Geoff King, Claire Molloy, and Yannis Tzioumakis (London: Routledge, 2012), 140–52.

44. Banes, *Terpsichore in Sneakers*.

45. This discussion would be incomplete without a nod to the "canon wars." Indeed, critiques of the canon are not at all new but have instead been leveled by many scholars across many disciplines. Such critiques are associated with the linguistic turn of the twentieth century in which artists, scholars, and cultural critics challenged the authority of the canon and deconstructed the power that institutions of all kinds had granted it for centuries. The so-called canon wars that resulted from these discussions prompted artists and scholars to rethink *what* and *who* they were canonizing and *why*. However, as Erica Hateley notes, the canon wars were fought "less over the idea of a canon . . . than over who or what is included in a given canon, or who or what determines such inclusion." We might surmise, then, that the canon wars concerned more the *content* of the canon than its structure as a hegemonic force.

46. Sherril Dodds effectively deconstructs the categories of "social dance" and "popular dance" in *Dancing on the Canon: Embodiments of Value in Popular Dance* (London: Palgrave Macmillan UK, 2011).

47. This shift that occurs through *nonchalant gestures* is linked to the ways in which value is constructed. Many scholars have emphasized the role of the body in shaping and negotiating value. In *Dancing on the Canon*, for instance, Sherril Dodds proposes the concept of "embodied value," maintaining that "those engaged in popular dance practice are not only produced by a framework of value, but also have the capacity to negotiate and re-imagine the values they encounter through their dancing bodies." Susan Leigh Foster extends this notion by demonstrating how value is not only sourced with and navigated through the body but also determined by its exchange between and among bodies. *Valuing Dance: Commodities and Gifts in Motion* (New York: Oxford, 2019). Harmony Bench notably applies the logic of the gift and commodity to circulations of performance on new media. Bench writes, "Digital platforms facilitate the slippage between gift and commodity, since posting and sharing content online have the effect of orphaning that content, stripping away affiliations and contextual information." Part of these affiliations and contextual information may very well be allusions to a canon or canonical figures, thereby stressing the remixing effect that new media has on the canon. *Perpetual Motion: Dance, Digital Cultures, and the Common* (Minneapolis: University of Minnesota Press, 2020), 176.

48. De Kosnik, *Rogue Archives*, 63.

49. Lewis Hyde, *A Primer for Forgetting: Getting Past the Past* (Edinburgh: Canongate Books, 2019), 4.

50. While such legislative action has taken effect primarily in the European Union, the ideas they reflect are recognized on a more global scale. For instance, debates around net neutrality in the United States and Canada reflect a similar public interest in the rights of internet users. In general, across these threads of international discourse, movements that promote online forgottenness tend to illustrate how new media denizens might find agency, comfort, and autonomy in a state or space of oblivion and how they are willing to stand for their right to be forgotten. For a comprehensive overview of legal policies dealing with net neutrality and the right to be forgotten, see Paul Lambert, *The Right to Be Forgotten* (London: Bloomsbury, 2019), and George Brock, *The Right to Be Forgotten: Privacy and the Media in the Digital Age* (London: I. B. Tauris, 2016).

51. Brock, *The Right to Be Forgotten*, 9. In this quote, Brock cites Verna Gehring, *The Internet in Public Life* (Lanham, MD: Rowman and Littlefield, 2004), 9.

52. In *Delete*, Viktor Mayer-Schönberger aptly articulates this shifting paradigm of forgetting: one from wanting technology to remember to wanting it to forget. *Delete: The Virtue of Forgetting in the Digital Age* (Princeton: Princeton University Press, 2009).

53. The bug bounty program is a deal that many websites, developers, and software companies offer to reward individuals who find bugs in their systems. After a bug is reported, the companies then fix the issue before it creates a wider problem.

54. It is important to acknowledge here that the "Data Download" feature that Pokherel used was not always part of Instagram's system. The company added it in 2018 in order to comply with European policies around data. Before this feature, users had no way of downloading and reusing their own content.

55. Zack Whittaker, "Instagram Wasn't Removing Photos and Direct Messages from Its Servers," *Tech Crunch*, August 13, 2020, https://techcrunch.com/2018/04/24/instagram-export/.

56. This idea of the home dance video performing in its own way reflects the argument of Isobel Harbison in *Performing Image*. Harbison writes, "Encounters and conversations that we have online are constituted, supplemented, or complemented with images: it becomes difficult to discern whether we are conversing with people through images or whether we are having encounters as images, differently dimensioned versions of ourselves interacting with others' different dimensions." *Performing Image* (Cambridge: MIT Press, 2019).

57. Henry Jenkins, *Fans, Bloggers, and Gamers: Exploring Participatory Culture* (New York: NYU Press), 155.

58. As Vincent Miller notes, "The main difference between industrial and informational society is that marginalisation in information society revolves specifically around (unsurprisingly) information and communication: access to it, the ability to use it effectively and the rights to produce it." *Understanding Digital Culture* (London: Sage, 2011), 96.

Also, for an investigation into the notion of the digital divide through a media studies perspective, see Jan van Dijk, *The Digital Divide* (Newark: Polity Press, 2020).

59. In this analysis van Dijk points to the Bourdieuian "forms of capital" (cultural, social, economic, and political, among others) that shape access. *The Deepening Divide: Inequality in the Information Society* (London: Sage, 2005).

60. Laura Robinson et al., "Digital Inequalities and Why They Matter," *Information, Communication & Society* 18, no. 5 (2015): 569–82. This notion of digital inequality is also the foundation of Safiya Noble's critique of algorithms in *Algorithms of Oppression: How Search Engines Reinforce Racism* (New York: NYU Press, 2018).

61. Mauve Shearlaw, "Facebook Lures Africa with Free Internet—But What Is the Hidden Cost?" *The Guardian*, August 1, 2016, https://www.theguardian.com/world/2016/aug/01/facebook-free-basics-internet-africa-mark-zuckerberg.

62. Sarah Banet-Weiser, *Authentic™: The Politics of Ambivalence in a Brand Culture* (New York: NYU Press, 2012); Harbison, *Performing Image*.

63. Harmony Bench and Simon Ellis, eds., "Editorial: Solo/Screen," *International Journal of Screendance* 8 (2017): 1, https://doi.org/10.18061/ijsd.v8i0.5891.

CHAPTER 4

1. At the time of writing this book, Declan and Gemma both have public accounts on Instagram with very robust followings. Despite the very public nature of their media, I have changed their names and removed any identifying information from this analysis of their work.

2. The theory of homophily describes the condition on social media in which "people's personal networks are homogeneous with regard to many sociodemographic, behavioral, and intrapersonal characteristics." See Miller McPherson, Lynn Smith-Lovin, and James Cook, "Birds of a Feather: Homophily in Social Networks," *Annual Review of Sociology* 27, no. 1 (2001): 415–44.

Many other scholars have published on a similar concept: that of the internet's cultivation of "echo chambers." See Elanor Colleoni, Aleessando Rozza, and Adam Arvidsson, "Echo Chamber or Public Sphere? Predicting Political Orientation and Measuring Political Homophily in Twitter Using Big Data," *Journal of Communication* 64, no. 2 (2014): 317–32; and Cass Sunstein, *Republic.com 2.0* (Princeton: Princeton University Press, 2007).

3. In alluding to the possibility that a home movie is an amateur production, I do not pass any value-based judgments of the form. Keeping with Patricia Zimmerman's view, home movies and other forms of amateur filmmaking deserve scholarly attention. Investigations of their formalistic qualities and cultures of production help to critically analyze distinctions between amateur and professional. *Reel Families: A Social History of Amateur Film* (Bloomington: Indiana University Press, 1995).

4. Richard Chalfen, *Snapshot Versions of Life* (Bowling Green, OH: Bowling Green State University Popular Press, 1987), 63.

5. Chalfen, *Snapshot Versions of Life*, 61–62.

6. Zimmermann, *Reel Families*, 113.

7. Indeed, much of the literature on home movies reflects a Euro-American perspective. Notable exceptions to this trend include *Mining the Home Movie: Excavations in Histories and Memories*, ed. Karen Ishizuka and Patricia Zimmerman (Berkeley: University of California Press, 2008).

8. The popularity of television programs like *America's Funniest Home Movies* is one exception to this culture of production. It may be argued that this show gave families the prospect of mass viewership through the possibility of selection for the show, and thus families determined its aesthetics of production.

9. While *Dance Moms* made a media sensation out of the competition dance stage mom, the show is not the sole source of cultural representations for the parents of young dancers. In fact, many television programs that followed *Dance Moms*, such as *Toddlers in Tiaras*, provided a similar look at the stage mom, while also extending that archetype into other fields of representation.

10. See, for instance, Karen Schupp, "Dance Competition Culture and Commercial Dance," *Journal of Dance Education* 19, no. 2 (2019): 58–67.

11. As discussed in subsequent sections of the chapter, most social media sites tend to enforce an age minimum of thirteen. Interestingly, these companies do not refer to this age restriction as an "age of majority," which makes it easier for them to exempt

themselves from the responsibility that other sectors of society perform (and are required by law to perform).

12. Jan van Dijk, *The Network Society: Social Aspects of New Media*, 2nd ed. (London: Sage, 2006), 131.

13. The discourse on child development is robust and beyond the confines of this discussion. Nonetheless, historiographic perspectives on this subject are helpful in understanding the shifts in how the physical and cognitive development of children has been understood over time and across cultural boundaries. A helpful resource in this regard is James Mourilyan Tanner, *A History of the Study of Human Growth* (Cambridge: Cambridge University Press, 1981).

14. Liz Jones, "Becoming Child/Becoming Dress," *Global Studies of Childhood* 3, no. 3 (2013): 289–96.

15. Social scientists refer to the process of an individual mirroring the codes of their surroundings as *acquisition*. Elliot Turiel notably mingles perspectives in psychology and anthropology to complicate the concept of acquisition. "A concern with acquisition," Turiel writes, "must go beyond assumptions to direct investigations and explication of the process of development. The nature of the individual's relationship to the broader social system, the ways in which behavior is influenced by social experience, and the genesis of the individual's social makeup are all issues requiring explanation. Are individuals shaped by the social world, or do they develop conceptual systems for understanding and transforming the social world?" *The Development of Social Knowledge: Morality and Convention* (Cambridge: Cambridge University Press, 1983).

16. Urie Bronfenbrenner, *The Ecology of Human Development: Experiments by Nature and Design* (Cambridge, MA: Harvard University Press, 1979); Leon Kuczynski, Sheila Marshall, and Kathleen Schell, "Value Socialization in a Bi-directional Context," in *Parenting and Children's Internalization of Values: A Handbook of Contemporary Theory*, ed. J. E. Grusec and L. Kuczynski, 23–50 (New York: Wiley, 1997); Elli P. Schachter and Jonathan J. Ventura, "Identity Agents: Parents as Active and Reflective Participants in their Children's Identity Formation," *Journal of Research on Adolescence* 18, no. 3 (2008): 449–76.

17. Andrew Hewitt defines "social choreography" as a kinesthetic ideology in which "social possibilities are both rehearsed and performed." Through dance, in particular, bodies may envision and perform "utopian social order." *Social Choreography: Ideology as Performance in Dance and Everyday Movement* (Durham: Duke University Press, 2005), 4. Imani Kai Johnson provides apt commentary on this theory by extending it to "outlaw culture" in 1970s and '80s New York City. Johnson claims that social choreography can be just as subversive as it is "utopian" and should also include improvisation. "Battling in the Bronx: Social Choreography and Outlaw Culture among Early Hip-Hop Streetdancers in New York City," *Dance Research Journal* 50, no. 2 (2018): 62–75.

18. One Instagram study featuring interviews with influencers claim how their parents are heavily involved in the productions of influencers: "One interesting finding we should take into account is how the parents work to guide their children through the process of becoming an influencer. Most influencers mention at least one of their parents at some point in the interview. One influencer (17, f) claims it was her mother who convinced her to start a blog. Further, we notice that parents play an important role in the creation of content as one influencer describes (11, f): 'Sometimes I forget making

photos because I have other things on my mind, and then my mom says 'Isn't it time to post a photo on Instagram?' A few influencers also indicate that their parents are the ones who take pictures of them." Marijke De Veirman, Steffi De Jans, Elisabeth Van den Abeele, and Liselot Hudders, "Unravelling the Power of Social Media Influencers: A Qualitative Study on Teenage Influencers as Commercial Content Creators on Social Media," in *The Regulation of Social Media Influencers*, ed. Catalina Goanta and Sofia Ranchordás (Cheltenham: Edward Elgar, 2020), 144.

19. Sara Ahmed, *Queer Phenomenology: Orientations, Objects, Others* (Durham: Duke University Press, 2006), 31–32.

20. Roland Barthes, *S/Z*, trans. Richard Miller (New York: Hill and Wang, 1974), 20.

Notably, Kelli Fuery applies Barthes's logic of the code to new media circulation of images. *New Media: Culture and Image* (Basingstoke: Palgrave Macmillan, 2009).

Of course, the codes through which new media objects are produced, circulated, and consumed are complex in their transmission and many nodes of connections. See Alexandra Harlig, "Social Texts, Social Audiences, Social Worlds: The Circulation of Popular Dance on YouTube," PhD diss., The Ohio State University, 2019.

21. Hewitt, *Social Choreography*, 6.

22. These orchestrations are the very reason why platform studies is a growing discourse in the investigation of new media production, circulation, and consumption. As Aubrey Anable writes, "By emphasizing the matter of media devices—their chips, wires, slots, sensors, plastic and anodized aluminum bodies—in other words, their *thingness*, platform studies considers what this matter can tell us about the forces and conditions that shape our media landscape." "Platform Studies," *Feminist Media Histories* 4, no. 2 (2018): 135–40.

23. For instance, see Rianka Singh, "Platform Feminism: Feminist Protest Space and the Politics of Spatial Organization," PhD diss., University of Toronto, 2020.

24. "Home in Global Literacies and Visual Cultures," in *Domestic Imaginaries: Navigating the Home in Global Literary and Visual Cultures*, ed. Bex Harper and Hollie Price (Berlin: Springer International Publishing, 2017).

25. This uncertainty points to a caveat of intimaesthetics: that a knowledge of the camera does not always mean a knowledge of the video's subsequent publicization and circulation online.

26. Of course, the ways in which Declan's and Gemma's performances log gender through new media do not foreclose their work with/through/on other social categories of their identities and public portraits. In this analysis, gender and class become prominent aspects of these children's respective semiotics, which helps to figure them as divergent examples of the modeling kids movement. These examples, as we situate them next to one another, however, do not foreground the performances of social categories beyond gender and class. We might imagine how a similar approach to the choreography of race, ethnicity, nationality, or sexuality, for example, might also lend itself to minor choreography. Indeed, these positionings certainly contribute to the cultivation of the children's digital identity. Thus, we must acknowledge how any analysis of minor choreography, both in online and offline instances, is inherently partial.

27. For example, one video starts with Danielle initiating a conversation from behind the camera: "Okay, so tell me everything." Declan, wearing his hair in a tight bun,

says, "I got to go on stage today. And I loved it." "You loved it?" repeated Danielle. "I LOVED it," says Declan, looking directly at the camera with an intensity in his eyes. "What did you love about it?" asks Danielle. Declan replies, "Because my shimmy!" Declan moves in closer to the camera as he subtly shimmies his shoulders. "Your shimmy? Did you do your shimmy on stage?" retorts Danielle. "Yassssss," says Declan, flicking his wrist as he brings his hand to his face. All of a sudden Declan changes his accent, "Yas, we're going to Italian," he states as he emphatically gestures with his hand before whipping around to strut away from the camera. "You're going where?" "I'm going to . . . I'm going to . . . Paris," Declan states as he turns back toward the camera and lifts his chin with his hand. "Paris?" Danielle says inquisitively before laughing. "I'm going to live in a hotel," says Declan as he continues walking away.

28. Declan's mother's name is made evident through the mentioning of her account in the bio of Declan's profile, and her account features her name, Danielle Shaffer.

29. Ramsay Burt, *The Male Dancer: Bodies, Spectacle, Sexualities* (London: Routledge, 2007); Jennifer Fisher, "Tulle as Tool: Embracing the Conflict of the Ballerina as Powerhouse," *Dance Research Journal* 39, no. 1 (Summer 2007): 3–24; Pirkko Markula and Marianne I. Clark, "Introduction," in *The Evolving Feminine Ballet Body*, ed. Pirkko Markula and Marianne I. Clark, xv–xxxiv (Edmonton: University of Alberta Press, 2018).

30. Roland Barthes, *Mythologies*, trans. Richard Howard and Annette Lavers (New York: Hill and Wang, 2012).

31. It should also be mentioned that Danielle's minor choreography has paid off. The attention that Declan has garnered on social media has led to his casting in music videos, his appearance on television programs, and his feature in a number of news publications. Declan now has a page on IMDb. As of February 2022, peopleai.com estimated Declan's net worth at $2.04 million, an estimation that is solely derived from his Instagram account.

32. While a user's socioeconomic status does not always transfer to social and cultural capital on a platform like Instagram, the relationship between economic security and new media literacy is compelling. The implication here is that the financial wealth of Declan's family has afforded them the time to learn about and hone the techniques of new media and also perhaps the aid of influential friends and family members who can boost their content. Moreover, the capability to purchase followers and likes from companies that create and operationalize bot accounts is also an option for those users who can afford it. Though it is difficult to discern if Declan's family took advantage of these possibilities, the fact that the techniques are available to them speaks to their new media privilege.

33. Another indication that Gemma is attending dance class from home is the use of #socialdisDANCING: a reference to the global shutdown and quarantine that began in 2020 as a result of the COVID-19 pandemic. The alignment of this media with such a momentous global movement toward the home is critically profound. For information on the meaning of dance during this period, see the special issue of the *International Journal of Screendance* regarding the COVID-19 pandemic. Harmony Bench and Alexandra Harlig, eds., "This Is Where We Dance Now: COVID-19 and the New and Next in Dance Onscreen," *International Journal of Screendance* 12 (2021).

34. An understanding of Miss Chelsea's name is based on the mention in the caption, as well as on the name "Chelsea Sebes" in the bio of the tagged account.

35. Karen Schupp, "Dance Competition Culture and Capitalism," *Congress on Research in Dance Conference Proceedings*, (Cambridge, UK: Cambridge University Press, 2016).

36. Susan Leigh Foster, "Dancing Bodies: An Addendum, 2009," *Theater* 40, no. 1 (2010): 25–29.

37. Elizabeth Schultz, "The Sexualization of Girls in Dance Competitions," PhD diss., University of California, Irvine, 2018; Lisa Sandlos, "'In the Land of Dance': Unpacking Sexualization and the Wellbeing of Girls in Competitive Dance," *Journal of Dance Education* 23, no. 3 (2023): 234–42.

38. Heather Harrington, "Consumer Dance Identity: The Intersection Between Competition Dance, Televised Dance Shows and Social Media," *Research in Dance Education* 21, no. 2 (2020): 169–87.

39. In 2024, Instagram made a change that made all teen accounts private by default. Of course, this designation of "teen account" is solely based on the user's disclosure of their age—a feature that can be easily circumvented.

It is also worth noting a level of access between public and private on Instagram, which is called "close friends." This feature was not always part of the platform's offerings; however, in 2018, Instagram added the ability for users to create a list of followers who are their "close friends." Once this list is defined, a user can share content with a select group of people rather than everyone who follows them. As opposed to the previous "all or nothing" approach to content dissemination, this update effectively creates two networks within one platform—two levels of publicity. Not every user takes advantage of this feature, but it does make it possible for users to nuance their audience and create two tiers of access.

40. *The Private Is Political: Networked Privacy and Social Media* (New Haven: Yale University Press, 2023), 63–98.

41. In a press release on September 27, 2021, Meta claimed that children are "getting phones younger and younger, misrepresenting their age, and downloading apps that are meant for those 13 or older." This acknowledgment suggests that the company's age-gating feature is merely symbolic. As we will find out, the company also uses the difficulties of effective age gating to rationalize its creation of a separate platform just for kids. Adam Mosseri, "Pausing 'Instagram Kids' and Building Parental Supervision Tools," Instagram, September 27, 2021, https://about.instagram.com/blog/announcements/pausing-instagram-kids.

42. Natasha Singer, "At Meta, Millions of Underage Users Were an 'Open Secret' States Say," *New York Times*, November 25, 2023, https://www.nytimes.com/2023/11/25/technology/instagram-meta-children-privacy.html.

43. When a user creates a new account while logged into an existing account, the system provides fine-print text at the bottom of the confirmation page that reads: "We'll add private information from [Existing Account] to [New Account]. See Terms and Data Policy." While the policy is linked from there, users do not have much information about how their separate accounts are linked and what information is shared between them.

44. While Instagram currently does not verify identity, the company has acknowledged their interest in doing so, particularly with the goal of preventing children from lying about their age in order to create their own account. An article that Instagram posted to its blog on March 17, 2021, reads: "While many people are honest about their age, we know that young people can lie about their date of birth. We want to do more to stop this from happening, but verifying people's age online is complex and something many in our industry are grappling with. To address this challenge, we're developing new artificial intelligence and machine learning technology to help us keep teens safer and apply new age-appropriate features," https://about.instagram.com/blog/announcements/continuing-to-make-instagram-safer-for-the-youngest-members-of-our-community#:~:text=We%20require%20everyone%20to%20be,an%20account%20for%20some%20time.

45. Eric Drott, "Fake Streams, Listening Bots, and Click Farms: Counterfeiting Attention in the Streaming Music Economy," *American Music* 38, no. 2 (2020): 153–75.

46. "The attorneys general urge Facebook to abandon these plans. Use of social media can be detrimental to the health and well-being of children, who are not equipped to navigate the challenges of having a social media account. Further, Facebook has historically failed to protect the welfare of children on its platforms. The attorneys general have an interest in protecting our youngest citizens, and Facebook's plans to create a platform where kids under the age of 13 are encouraged to share content online is contrary to that interest," https://ag.ny.gov/sites/default/files/naag_letter_to_facebook_-_final.pdf.

47. Mosseri, "Pausing 'Instagram Kids' and Building Parental Supervision Tools," September 27, 2021, https://about.instagram.com/blog/announcements/pausing-instagram-kids.

48. My use of alienation here refers to the loss of a sense of labor that occurs through commodity fetishism. For a helpful review of the ways in which social media enables alienation, see Kane X. Faucher, *Social Capital Online: Alienation and Accumulation* (London: University of Westminster Press, 2018). For a broader discussion of a Marxist approach to new media, see Christian Fuchs, *Digital Labour and Karl Marx* (New York: Routledge, 2014).

CONCLUSION

1. Roy Boyne, "Post-Panopticism," *Economy and Society* 29, no. 2 (2000): 285–307.

2. I borrow the phrase "culture of consent" from David Harvey, *A Brief History of Neoliberalism* (New York: Oxford University Press, 2005), 39.

3. The concept of "jumping scales," mentioned throughout the book, is sourced with Neil Smith, "Contours of a Spatialized Politics: Homeless Vehicles and the Production of Geographical Scale," *Social Text* 33 (1992): 19–33.

4. We might argue, on the other hand, that an uber private Instagram user is an oxymoron and that no such person exists. Even if no other users see their content, it still lives on a platform that stores, tracks, and analyzes their data. Nonetheless, this phantom user is an interesting subject of consideration.

References

Abidin, Crystal. "'Aren't These Just Young, Rich Women Doing Vain Things Online?': Influencer Selfies as Subversive Frivolity." *Social Media + Society* 2, no. 2 (2016): 1–17.

Abidin, Crystal. "#familygoals: Family Influencers, Calibrated Amateurism, and Justifying Young Digital Labor." *Social Media + Society* 3, no. 2 (2017): 205630511770719–.

Abidin, Crystal. "#In$tagLam: Instagram as a Repository of Taste, a Brimming Marketplace, a War of Eyeballs." In *Mobile Media Making in the Age of Smartphones*, edited by M. Berry and M. Schleser, 119–28. New York: Palgrave Pivot, 2014.

Ahmed, Sara. *Queer Phenomenology: Orientations, Objects, Others*. Durham: Duke University Press, 2008.

Anable, Aubrey. "Platform Studies." *Feminist Media Histories* 4, no. 2 (2018): 135–40.

Antunes, Joana, Maria de Lurdes Craveiro, and Carla Alexandra Gonçalves, eds. *The Centre as Margin: Eccentric Perspectives on Art*. Wilmington, DE: Vernon Press, 2019.

Appadurai, Arjun. "Introduction." In *The Social Life of Things: Commodities in Cultural Perspective*, edited by Arjun Appadurai, 3–63. Cambridge: Cambridge University Press, 1986.

Apter, Emily S. *Feminizing the Fetish: Psychoanalysis and Narrative Obsession in Turn-of-the-Century France*. Ithaca: Cornell University Press, 1991.

Augé, Marc. *Oblivion*. Translated by Marjolijn de Jager. Minneapolis: University of Minnesota Press, 2004.

Austin, J. L. *How to Do Things with Words*. Oxford: Clarendon Press, 1962.

Babak, Elahi, and Persis M. Karim. "Introduction: Iranian Diaspora." *Comparative Studies of South Asia, Africa and the Middle East* 31, no. 2 (2011): 381–87.

Bachelard, Gaston. *The Poetics of Space*. Translated by Maris Jolas. New York: Penguin Books, 2014.

Banes, Sally. *Terpsichore in Sneakers: Post-Modern Dance*. Boston: Houghton Mifflin, 1980.

Banet-Weiser, Sarah. *Authentic™: The Politics of Ambivalence in a Brand Culture*. New York: NYU Press, 2012.

Banet-Weiser, Sarah. "Postfeminism and Popular Feminism." *Feminist Media Histories* 4, no. 2 (2018): 152–56.

Barthes, Roland. *Image-Music-Text*. Translated by Stephen Heath. New York: Hill and Wang, 1978.

Barthes, Roland. *Mythologies*. Translated by Richard Howard and Annette Lavers. New York: Hill and Wang, 2012.

Barthes, Roland. *S/Z*. Translated by Richard Miller. New York: Hill and Wang, 1974.

Bench, Harmony. "Media and the No-Place of Dance." *Forum Modernes Theater* 23, no. 1 (2008): 37–47.

Bench, Harmony. *Perpetual Motion: Dance, Digital Cultures, and the Common*. Minneapolis: University of Minnesota Press, 2020.

Bench, Harmony, and Simon Ellis, eds. "Editorial: Solo/Screen." *International Journal of Screendance* 8 (2017).

Bench, Harmony, and Alexandra Harlig, eds. "This Is Where We Dance Now: COVID-19 and the New and Next in Dance Onscreen." *International Journal of Screendance* 12 (2021).

Benjamin, Walter. "The Work of Art in the Age of Mechanical Reproduction." In *Aesthetics*, 66–69. London: Routledge, 2017.

Boltanski, Luc, and Eve Chiapello. *The New Spirit of Capitalism*. London: Verso, 2005.

Bolter, Jay David, and Richard Grusin. *Remediation: Understanding New Media*. Cambridge, MA: MIT Press, 1999.

Bordo, Susan, ed. *Feminist Interpretations of René Descartes*. University Park: Pennsylvania State University Press, 1999.

Bordwell, David. *Figures Traced in Light: On Cinematic Staging*. Berkeley: University of California Press, 2005.

Bourdieu, Pierre. "Structures and the Habitus." In *Outline of a Theory of Practice*, 72–95. Cambridge: Cambridge University Press, 1977.

Boyne, Roy. "Post-Panopticism." *Economy and Society* 29, no. 2 (2000): 285–307.

Brock, George. *The Right to Be Forgotten: Privacy and the Media in the Digital Age*. London: I. B. Tauris, 2016.

Bronfenbrenner, Urie. *The Ecology of Human Development: Experiments by Nature and Design*. Cambridge, MA: Harvard University Press, 1979.

Brown, Tom. *Breaking the Fourth Wall: Direct Address in Cinema*. Edinburgh: Edinburgh University Press, 2012.

Bucher, Taina. *If . . . Then: Algorithmic Power and Politics*. New York: Oxford, 2018.

Bucher, Taina. "Nothing to Disconnect From? Being Singular Plural in an Age of Machine Learning." *Media, Culture & Society* 42, no. 4 (2020): 610–17.

Bucher, Taina. "Want to Be on the Top? Algorithmic Power and the Threat of Invisibility on Facebook." *New Media & Society* 14, no. 7 (November 2012): 1164–80.

Burke, Siobhan. "A Graveyard? She's Danced There. Just Check Instagram." *New York Times*, August 1, 2017. https://www.nytimes.com/2017/08/01/arts/dance/Mar-Mar -instagram-project-personal-practice.html

Burt, Ramsay. *The Male Dancer: Bodies, Spectacle, Sexualities*. London: Routledge, 2007.

Butler, Judith. *Gender Trouble: Feminism and the Subversion of Identity*. New York: Routledge, 2006.

Calvert, Clay. *Voyeur Nation: Media, Privacy, and Peering in Modern Culture*. Boulder, CO: Westview Press.

Carah, Nicholas, and Daniel Angus. "Algorithmic Brand Culture: Participatory Labour, Machine Learning and Branding on Social Media." *Media, Culture & Society* 40, no. 2 (2018): 178–94.

Carey, Robert, and Jacquelyn Ann Burkell. "A Heuristics Approach to Understanding Privacy-Protecting Behaviors in Digital Social Environments." In *Lessons from the Identity Trail: Anonymity, Privacy and Identity in a Networked Society*, edited by Ian Kerr, Valerie Steeves, and Carole Lucock, 65–82. Oxford: Oxford University Press, 2009.

Catlow, Ruth, Marc Garrett, Nathan Jones, and Sam Skinner. *Artists Re:thinking the Blockchain*. N.p.: Furtherfield and Torque Editions, 2017.

Chalfen, Richard. *Snapshot Versions of Life*. Bowling Green, OH: Bowling Green State University Popular Press, 1987.

Chatzichristodoulou, Maria, and Rachel Zerihan, eds. *Intimacy Across Visceral and Digital Performance*. Basingstoke: Palgrave Macmillan, 2012.

Chomsky, Noam. *Profit over People: Neoliberalism and Global Order*. New York: Seven Stories Press, 1999.

Chun, Wendy Hui Kyong. *Programmed Visions: Software and Memory*. Cambridge, MA: MIT Press, 2011.

Chun, Wendy Hui Kyong. *Updating to Remain the Same: Habitual New Media*. Cambridge, MA: MIT Press, 2016.

Clissold, Bradley. "Candid Camera and the Origins of Reality TV: Contextualizing a Historical Precedent." In *Understanding Reality Television*, edited by Su Holmes and Deborah Jermyn, 33–53. New York: Routledge, 2004.

Coaffee, Jon, David Murakami Wood, and Peter Rogers. "Controlling the Risky City." In *The Everyday Resilience of the City: How Cities Respond to Terrorism and Disaster*, edited by Jon Coaffee, David Murakami Wood, and Peter Rogers, 67–86. Basingstoke: Palgrave Macmillan, 2009.

Cock, Jacklyn. *Maids and Madams: A Study in the Politics of Exploitation*. Johannesburg: Raven Press, 1980.

Colleoni, Elanor, Alessandro Rozza, and Adam Arvidsson. "Echo Chamber or Public Sphere? Predicting Political Orientation and Measuring Political Homophily in Twitter Using Big Data." *Journal of Communication* 64, no. 2 (2014): 317–32.

Constine, Josh. "How Instagram's Algorithms Work." *Tech Crunch*, June 1, 2018. https://tcrn.ch/2LN5kDX

Couldry, Nick. *Why Voice Matters: Culture and Politics after Neoliberalism*. London: SAGE, 2010.

Davidson, Donald. "Events as Particulars." *Noûs* 4, no. 1 (1970): 25–32.

De Kosnik, Abigail. "Fandom as Free Labor." In *Digital Labor: The Internet as Playground and Factory*, edited by Trevor Scholtz, 98–111. New York: Routledge, 2012.

De Kosnik, Abigail. *Rogue Archives: Digital Cultural Memory and Media Fandom*. Cambridge, MA: MIT Press, 2016.

De Veirman, Marijke, Steffi De Jans, Elisabeth Van den Abeele, and Liselot Hudders. "Unravelling the Power of Social Media Influencers: A Qualitative Study on Teenage Influencers as Commercial Content Creators on Social Media." In *The Regulation of Social Media Influencers*, ed. Catalina Goanta and Sofia Ranchordás, 126–66. Cheltenham: Edward Elgar, 2020.

Deleuze, Gilles. *The Logic of Sense*. Translated by Mark Lester and Charles Stivale. Edited by Constantin V. Boundas. New York: Columbia University Press, 1990.

Derrida, Jacques. "Signature, Event, Context." In *Limited, Inc.*, 1–23. Evanston: Northwestern University Press, 1988.

Dobson, Amy, Nicholas Carah, and Brady Robarbs. "Digital Intimate Publics and Social Media: Towards Theorising Public Lives on Private Platforms." In *Digital Intimate Publics and Social Media*, edited by Amy Dobson, Brady Robarbs, and Nicholas Carah, 3–28. Cham: Springer, 2018.

Dodds, Sherril. *Dancing on the Canon*. London: Palgrave Macmillan, 2011.

Dodds, Sherril, and Colleen Hooper. "Faces, Close-Ups and Choreography: A Deleuzian Critique of *So You Think You Can Dance*." *International Journal of Screendance* 4, no. 1 (2014): 93–113.

Double, Oliver. "Introduction." In *Popular Performance*, edited by Adam Ainsworth, Oliver Double, and Louise Peacock. London: Bloomsbury, 2017.

Douglas, Mary. "The Idea of a Home: A Kind of Space." *Social Research* (1991): 287–307.

Drake, Philip. "Reputational Capital, Creative Conflict and Hollywood Independence: The Case of Hal Ashby." In *American Independent Cinema: Indie, Indiewood and Beyond*, edited by Geoff King, Claire Molloy, and Yannis Tzioumakis, 140–52. London: Routledge, 2012.

Droitcour, Brian. "A Selfie Is Not a Portrait." *Culturetwo*, October 24, 2013. Accessed July 1, 2020. https://culturetwo.wordpress.com/2013/10/24/a-selfie-is-not-a-portrait

Drott, Eric. "Fake Streams, Listening Bots, and Click Farms: Counterfeiting Attention in the Streaming Music Economy." *American Music* 38, no. 2 (2020): 153–75.

Duke, Shaul A. "Nontargets: Understanding the Apathy Towards the Israeli Security Agency's COVID-19 Surveillance." *Surveillance & Society* 19, no. 1 (2021): 114–29.

Dunagan, Colleen T. *Consuming Dance: Choreography and Advertising*. New York: Oxford University Press, 2018.

Eckel, Julia. "Selfies and Authorship: On the Displayed Authorship and the Author Function of the Selfie." In *Exploring the Selfie: Historical, Theoretical, and Analytical Approaches to Digital Self-Photography*, edited by Julia Eckel, Jens Ruchatz, and Sabine Wirth, 131–65. Cham: Palgrave Macmillan, 2018.

Edwards, Leigh. "Chasing the Real: Reality Television and Documentary Forms." In *Docufictions: Essays on the Intersection of Documentary and Fictional Filmmaking*, edited by Gary D. Rhodes and John Parris Springer. Jefferson, NC: McFarland, 2006.

Esfandiari, Haleh. *Restructured Lives: Women and Iran's Islamic Revolution*. Washington, DC: Woodrow Wilson Center Press, 1997.

Fadda, Reema. "Playing Against Invisibility: Negotiating the Institutional Politics of Cultural Production in Palestine." In *Future Imperfect: Contemporary Art Practices and Cultural Institutions in the Middle East*, edited by Anthony Downey, 149–66. Sternberg Press, 2016.

Fanon, Franz. *Black Skin, White Masks*. Translated by R. Philcox. New York: Grove Press, 2008.

Faucher, Kane X. *Social Capital Online: Alienation and Accumulation*. London: University of Westminster Press, 2018.

Fidler, Roger. *Mediamorphosis: Understanding New Media*. Thousand Oaks, CA: Pine Forge Press, 1997.

Finn, Jonathan. "Seeing Surveillantly: Surveillance as Social Practice." In *Eyes Everywhere*, edited by Randy Lippert, Aaron Doyle, and David Lyon, 67–80. London: Routledge, 2012.

Fisher, Jennifer. "Tulle as Tool: Embracing the Conflict of the Ballerina as Powerhouse." *Dance Research Journal* 39, no. 1 (Summer 2007): 3–24.

Foster, Susan Leigh. "The Ballerina's Phallic Pointe." In *Corporealities: Dancing Knowledge, Culture, and Power*, edited by Susan Leigh Foster, 1–25. London: Routledge, 2004.

Foster, Susan Leigh. "Choreographies of Gender." *Signs: Journal of Women in Culture & Society* 24, no. 1 (1998): 1–33.

Foster, Susan Leigh. *Choreographing Empathy: Kinesthesia in Performance*. New York: Routledge, 2010.

Foster, Susan Leigh. "Dancing Bodies: An Addendum, 2009." *Theater* 40, no. 1 (2010): 25–29.

Foster, Susan Leigh. *Reading Dancing: Bodies and Subjects in Contemporary American Dance*. Berkeley: University of California Press, 1986.

Foster, Susan Leigh. *Valuing Dance: Commodities and Gifts in Motion*. New York: Oxford University Press, 2019.

Foucault, Michel. *The Birth of the Clinic*. New York: Vintage Press, 1994 (1963).

Foucault, Michel. *Discipline and Punish: The Birth of the Prison*. Translated by Alan Sheridan. New York: Vintage Books, 1995.

Francisco, Valerie. "'The Internet Is Magic': Technology, Intimacy and Transnational Families." *Critical Sociology* 41, no. 1 (2015): 173–90.

Frosh, Paul. "The Gestural Image: The Selfie, Photography Theory, and Kinesthetic Sociability." *International Journal of Communication* 9 (2015): 1607–28.

Fuchs, Christian. *Digital Labour and Karl Marx*. New York: Routledge, 2014.

Fuchs, Christian. "Digital Prosumption Labour on Social Media in the Context of the Capitalist Regime of Time." *Time & Society* 23, no. 1 (2014): 97–123.

Fuchs, Christian. "New Media, Web 2.0 and Surveillance." *Sociology Compass* 5, no. 2 (2011): 134–47.

Fuery, Kelli. *New Media: Culture and Image*. Basingstoke: Palgrave Macmillan, 2009.

Funt, Allen, and Philip Reed. *Candidly, Allen Funt: A Million Smiles Later*. Fort Lee, NJ: Barricade Books, 1994.

Garcia, Megan. "Racist in the Machine: The Disturbing Implications of Algorithmic Bias." *World Policy Journal* 33, no. 4 (2016): 111–17.

Gehring, Verna V. *The Internet in Public Life*. Lanham, MD: Rowman and Littlefield, 2004.

George, Doran, and Susan Leigh Foster. *The Natural Body in Somatics Dance Training.* New York: Oxford University Press, 2020.

Gerber, Nina, Paul Gerber, and Melanie Volkamer. "Explaining the Privacy Paradox: A Systematic Review of Literature Investigating Privacy Attitude and Behavior." *Computers & Security* 77 (2018): 226–61.

Gibbs, Martin, James Meese, Michael Arnold, Bjorn Nansen, and Marcus Carter. "#Funeral and Instagram: Death, Social Media, and Platform Vernacular." Information, Communication & Society 18, no. 3 (2015): 255–268.

Gill, Rosalind. "Post-Postfeminism? New Feminist Visibilities in Postfeminist Times." *Feminist Media Studies* 16, no. 4 (2016): 610–30.

Gopinath, Sumanth, and Jason Stanyek. "Technologies of the Musical Selfie." In *The Cambridge Companion to Music in Digital Culture*, edited by David Trippett, Monique M. Ingalls, and Nicholas Cook, 89–118. Cambridge: Cambridge University Press, 2019.

Gravari-Barbas, Maria, and Sébastien Jacquot. "Mechanisms, Actors and Impacts of the Touristification of a Tourism Periphery: The Saint-Ouen Flea Market, Paris." *International Journal of Tourism Cities* 5, no. 3 (1AD): 370–91.

Guins, Raiford. "Morality Settings: New Generation Game Systems and Parental Controls." *Design Issues* 31, no. 3 (2015): 55–65.

Hakim, Catherine. *Erotic Capital: The Power of Attraction in the Boardroom and the Bedroom.* New York: Basic Books, 2011.

Hanna, Robert. "Kant's Non-Conceptualism, Rogue Objects, and the Gap in the B Deduction." *International Journal of Philosophical Studies* 19, no. 3 (2011): 399–415.

Harbison, Isobel. *Performing Image.* Cambridge, MA: MIT Press, 2019.

Harlig, Alexandra. "Social Texts, Social Audiences, Social Worlds: The Circulation of Popular Dance on YouTube." PhD diss., The Ohio State University, 2019.

Harrington, Heather. "Consumer Dance Identity: The Intersection Between Competition Dance, Televised Dance Shows and Social Media." *Research in Dance Education* 21, no. 2 (2020): 169–87.

Harvey, David. *A Brief History of Neoliberalism.* New York: Oxford University Press, 2005.

Hearn, Alison. "Meat, Mask, Burden: Probing the Contours of the Branded 'Self.'" *Journal of Consumer Culture* 8, no. 2 (2008): 197–217.

Heidegger, Martin. *Basic Writings: Revised and Expanded Edition.* New York: Harper Collins, 1993.

Hewitt, Andrew. *Social Choreography: Ideology as Performance in Dance and Everyday Movement.* Durham: Duke University Press, 2005.

Hier, Sean. "Risky Spaces and Dangerous Faces: Urban Surveillance Social Disorder and CCTV." *Social & Legal Studies* 13, no. 4 (2004): 541–54.

Hoskins, Andrew. "Digital Network Memory." In *Mediation, Remediation, and the Dynamics of Cultural Memory*, edited by Astrid Erll and Ansgar Nünning, 91–106. Berlin: Walter de Gruyter, 2009.

Huang, Ya-Rong. "Identity and Intimacy Crises and Their Relationship to Internet Dependence among College Students." *CyberPsychology & Behavior* 9, no. 5 (2006): 571–76.

Hyde, Lewis. *A Primer for Forgetting: Getting Past the Past*. Edinburgh: Canongate Books, 2019.

Instagram. "Continuing to Make Instagram Safer for the Youngest Members of Our Community." March 17, 2021. https://about.instagram.com/blog/announcements /continuing-to-make-instagram-safer-for-the-youngest-members-of-our-communi ty#:~:text=We%20require%20everyone%20to%20be,an%20account%20for%20 some%20time

Instagram. "See Posts You Care about First in Your Feed." March 15, 2016. https://abo ut.instagram.com/blog/announcements/see-posts-you-care-about-first-in-your-fe ed#:~:text=The%20order%20of%20photos%20and,just%20in%20a%20differe nt%20order

Ishizuka, Karen L., and Patricia Rodden Zimmermann, eds. *Mining the Home Movie: Excavations in Histories and Memories*. Berkeley: University of California Press, 2008.

Jansen, Ena. *Like Family: Domestic Workers in South African History and Literature*. Johannesburg: Wits University Press.

Jansson, André, and Karin Fast. "Transmedia Identities: From Fan Cultures to Liquid Lives." In *The Routledge Companion to Transmedia Studies*, edited by Matthew Freeman and Renira Rampazzo Gambarato, 340–49. London: Routledge, 2019.

Jenkins, Henry. *Convergence Culture: Where Old and New Media Collide*. New York: NYU Press, 2006.

Jenkins, Henry. *Fans, Bloggers, and Gamers: Exploring Participatory Culture*. New York: NYU Press, 2006.

Jenkins, Henry. *Textual Poachers: Television Fans and Participatory Culture*. New York: Routledge, 1992.

Jermyn, Deborah. "Video Technologies, Actuality and Affect in the Television Crime Appeal." In *Understanding Reality Television*, edited by Su Holmes and Deborah Jermyn, 71–90. London: Routledge, 2004.

Johnson, Imani Kai. "Battling in the Bronx: Social Choreography and Outlaw Culture among Early Hip-Hop Streetdancers in New York City." *Dance Research Journal* 50, no. 2 (2018): 62–75.

Jones, Liz. "Becoming Child/Becoming Dress." *Global Studies of Childhood* 3, no. 3 (2013): 289–96.

Kaplan, E. Ann. *Looking for the Other: Feminism, Film, and the Imperial Gaze*. New York: Routledge, 1997.

Kenaan, Hagi. "The Selfie and the Face." In *Exploring the Selfie: Historical, Theoretical, and Analytical Approaches to Digital Self-Photography*, edited by Julia Eckel, Jens Ruchatz, and Sabine Wirth, 113–30. Cham: Palgrave Macmillan, 2018.

Keutelian, Mary. "The Best Times to Post on Social Media in 2022." *SproutSocial*, April 13, 2022. Accessed April 15, 2022. https://sproutsocial.com/insights/best-times-to -post-on-social-media/

Kleinberg-Levin, David Michael. *Heidegger's Phenomenology of Perception*. London: Rowman and Littlefield International, 2020.

Kozel, Susan. *Closer: Performance, Technologies, Phenomenology*. Cambridge, MA: MIT Press, 2008.

Krautkrämer, Florian, and Matthias Thiele. "The Video Selfie as Act and Artifact of

Recording." In *Exploring the Selfie: Historical, Theoretical, and Analytical Approaches to Digital Self-Photography*, edited by Julia Eckel, Jens Ruchatz, and Sabine Wirth, 239–59. Cham: Palgrave Macmillan, 2018.

Kruspit, Donald. "The Appropriation of Modern Art in the 1980s." *American Art* 5, no. 1/2 (1991): 132–41.

Kuczynski, Leon, Sheila Marshall, and Kathleen Schell. "Value Socialization in a Bi-directional Context." In *Parenting and Children's Internalization of Values: A Handbook of Contemporary Theory*, edited by Joan E. Grusec and Leon Kuczynski, 23–50. New York: Wiley, 1997.

Laing, Morna, and Jacki Willson. *Revisiting the Gaze: The Fashioned Body and the Politics of Looking*. London: Bloomsbury, 2020.

Lambert, Alex. *Intimacy and Friendship on Facebook*. London: Palgrave MacMillan, 2013.

Lambert, Paul. *The Right to Be Forgotten*. London: Bloomsbury, 2019.

Leddy, Thomas. *The Extraordinary in the Ordinary: Aesthetics of Everyday Life*. Toronto: Broadview Press, 2012.

Lefait, Sebastien. *Surveillance on Screen: Monitoring Contemporary Films and Television Programs*. Lanham, MD: Scarecrow Press, 2013.

Lefebvre, Henri. *The Production of Space*. Translated by Donald Nicholson-Smith. Oxford: Blackwell, 1991.

Lehnur, Ace, ed. *Self-Representation in an Expanded Field: From Self-Portraiture to Selfie, Contemporary Art in the Social Media Age*. Basel: MDPI, 2021.

Leiendecker, Bernd. "Of Duck Faces and Cat Beards: Why Do Selfies Need Genres?" In *Historical, Theoretical, and Analytical Approaches to Digital Self-Photography*, edited by Julia Eckel, Jens Ruchatz, and Sabine Wirth, 189–209. Cham: Palgrave Macmillan, 2018.

Lejeune, Philippe. "The Autobiographical Pact." In *On Autobiography*, edited by P. J. Eakin, 3–30. Minneapolis: University of Minnesota Press, 1989.

Lepecki, André. *Exhausting Dance Performance and the Politics of Movement*. New York: Routledge, 2006.

Lomanowska, Anna M., and Matthieu J. Guitton. "Online Intimacy and Well-Being in the Digital Age." *Internet Interventions* 4 (2016): 138–44.

Lyon, David. *The Electronic Eye: The Rise of Surveillance Society*. Cambridge: Polity Press, 1994.

Lyon, David. *Surveillance Society: Monitoring Everyday Life*. Buckingham: Open University Press, 2001.

Lyon, David. *Surveillance Studies: An Overview*. Cambridge: Polity, 2007.

Lyon, David. *Theorizing Surveillance*. London: Routledge, 2006.

Machon, Josephine. *Immersive Theatres Intimacy and Immediacy in Contemporary Performance*. London: Palgrave MacMillan, 2013.

Madej, Krystina. *Interactivity, Collaboration, and Authoring in Social Media*. New York: Springer, 2016.

Mann, Steve. "'Sousveillance': Inverse Surveillance in Multimedia Imaging." *Proceedings of the 12th Annual ACM International Conference on Multimedia*, 620–27.

Mann, Steve, and Joseph Ferenbok. "New Media and the Power Politics of Sousveillance in a Surveillance-Dominated World." *Surveillance & Society* 11, no. 1/2 (2013): 18–34.

Manovich, Lev. *The Language of New Media*. Cambridge, MA: MIT Press, 2002.

Marks, Laura. *Touch: Sensuous Theory and Multisensory Media*. Minneapolis: University of Minnesota Press, 2002.

Markula, Pirkko, and Marianne I. Clark. "Introduction." In *The Evolving Feminine Ballet Body*, edited by Pirkko Markula and Marianne I. Clark, xv–xxxiv. Edmonton: University of Alberta Press, 2018.

Marwick, Alice E. *The Private Is Political: Networked Privacy and Social Media*. New Haven: Yale University Press, 2023.

Mayer-Schönberger, Viktor. *Delete: The Virtue of Forgetting in the Digital Age*. Princeton: Princeton University Press, 2009.

Mbembe, Achille. *Necropolitics*. Translated by Steven Corcoran. Durham: Duke University Press, 2019.

McDowell, Linda. "Rethinking Place: Thoughts on Spaces of the Home, Absence, Presence, New Connections and New Anxieties." In *The Domestic Space Reader*, edited by Chiara Briganti and Kathy Mezei, 54–58. Toronto: University of Toronto Press, 2012.

McPherson, Miller, Lynn Smith-Lovin, and James M. Cook. "Birds of a Feather: Homophily in Social Networks." *Annual Review of Sociology* 27, no. 1 (2001): 415–44.

McRobbie, Angela. "Post-Feminism and Popular Culture." *Feminist Media Studies* 4, no. 3 (2004): 255–64.

Mercer, Kobena. "Unburying the Dismembered." In *New Histories: Institute of Contemporary Art*. Boston: Institute of Contemporary Art, 1996.

Milgram, Stanley, and John Sabini. "Candid Camera." *Society* (New Brunswick) 16, no. 6 (1979): 72–75.

Miller, Jacques-Alain. "Extimité." In *Lacanian Theory of Discourse: Subject, Structure, and Society*, edited by Mark Bracher et al., 74–87. New York: NYU Press, 1994.

Miller, Kiri. *Playable Bodies: Dance Games and Intimate Media*. New York: Oxford University Press, 2017.

Miller, Kiri. *Playing Along: Digital Games, YouTube, and Virtual Performance*. Oxford: Oxford University Press, 2012.

Miller, Vincent. *Understanding Digital Culture*. London: Sage, 2011.

Montoya, Peter. *The Personal Branding Phenomenon: Realize Greater Influence, Explosive Income Growth and Rapid Career Advancement by Applying the Branding Techniques of Michael, Martha and Oprah*. Santa Ana, CA: Peter Montoya, 2002.

Moore, Henrietta. "If Intimacy Is the Answer, Then What Is the Question?" Keynote address at "Probing the Intimate: Cross-Cultural Queries of Proximity and Beyond" workshop, University of Cambridge, May 2014.

Moran, James M. *There's No Place Like Home Video*. Minneapolis: University of Minnesota Press, 2002.

Morelock, Jeremiah, and Felipe Ziotti Narita. "Introduction: Information Technology and Authoritarian Populism." In *The Society of the Selfie: Social Media and Liberal Democracy*, 1–14. London: University of Westminster Press, 2021.

Morse, Nicole Erin. *Selfie Aesthetics: Seeing Trans Feminist Futures in Self-Representational Art*. Durham: Duke University Press, 2022.

Motrescu-Mayes, Annamaria, and Susan Aasman. *Amateur Media and Participatory Cultures: Film, Video, and Digital Media*. Abingdon, Oxon: Routledge, 2019.

Mulvey, Laura. *Visual and Other Pleasures*. Bloomington: Indiana University Press, 1989.

Muñoz, José Esteban. *Disidentifications: Queers of Color and the Performance of Politics*. Minneapolis: University of Minnesota Press, 1999.

Nadis, Fred. "Citizen Funt: Surveillance as Cold War Entertainment." *Film & History* 37, no. 2 (2007): 13–22.

Najmabadi, Afsaneh. *Professing Selves: Transsexuality and Same-Sex Desire in Contemporary Iran*. Durham: Duke University Press, 2014.

National Association of Attorneys General. "Facebook's Plans to Develop Instagram for Children Under the Age of 13." May 10, 2021. Accessed December 15, 2021. https://ag.ny.gov/sites/default/files/naag_letter_to_facebook_-_final.pdf

Newmahr, Staci. *Playing on the Edge: Sadomasochism, Risk, and Intimacy*. Bloomington: Indiana University Press, 2011.

Ngai, Sianne. *Our Aesthetic Categories: Zany, Cute, Interesting*. Cambridge, MA: Harvard University Press, 2012.

Noble, Safiya Umoja. *Algorithms of Oppression: How Search Engines Reinforce Racism*. New York: NYU Press, 2018.

Norris, Clive, and Gary Armstrong. *The Maximum Surveillance Society: The Rise of CCTV*. Oxford: Berg, 1999.

Norris, Clive, and Michael McCahill. "CCTV: Beyond Penal Modernism?" *British Journal of Criminology* 46, no. 1 (2006): 97–118.

O'Neil, Cathy. *Weapons of Math Destruction: How Big Data Increases Inequality and Threatens Democracy*. New York: Crown, 2016.

Ortner, Sherry B. "Is Female to Male as Nature Is to Culture?" *Feminist Studies* 1, no. 2 (1972): 5–31.

Pasquale, Frank. *The Black Box Society: The Secret Algorithms That Control Money and Information*. Cambridge, MA: Harvard University Press, 2015.

Peters, John Durham. "Calendar, Clock, Tower." In *Deus in Machina: Religion and Technology in Historical Perspective*, edited by Jeremy Stolow, 25–42. New York: Fordham University Press, 2013.

Peters, Tom. "The Brand Called You." *Fast Company* 10, no. 10 (1997): 83–90.

Petre, Caitlin, Brooke Erin Duffy, and Emily Hund. "'Gaming the System': Platform Paternalism and the Politics of Algorithmic Visibility." *Social Media + Society* 5, no. 5 (2019): 1–12.

Pink, Sarah. *Home Truths: Gender, Domestic Objects and Everyday Life*. London: Taylor and Francis, 2020.

Raley, Rita. "Dataveillance and Countervailance." In *Raw Data Is an Oxymoron*, edited by Lisa Gitelman, 121–45. Cambridge, MA: MIT Press, 2013.

Razaghpanah, Abbas, et al. "Apps, Trackers, Privacy, and Regulators: A Global Study of the Mobile Tracking Ecosystem." Paper presented at the 25th Annual Network and Distributed System Security Symposium, 2018.

Reilly, Ian. *Media Hoaxing: The Yes Men and Utopian Politics*. Lanham, MD: Lexington Books, 2018.

Reiss, Julie. *From Margin to Center: The Spaces of Installation Art.* Cambridge, MA: MIT Press, 1999.

Rettberg, Jill Walker. "Snapchat: Phatic Communication and Ephemeral Social Media." In *Appified: Culture in the Age of Apps,* edited by Jeremy Wade Morris and Sarah Murray, 188–96. Ann Arbor: University of Michigan Press, 2018.

Reviglio, Urbano, and Claudio Agosti. "Thinking Outside the Black-Box: The Case for 'Algorithmic Sovereignty' in Social Media." *Social Media + Society* 6, no. 2 (2020): 1–12.

Roach, Joseph R. *Cities of the Dead: Circum-Atlantic Performance.* New York: Columbia University Press, 1996.

Robinson, Laura, et al. "Digital Inequalities and Why They Matter." *Information, Communication & Society* 18, no. 5 (2015): 569–82.

Roche, David, and Isabelle Schmitt-Pitiot. *Intimacy in Cinema: Critical Essays on English Language Films.* Jefferson, NC: McFarland, 2014.

Rosewarne, Lauren. *Intimacy on the Internet: Media Representations of Online Connections.* London: Routledge, 2016.

Rowner, Ilai. *The Event: Literature and Theory.* Lincoln: University of Nebraska Press, 2015.

Rushkoff, Douglas. *Open Source Democracy: How Online Communication Is Changing Offline Politics.* London: Demos, 2003.

Saito, Yuriko. *Everyday Aesthetics.* Oxford: Oxford University Press, 2007.

Sandlos, Lisa. "'In the Land of Dance': Unpacking Sexualization and the Wellbeing of Girls in Competitive Dance." *Journal of Dance Education* 23, no. 3 (2023): 234–42.

Schneider, Rebecca. *Performing Remains: Art and War in Times of Theatrical Reenactment.* New York: Routledge, 2011.

Scholz, Trebor. *Digital Labor: The Internet as Playground and Factory.* New York: Routledge, 2013.

Schultz, Elizabeth Gough. "The Sexualization of Girls in Dance Competitions." PhD diss., University of California, Irvine, 2018.

Schupp, Karen. "Dance Competition Culture and Capitalism." *Congress on Research in Dance Conference Proceedings,* 2016.

Schupp, Karen. "Dance Competition Culture and Commercial Dance." *Journal of Dance Education* 19, no. 2 (2019): 58–67.

Schwab, Klaus, and Peter Vanham. *Stakeholder Capitalism: A Global Economy That Works for Progress, People and Planet.* London: Wiley, 2021.

Senft, Theresa. "Microcelebrity and the Branded Self." *A Companion to New Media Dynamics* 11 (2013): 346–54.

Sharzer, Greg. *Late Escapism and Contemporary Neoliberalism: Alienation, Work and Utopia.* Milton: Taylor and Francis, 2021.

Shearlaw, Maeve. "Facebook Lures Africa with Free Internet—But What Is the Hidden Cost?" *The Guardian,* August 1, 2016.

Shefer, Tamara. "Fraught Tenderness: Narratives on Domestic Workers in Memories of Apartheid." *Peace and Conflict: Journal of Peace Psychology* 18, no. 3 (2012): 307–17.

Singh, Rianka. "Platform Feminism: Feminist Protest Space and the Politics of Spatial Organization." PhD diss., University of Toronto, 2020.

Smith, Neil. "Contours of a Spatialized Politics: Homeless Vehicles and the Production of Geographical Scale." *Social Text* 33 (1992): 19–33.

Smith, Sidonie, and Julia Watson. "Virtually Me: A Toolbox about Online Self-Presentation." In *Identity Technologies: Constructing the Self Online,* edited by Anna Poletti and Julie Rak, 70–95. Madison: University of Wisconsin Press, 2014.

Sontag, Susan. *On Photography.* New York: Farrar, Straus, and Giroux, 1973.

Sontag, Susan. *Regarding the Pain of Others.* New York: Farrar, Straus and Giroux, 2003.

Sunstein, Cass R. *Republic.com 2.0.* Princeton: Princeton University Press, 2007.

Szabo, Gabor, et al. "Temporal Processes: The When of Social Media." In *Social Media Data Mining and Analytics,* 77–121. Indianapolis: Wiley, 2019.

Tanner, James Mourilyan. *A History of the Study of Human Growth.* Cambridge: Cambridge University Press, 1981.

Terzis, Gillian. "Death Trends: Hashtag Activism and the Rise of Online Grief." *Kill Your Darlings* 22 (2015): 9–24.

Thomas, Bronwen. *Literature and Social Media.* New York: Routledge, 2020.

Tinel-Temple, Muriel, Laura Busetta, and Marlène Monteiro, eds. *From Self-Portrait to Selfie: Representing the Self in Moving Image.* Oxford: Peter Lang, 2019.

Toffler, Alvin. *The Third Wave.* New York: Morrow, 1980.

Turiel, Elliot. *The Development of Social Knowledge: Morality and Convention.* Cambridge: Cambridge University Press, 1983.

Turkle, Sherry. *Alone Together: Why We Expect More from Technology and Less from Each Other.* New York: Basic Books, 2011.

Van Dijk, Jan. "Datafication, Dataism and Dataveillance: Big Data Between Scientific Paradigm and Ideology." *Surveillance & Society* 12, no. 2 (2014): 197–208.

Van Dijk, Jan. *The Digital Divide.* Newark: Polity Press, 2020.

Van Dijk, Jan. *The Network Society: Social Aspects of New Media.* 2nd ed. London: Sage, 2006.

Vo, Lam Thuy. *Mining Social Media: Finding Stories in Internet Data.* San Francisco: No Starch Press, 2019.

Wee, Lionel, and Ann Brooks. "Personal Branding and the Commodification of Reflexivity." *Cultural Sociology* 4, no. 1 (2010): 45–62.

Whitmer, Jennifer. "You Are Your Brand: Self-Branding and the Marketization of Self." *Sociology Compass* 13, no. 3 (2019): 1–10.

Whittaker, Zack. "Instagram Wasn't Removing Photos and Direct Messages from Its Servers." *Tech Crunch,* August 13, 2020. Accessed November 16, 2020. https://techcrunch.com/2018/04/24/instagram-export/

Wolff, Richard. *Democracy at Work: A Cure for Capitalism.* Chicago: Haymarket Books, 2012.

Wrenn, Mary V. "Agency and Neoliberalism." *Cambridge Journal of Economics* 39, no. 5 (2015): 1231–43.

WSJ Noted. "How Instagram Is Hurting Teen Girls; A Wall Street Journal Investigation Reveals That Facebook's Own Research Shows a Significant Teen Mental-Health Issue That the Company Plays Down in Public." *Wall Street Journal.* Eastern ed. September 29, 2021. https://www.wsj.com/articles/how-instagram-is-hurting-teen-girls-11632940937

Zimmerman, Patricia. *Reel Families: A Social History of Amateur Film.* Bloomington: Indiana University Press, 1995.

Žižek, Slavoj. *The Courage of Hopelessness: Chronicles of a Year of Acting Dangerously.* London: Allen Lane, 2017.

Zuboff, Shoshana. *Surveillance Capitalism: The Fight for a Human Future at the New Frontier of Power.* New York: Public Affairs, 2019.

Index

New Spirit of Capitalism (Boltanski and
  Chiapello), 11. *See also* Boltanski,
  Luc; Chiapello, Éve
Ngai, Sianne, 3
nontarget, 117–18, 145, 214n15

oblivion
  choreography of (*see* choreography: of
    oblivion)
  paradox of, 121–23
ontology, 123, 205n38
original post, 56–58
Our Aesthetic Categories, 3, 198n7. *See
  also* Sianne, Ngai

pandemic. See Covid-19 pandemic
parental control, 162, 182
Performing Remains, 203n2. *See also*
  Schneider, Rebecca; ontology.
performativity, 123, 172, 189
personal brand, 11, 15, 21, 65, 98–101,
  106, 108, 164, 169, 211n42
platform control, 2, 13, 19, 162, 183. See
  also parental control, intimaesthetics: circulations of
platform specificity, 161, 193
platform affordances, 96, 132, 194
Point-of-view shot, 70–71
politics of ambivalence. *See* ambivalence
post-panoptic
  -ism, 12, 34, 192, 200n31. *See also*
    Boyne, Roy.
  surveillance society, 12, 20. *See also*
    surveillance: society.
postmodern dance, 89, 113, 134–39, 165
POV. *See* point-of-view shot
privacy work, 183. See also Marwick,
  Alice
prosumer, 216n35

reality TV, 6, 98, 153, 157, 202n7. *See also
  Dance Moms*
relevancy sorting. *See* algorithms: relevancy sorting
reproduction
  of art, 199n21, 205n38

of gender, 26, 41–47, 151, 166–82
of values, 160–161, 180, 187–88
research methodology, 14–19
reverse exnomination, 172
Roach, Joseph, 122
Robarbs, Brady, 200n28
rogue archives, 125–26, 133
rogue-ness, 21, 112–14, 121, 124–26, 133–
  34, 140, 145–47, 193, 215n29

Saito, Yuriko, 3
self brand. *See* personal brand
self reflexivity, 70
selfie. *See also* moving selfie
  culture, 66–68, 98, 119, 193
  frivolity of (*see* subversion frivolity)
  historicity of, 69
  ontology of, 67–69
  subversiveness of (*see* subversive
    frivolity)
Schneider, Rebecca, 122–23, 203n21
social choreography, 160, 220n17
social media
  archives (*see* archives: digital)
  authorship, 27, 58, 74–78, 88, 151–53,
    164, 174, 178–81, 184, 208n13
  bait-and-switch logic of, 2, 13, 62, 144,
    183
  collaboration on, 58–59, 150. *See also*
    social media: authorship; social
    media: consent
  consent, 37–39, 59–61, 117, 148, 157,
    164, 193, 200n35
  feed, 67, 92–96, 107, 114, 116, 194. *See
    also* algorithms: relevancy sorting,
    currency.
  humor in (*see* affective registers:
    humor)
  like-for-like strategy on, 94
  originality (*see* original post)
  ownership, 27, 54–58, 61, 141,
    200n28
  settings, 14–15, 161, 182–84, 188,
    194–95
  tacit knowledge of, 94
  time stamp, 55–57, 61